Graphic Classics:
BRAM STOKER

Graphic Classics Volume Seven
2003

©2002 KIRSTEN ULVE

EUREKA PRODUCTIONS
8778 Oak Grove Road, Mount Horeb, Wisconsin 53572
www.graphicclassics.com

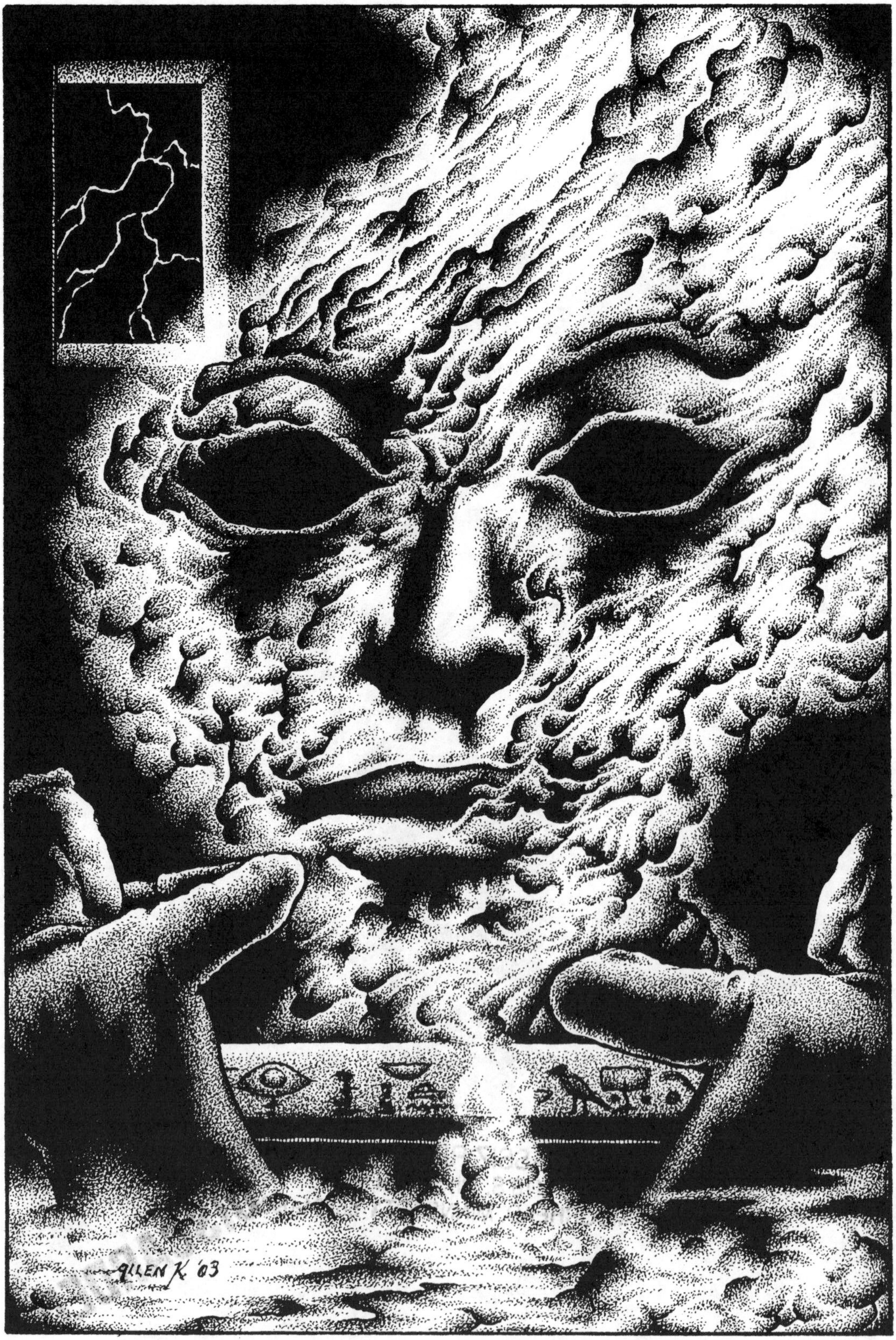
ALLEN K. '03

from THE JEWEL OF SEVEN STARS ©2003 ALLEN KOSZOWSKI

CONTENTS

Graphic Classics:
BRAM STOKER

©2003 HUNT EMERSON

Introduction *by Mort Castle* 5

Lair of the White Worm *adapted & illustrated by Rico Schacherl* 8

Torture Tower *adapted & illustrated by Onsmith Jeremi* 40

The Wondrous Child *illustrated by Evert Geradts* 50

The Funeral Party *illustrated by Richard Sala* 56

Dracula's Voyage *adapted & illustrated by John W. Pierard* 58

The Dracula Gallery *illustrated by Brandon Ragnar Johnson, Kostas Aronis, Neale Blanden,*
   Skot Olsen, Michael Manning, Jeff Gaither, Maxon Crumb, Lisa K. Weber, Spain Rodriguez,
   Todd Schorr, Anton Emdin & Todd Lovering 76

The Vampire Hunter's Guide *illustrated by Hunt Emerson* 89

The Dualitists *illustrated by Lesley Reppeteaux* 94

The Judge's House *adapted & illustrated by Gerry Alanguilan* 102

The Bridal of Death *adapted & illustrated by J.B.Bonivert* 119

About the Artists & Writers 140

Cover illustration by Glenn Barr / Back cover illustration by Christopher Miscik
Additional illustrations by Kirsten Ulve, Allen Koszowski and Mitch O'Connell

Graphic Classics: Bram Stoker is published by Eureka Productions. ISBN #0-9712464-7-5. Price US $9.95. Available from Eureka Productions, 8778 Oak Grove Road, Mount Horeb, WI 53572. The Graphic Classics website is at http://www.graphicclassics.com. Tom Pomplun, designer and publisher, tom@graphicclassics.com. Eileen Fitzgerald, editorial assistant. This compilation and all original works ©2003 Eureka Productions. All rights revert to creators after publication. Graphic Classics is a trademark of Eureka Productions. Printed in Canada.

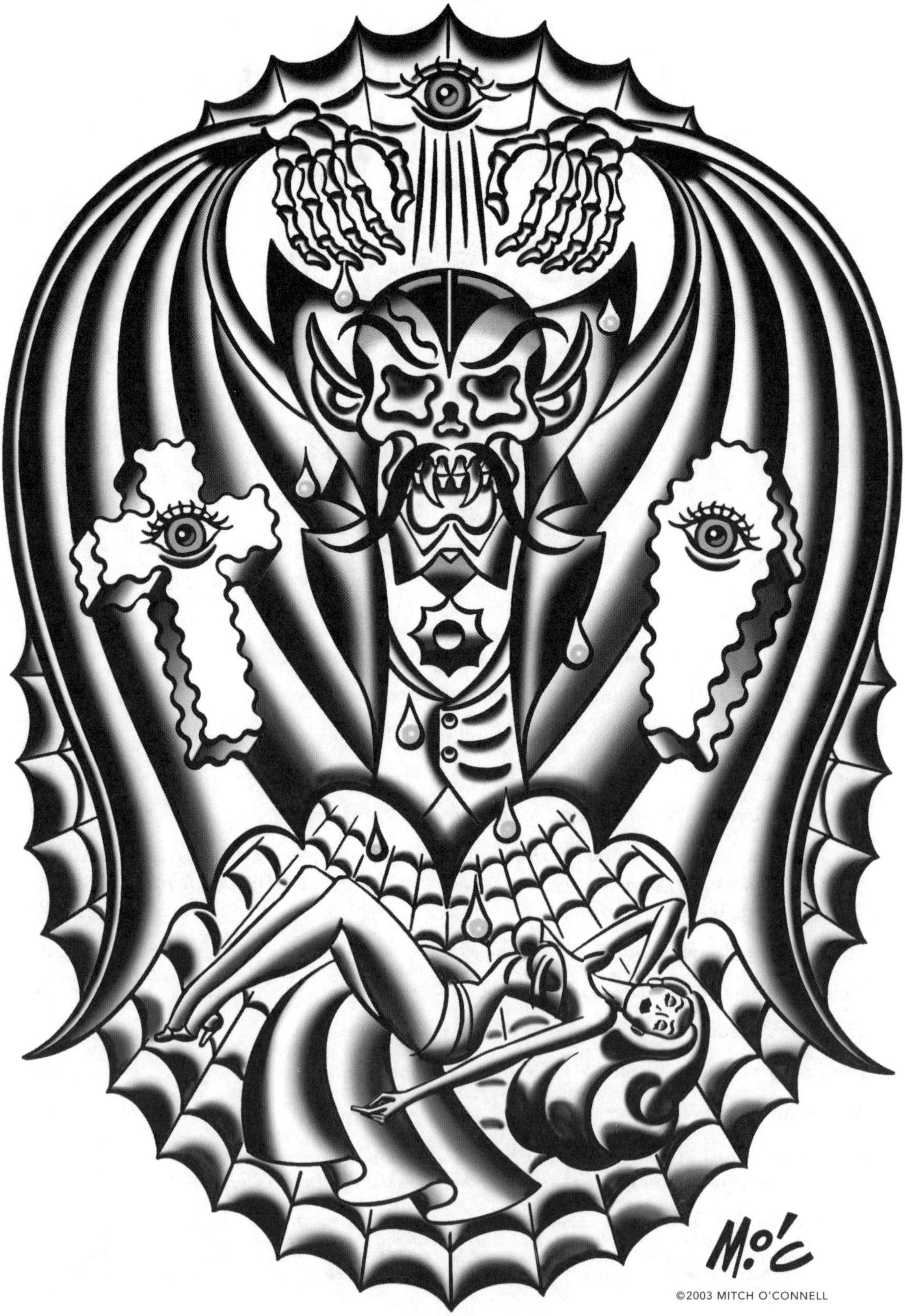
M.O'C

June 13, 2003

To: Abraham "Bram" Stoker, Esq.
Perhaps c/o The Lyceum Theatre, London, England
or The Borgo Pass in the Carpathian Mountains, Transylvania
or Somewhere Out There

My Very Dear Mr. Stoker,

Please regard this as my Modest Proposal for a *New Dramatic Presentation of Dracula:*

By way of preface, my good sir, I deem this an opportune time to write you, in that today is Friday the 13th, a day upon which it well might be that "the powers of evil are exalted" (to quote your acquaintance Sir Arthur Conan Doyle). I have only this week returned from New York City, New York, where I was in attendance at the Sixteenth Annual Bram Stoker Awards Ceremony of the Horror Writers Association. Recognizing the *possibility* that news of these awards has not reached you in your current abode, I wish you to know that the Horror Writers Association (HWA), nearly 1,000 members strong, annually presents Stoker awards for outstanding horror writing in 12 different categories. I think it might please you to learn that this year the HWA bestowed its highest honor, the Lifetime Achievement Award, on a Mr. Stephen King, author of numerous works, among them *Salem's Lot*, a chronicle of vampiric doings in Maine, and Mr. J.N. Williamson, author of almost 40 novels, among them *Death Coach*, relating a tale of vampires in the state of Indiana.

It seems that your creation, Count Dracula, is indeed eternally undead and immortal and that he and his literary descendants (if not exactly blood kin!) are surviving ever so nicely in an age which thinks itself even more rational and scientific than your own Victorian era.

Of course, *Dracula*, the "Gothic chiller" you published in 1897, had initial critical success: "It is splendid. No book since Mrs. Shelley's *Frankenstein* or indeed any other at all has come near yours in originality, or terror." That was the opinion of one reviewer, your mother, she who shared with you the lore and legend of your native Ireland (might not some leprechauns have very sharp teeth, Little Abraham).

Sir Arthur Conan Doyle concurred: "I think it is the very best story of *diablerie* which I have read for many years. It is really wonderful how with so much exciting interest over so long a book there is never an anti-climax."

Despite such unbiased positive responses, while *Dracula* sold well enough in England, it was at best considered a "potboiler." And though sales were better in the United States, your "penny dreadful" had not been properly copyrighted, and so you saw no Yankee coppers for your efforts.

You had other hopes for your creation, did you not, my dear Mr. Stoker? Yours was the vision that clearly saw the *dramatic* possibilities of Count Dracula, Van Helsing, and Misses Mina and Lucy (and the comically revolting *Renfield*).

Alas, despite your best of endeavors, you never did see Dracula step and strut upon the stage, and this despite your modeling the diabolical Count upon your employer/friend/master Henry Irving, for whom you labored in the role of acting manager at the Lyceum Theatre for so many years. (And many would say labored with little appreciation and less recompense!)

Not that you admitted to that: Indeed, you've obfuscated the origins of your tale, having written that it came from your research into the history and superstitions of Eastern Europe, to wit: "Having some time at my disposal when in London, I had visited the British Museum, and made search among the books and maps in the library regarding Transylvania..." You've also credited your acquaintance, the Hungarian professor Arminius Vanbéry, with telling you the history of the Romanian prince Vlad Tepes, better known as Dracula. And of course, there was that "inspiration" claimed by other writers: "The idea for the tale comes from a...nightmare!"

Yet here is your description of Count Dracula:

> *"His face was a strong, a very strong, aquiline, with high bridge of the thin nose and peculiarly arched nostrils, with lofty domed forehead, and hair growing scantily round the temples but profusely elsewhere. His eyebrows were very massive, almost meeting over the nose, and with bushy hair that seemed to curl in its own profusion. The mouth, so far as I could see it under the heavy moustache, was fixed and rather cruel-looking, with peculiarly sharp white teeth. These protruded over the lips, whose remarkable ruddiness showed astonishing vitality in a man of his years. For the rest, his ears were pale, and at the tops extremely pointed. The chin was broad and strong, and the cheeks firm though thin. The general effect was one of extraordinary pallor."*

This is almost identical to that found in your biographical study of Henry Irving. And I don't think this recent quote would be in the least remarkable to you: "Irving allowed his audiences the perverse pleasure of recoiling themselves to his double guise as a kind of 'Sacred Monster.'"' But Irving (the monster, sacred or otherwise!) refused you, left you bitter, and that bitterness went with you to your grave.

Dracula did not.

Can you know of and do you note with irony the innumerable times the Lord of the Undead has taken to the boards and to the ether and to the silver and the cathode ray screens (gas plasma coming soon)? Called *Count Orlock* in F.W. Murnau's **Nosferatu**, he was enacted by Max Shrek in 1922 and appeared no less hideously made up in the remake of that film by Werner Herzog; turned into a lacquer-haired nobleman who spoke English as an Unknown Language by Bela Lugosi, anemically portrayed by John Carradine, brought to plodding motion by Lon Chaney Jr. who intoned "I want to drink your blood" in the same manner he had "I want ketchup on my beans, George," transformed into a wordless menace with a long stride and red contact lenses by Christopher Lee, and... Truly, I hope you did not see Gary Oldham with what looked like a plastic buttock enhancer on his head.

Oh, thanks to your wife, your *widow's*, sound business sense, your creation provided more than adequately for the Stoker family; the dramatic rights brought in the proverbial handsome income when you, being dead, could earn nothing.

But Mr. Stoker, I feel obliged to say to you that throughout much of the Twentieth Century and these early years of the Twenty-first, too numerous enactments of *Dracula* have ranged from dismal to depraved to (mildly) diverting.

Might I therefore beg to propose that the Count's tale be enacted in a new medium: The ballet!

Consider, Mr. Stoker, a ballet! Consider the ballet in which great effort is made effortless, in which, although the laws of gravity cannot be repealed, they can be amended, in which pose and poise and time are melted and transformation is the abiding natural principle as all becomes a surrealistic kaleidoscope...

To at last become your *vision*,

> *all sorts of queer dreams. There was a dog howling all night under my window*

the vision you had as a child

> *unnatural, horrible net of gloom and mystery which seemed closing around me*

a desperately ill little boy

> *In the moonlight opposite me were three young women, ladies by their dress and manner. I thought... I must be dreaming... they threw no shadow on the floor. They came close to me, and looked at me for some time, and then whispered together*

who lay bedridden, incapable of even standing by yourself for the first seven years of your life, when monsters manifested themselves in your fever dream

> *we must either capture or kill this monster in his lair, or we must... sterilize the earth*

Little boys grow up, find a profession, and discover, as did you, the face of the monster.

Mr. Stoker, I entreat you, let your monster now dance for us all, dance in the liquid tones of angled dreamscape as vividly as he did in your mind and in all our minds.

Mr. Stoker, I eagerly, yet with all patience, await your response to what I pray will be my greatly favored proposal.

Yours Most Sincerely,

Mort Castle
Four Times Bram Stoker Award Nominee

NOTE: Last month there debuted in New York a motion picture by Canadian director Guy Maddin: Dracula: Pages from a Virgin's Diary. It's a filmed ballet. It's damned good.

˙(Salter, Denis. "Henry Irving, the 'Dr. Freud' of Melodrama." In *Melodrama*. Ed. James Redmond. Cambridge: Cambridge University Press, 1992. 161-82.)

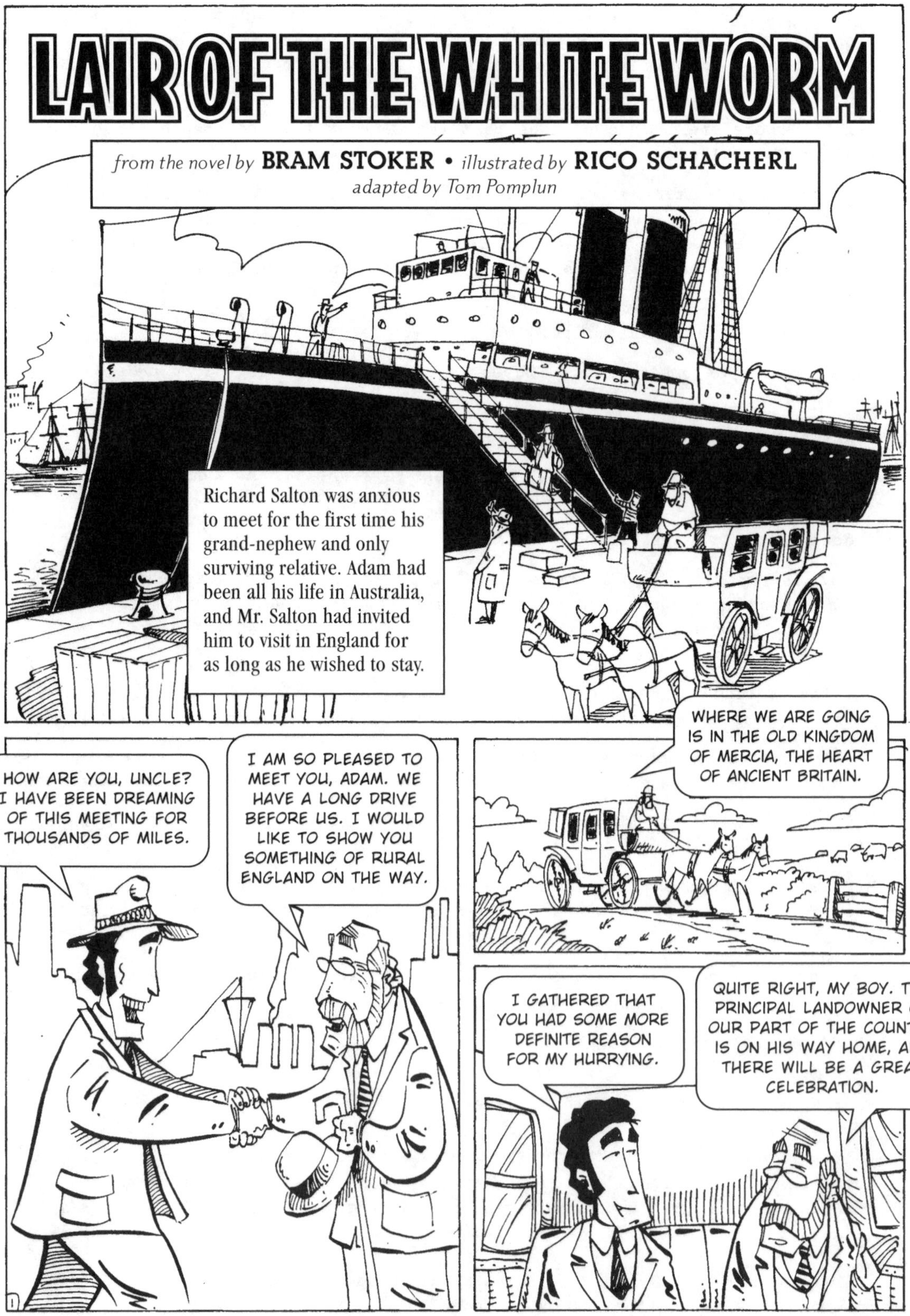
LAIR OF THE WHITE WORM
from the novel by BRAM STOKER • illustrated by RICO SCHACHERL
adapted by Tom Pomplun
Richard Salton was anxious to meet for the first time his grand-nephew and only surviving relative. Adam had been all his life in Australia, and Mr. Salton had invited him to visit in England for as long as he wished to stay.
HOW ARE YOU, UNCLE? I HAVE BEEN DREAMING OF THIS MEETING FOR THOUSANDS OF MILES.
I AM SO PLEASED TO MEET YOU, ADAM. WE HAVE A LONG DRIVE BEFORE US. I WOULD LIKE TO SHOW YOU SOMETHING OF RURAL ENGLAND ON THE WAY.
WHERE WE ARE GOING IS IN THE OLD KINGDOM OF MERCIA, THE HEART OF ANCIENT BRITAIN.
I GATHERED THAT YOU HAD SOME MORE DEFINITE REASON FOR MY HURRYING.
QUITE RIGHT, MY BOY. THE PRINCIPAL LANDOWNER OF OUR PART OF THE COUNTRY IS ON HIS WAY HOME, AND THERE WILL BE A GREAT CELEBRATION.

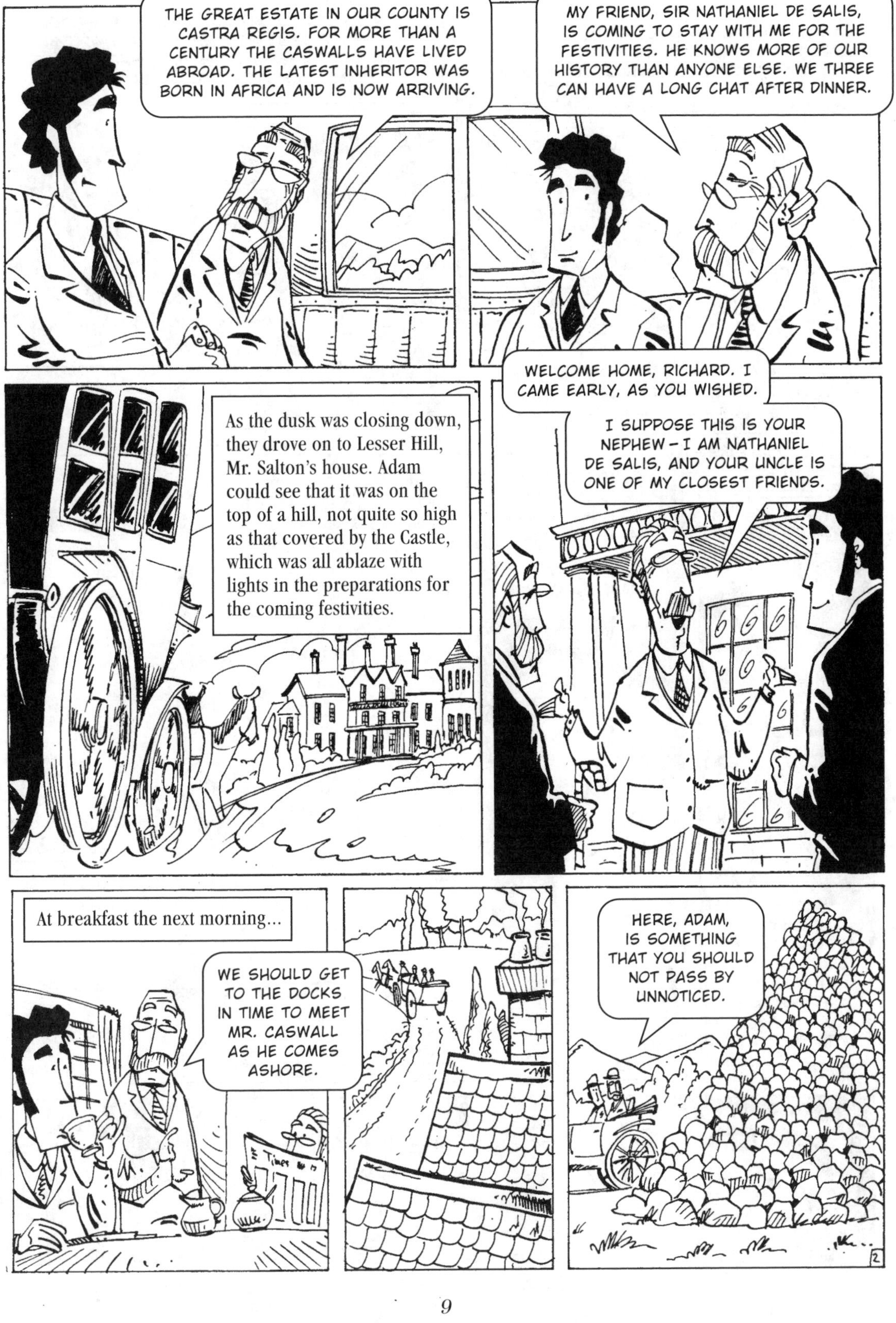
THE GREAT ESTATE IN OUR COUNTY IS CASTRA REGIS. FOR MORE THAN A CENTURY THE CASWALLS HAVE LIVED ABROAD. THE LATEST INHERITOR WAS BORN IN AFRICA AND IS NOW ARRIVING.
MY FRIEND, SIR NATHANIEL DE SALIS, IS COMING TO STAY WITH ME FOR THE FESTIVITIES. HE KNOWS MORE OF OUR HISTORY THAN ANYONE ELSE. WE THREE CAN HAVE A LONG CHAT AFTER DINNER.
As the dusk was closing down, they drove on to Lesser Hill, Mr. Salton's house. Adam could see that it was on the top of a hill, not quite so high as that covered by the Castle, which was all ablaze with lights in the preparations for the coming festivities.
WELCOME HOME, RICHARD. I CAME EARLY, AS YOU WISHED.
I SUPPOSE THIS IS YOUR NEPHEW – I AM NATHANIEL DE SALIS, AND YOUR UNCLE IS ONE OF MY CLOSEST FRIENDS.
At breakfast the next morning...
WE SHOULD GET TO THE DOCKS IN TIME TO MEET MR. CASWALL AS HE COMES ASHORE.
Times
HERE, ADAM, IS SOMETHING THAT YOU SHOULD NOT PASS BY UNNOTICED.
2

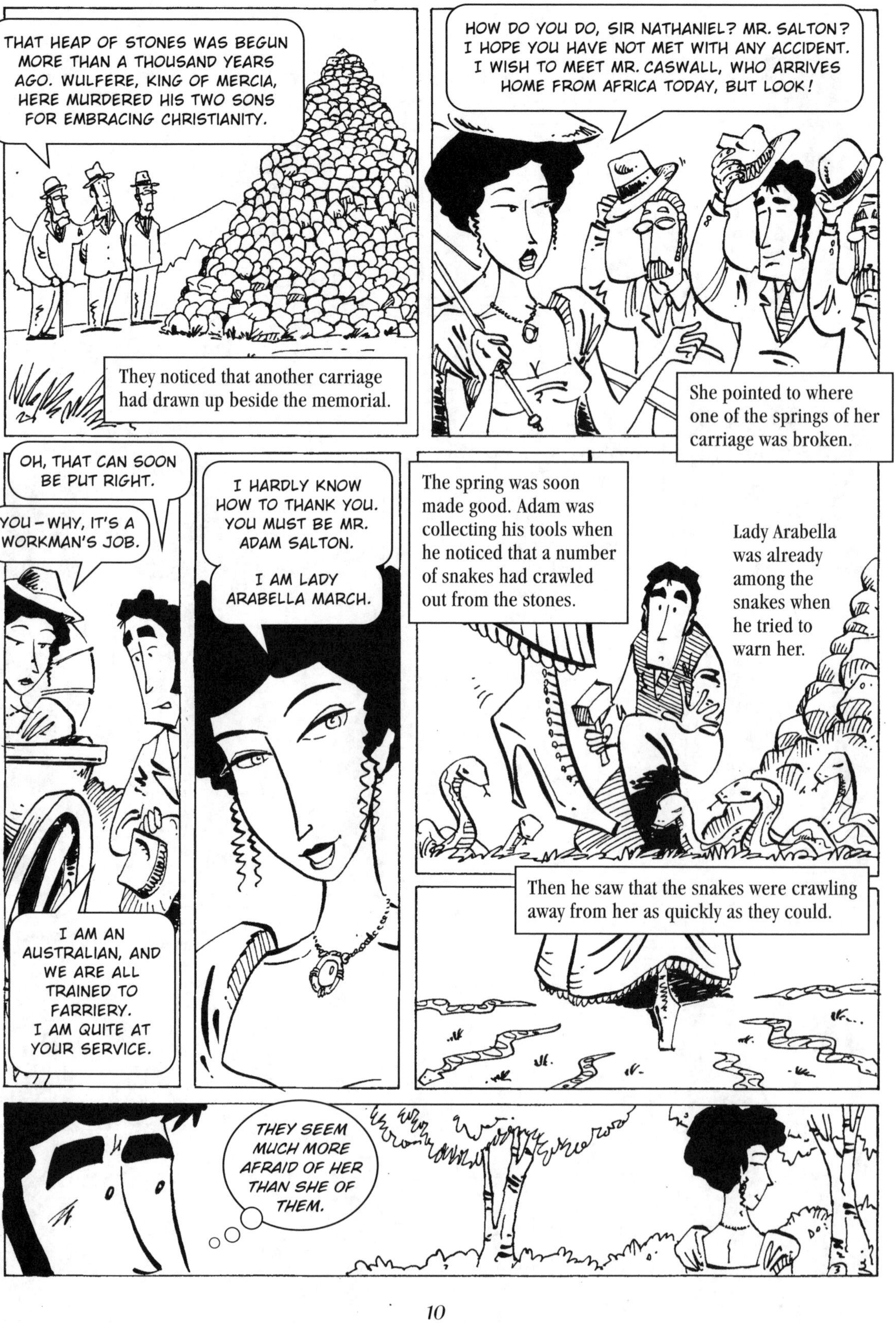
THAT HEAP OF STONES WAS BEGUN MORE THAN A THOUSAND YEARS AGO. WULFERE, KING OF MERCIA, HERE MURDERED HIS TWO SONS FOR EMBRACING CHRISTIANITY.
They noticed that another carriage had drawn up beside the memorial.
HOW DO YOU DO, SIR NATHANIEL? MR. SALTON? I HOPE YOU HAVE NOT MET WITH ANY ACCIDENT. I WISH TO MEET MR. CASWALL, WHO ARRIVES HOME FROM AFRICA TODAY, BUT LOOK!
She pointed to where one of the springs of her carriage was broken.
OH, THAT CAN SOON BE PUT RIGHT.
YOU—WHY, IT'S A WORKMAN'S JOB.
I AM AN AUSTRALIAN, AND WE ARE ALL TRAINED TO FARRIERY. I AM QUITE AT YOUR SERVICE.
I HARDLY KNOW HOW TO THANK YOU. YOU MUST BE MR. ADAM SALTON.
I AM LADY ARABELLA MARCH.
The spring was soon made good. Adam was collecting his tools when he noticed that a number of snakes had crawled out from the stones.
Lady Arabella was already among the snakes when he tried to warn her.
Then he saw that the snakes were crawling away from her as quickly as they could.
THEY SEEM MUCH MORE AFRAID OF HER THAN SHE OF THEM.

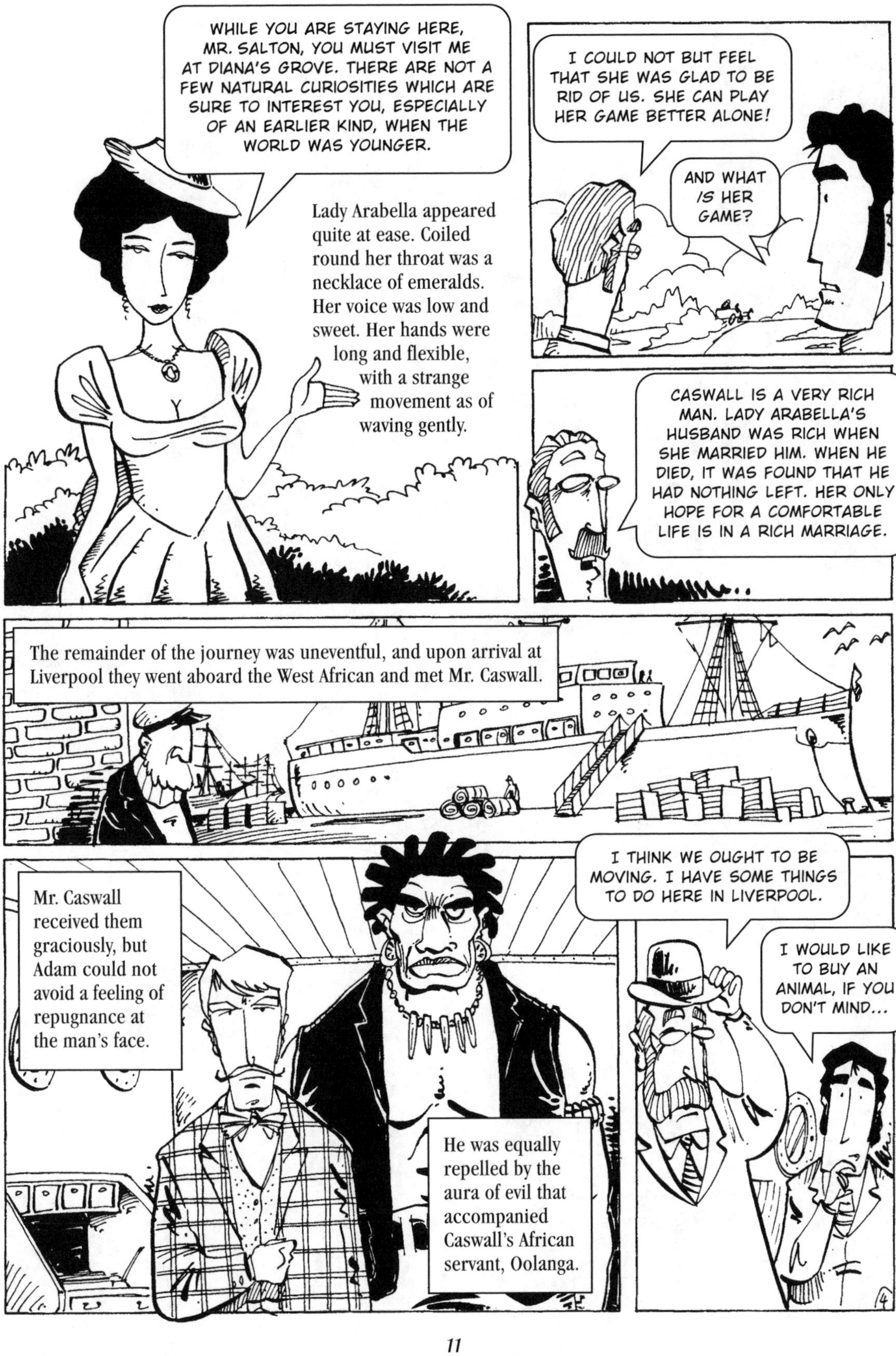
WHILE YOU ARE STAYING HERE, MR. SALTON, YOU MUST VISIT ME AT DIANA'S GROVE. THERE ARE NOT A FEW NATURAL CURIOSITIES WHICH ARE SURE TO INTEREST YOU, ESPECIALLY OF AN EARLIER KIND, WHEN THE WORLD WAS YOUNGER.
Lady Arabella appeared quite at ease. Coiled round her throat was a necklace of emeralds. Her voice was low and sweet. Her hands were long and flexible, with a strange movement as of waving gently.
I COULD NOT BUT FEEL THAT SHE WAS GLAD TO BE RID OF US. SHE CAN PLAY HER GAME BETTER ALONE!
AND WHAT IS HER GAME?
CASWALL IS A VERY RICH MAN. LADY ARABELLA'S HUSBAND WAS RICH WHEN SHE MARRIED HIM. WHEN HE DIED, IT WAS FOUND THAT HE HAD NOTHING LEFT. HER ONLY HOPE FOR A COMFORTABLE LIFE IS IN A RICH MARRIAGE.
The remainder of the journey was uneventful, and upon arrival at Liverpool they went aboard the West African and met Mr. Caswall.
Mr. Caswall received them graciously, but Adam could not avoid a feeling of repugnance at the man's face.
He was equally repelled by the aura of evil that accompanied Caswall's African servant, Oolanga.
I THINK WE OUGHT TO BE MOVING. I HAVE SOME THINGS TO DO HERE IN LIVERPOOL.
I WOULD LIKE TO BUY AN ANIMAL, IF YOU DON'T MIND...

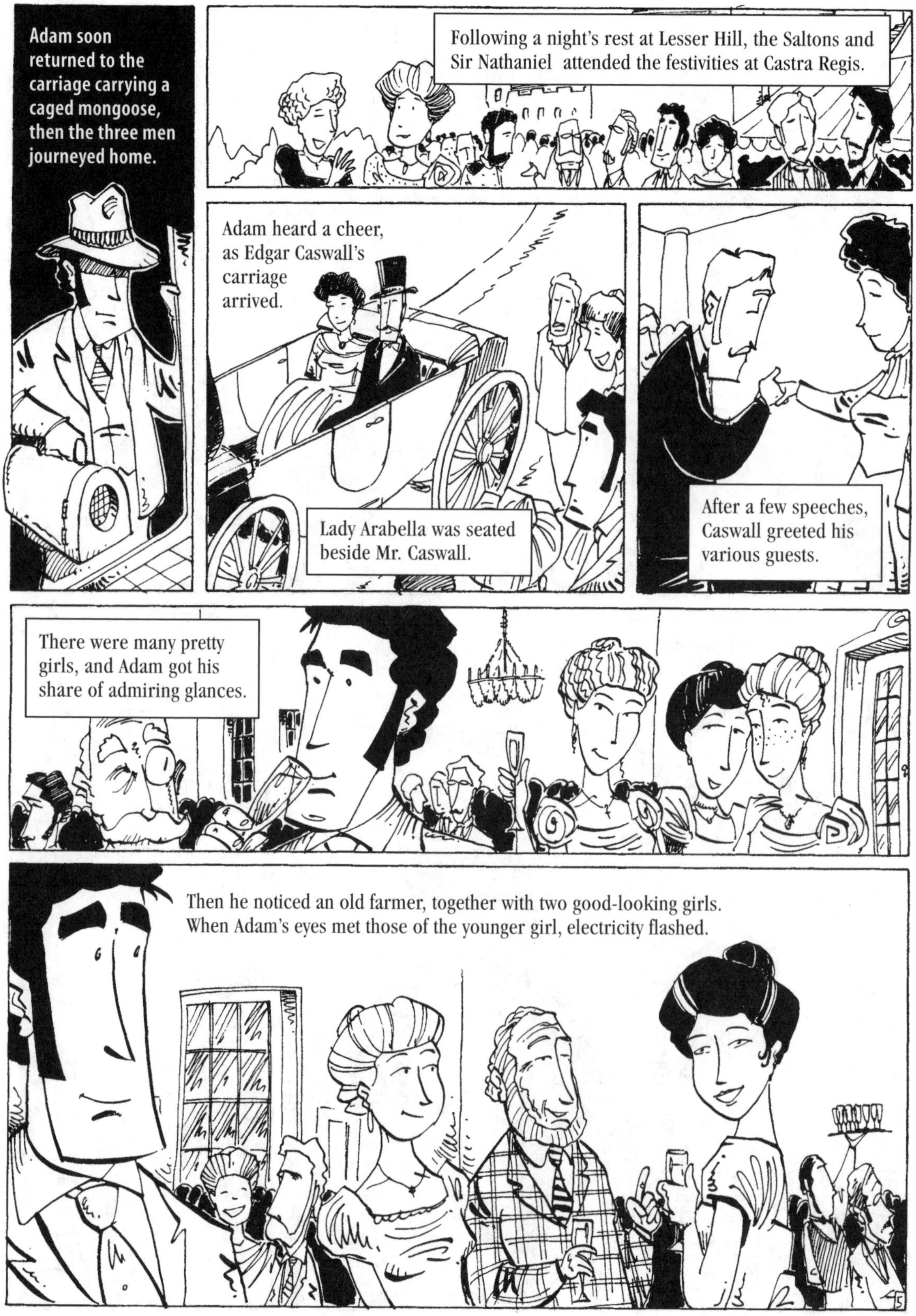
Adam soon returned to the carriage carrying a caged mongoose, then the three men journeyed home.
Following a night's rest at Lesser Hill, the Saltons and Sir Nathaniel attended the festivities at Castra Regis.
Adam heard a cheer, as Edgar Caswall's carriage arrived.
Lady Arabella was seated beside Mr. Caswall.
After a few speeches, Caswall greeted his various guests.
There were many pretty girls, and Adam got his share of admiring glances.
Then he noticed an old farmer, together with two good-looking girls. When Adam's eyes met those of the younger girl, electricity flashed.

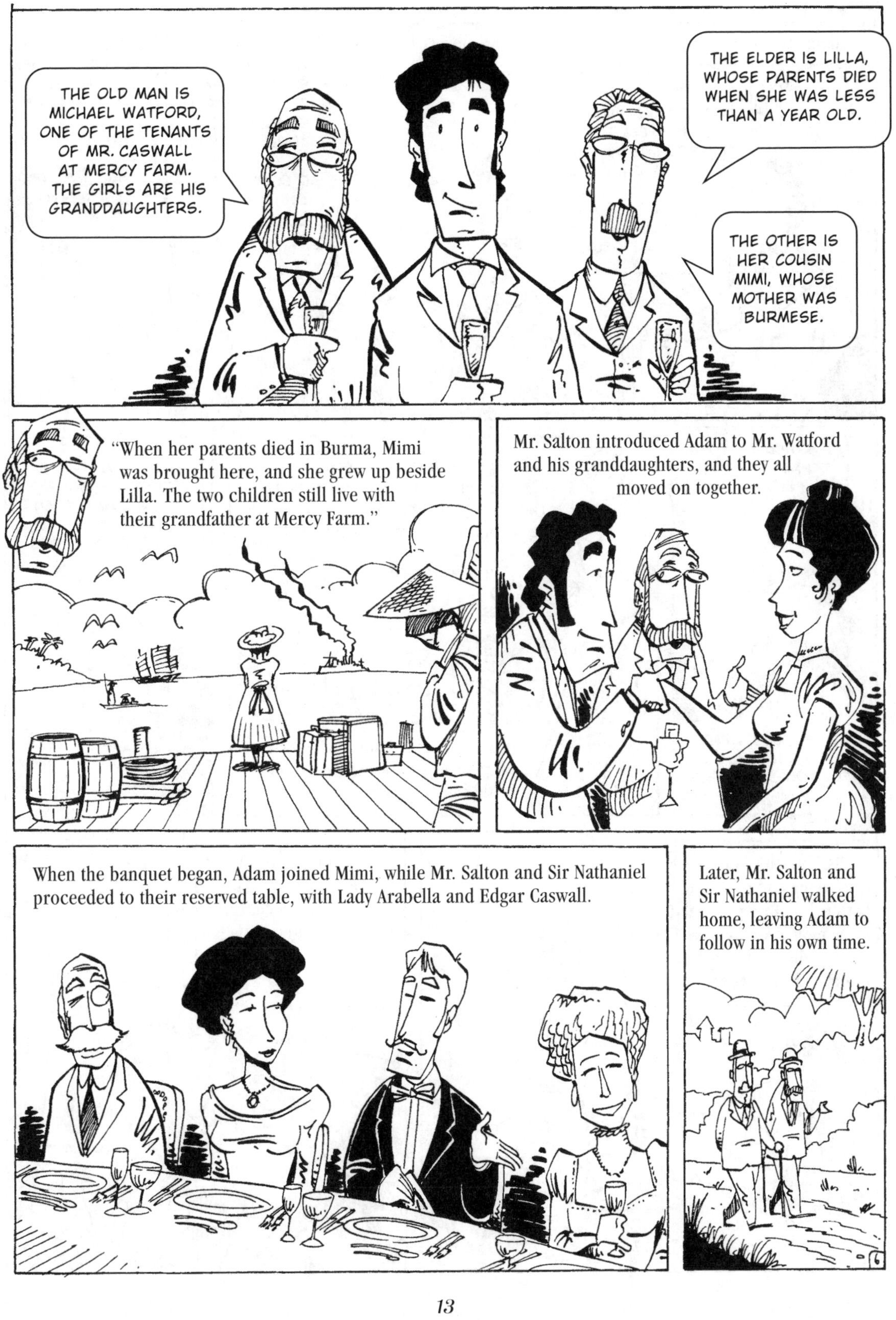
THE OLD MAN IS MICHAEL WATFORD, ONE OF THE TENANTS OF MR. CASWALL AT MERCY FARM. THE GIRLS ARE HIS GRANDDAUGHTERS.
THE ELDER IS LILLA, WHOSE PARENTS DIED WHEN SHE WAS LESS THAN A YEAR OLD.
THE OTHER IS HER COUSIN MIMI, WHOSE MOTHER WAS BURMESE.
"When her parents died in Burma, Mimi was brought here, and she grew up beside Lilla. The two children still live with their grandfather at Mercy Farm."
Mr. Salton introduced Adam to Mr. Watford and his granddaughters, and they all moved on together.
When the banquet began, Adam joined Mimi, while Mr. Salton and Sir Nathaniel proceeded to their reserved table, with Lady Arabella and Edgar Caswall.
Later, Mr. Salton and Sir Nathaniel walked home, leaving Adam to follow in his own time.

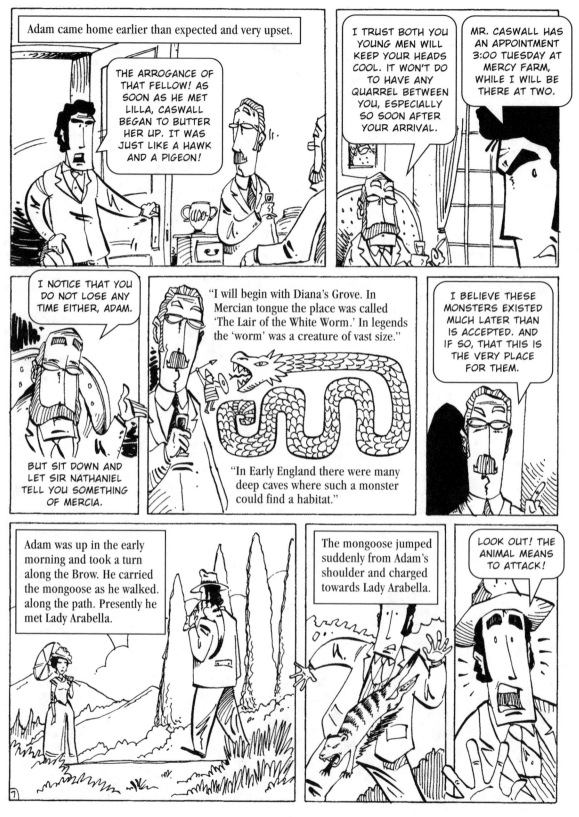

Adam came home earlier than expected and very upset.

THE ARROGANCE OF THAT FELLOW! AS SOON AS HE MET LILLA, CASWALL BEGAN TO BUTTER HER UP. IT WAS JUST LIKE A HAWK AND A PIGEON!

I TRUST BOTH YOU YOUNG MEN WILL KEEP YOUR HEADS COOL. IT WON'T DO TO HAVE ANY QUARREL BETWEEN YOU, ESPECIALLY SO SOON AFTER YOUR ARRIVAL.

MR. CASWALL HAS AN APPOINTMENT 3:00 TUESDAY AT MERCY FARM, WHILE I WILL BE THERE AT TWO.

I NOTICE THAT YOU DO NOT LOSE ANY TIME EITHER, ADAM.

BUT SIT DOWN AND LET SIR NATHANIEL TELL YOU SOMETHING OF MERCIA.

"I will begin with Diana's Grove. In Mercian tongue the place was called 'The Lair of the White Worm.' In legends the 'worm' was a creature of vast size."

"In Early England there were many deep caves where such a monster could find a habitat."

I BELIEVE THESE MONSTERS EXISTED MUCH LATER THAN IS ACCEPTED. AND IF SO, THAT THIS IS THE VERY PLACE FOR THEM.

Adam was up in the early morning and took a turn along the Brow. He carried the mongoose as he walked. along the path. Presently he met Lady Arabella.

The mongoose jumped suddenly from Adam's shoulder and charged towards Lady Arabella.

LOOK OUT! THE ANIMAL MEANS TO ATTACK!

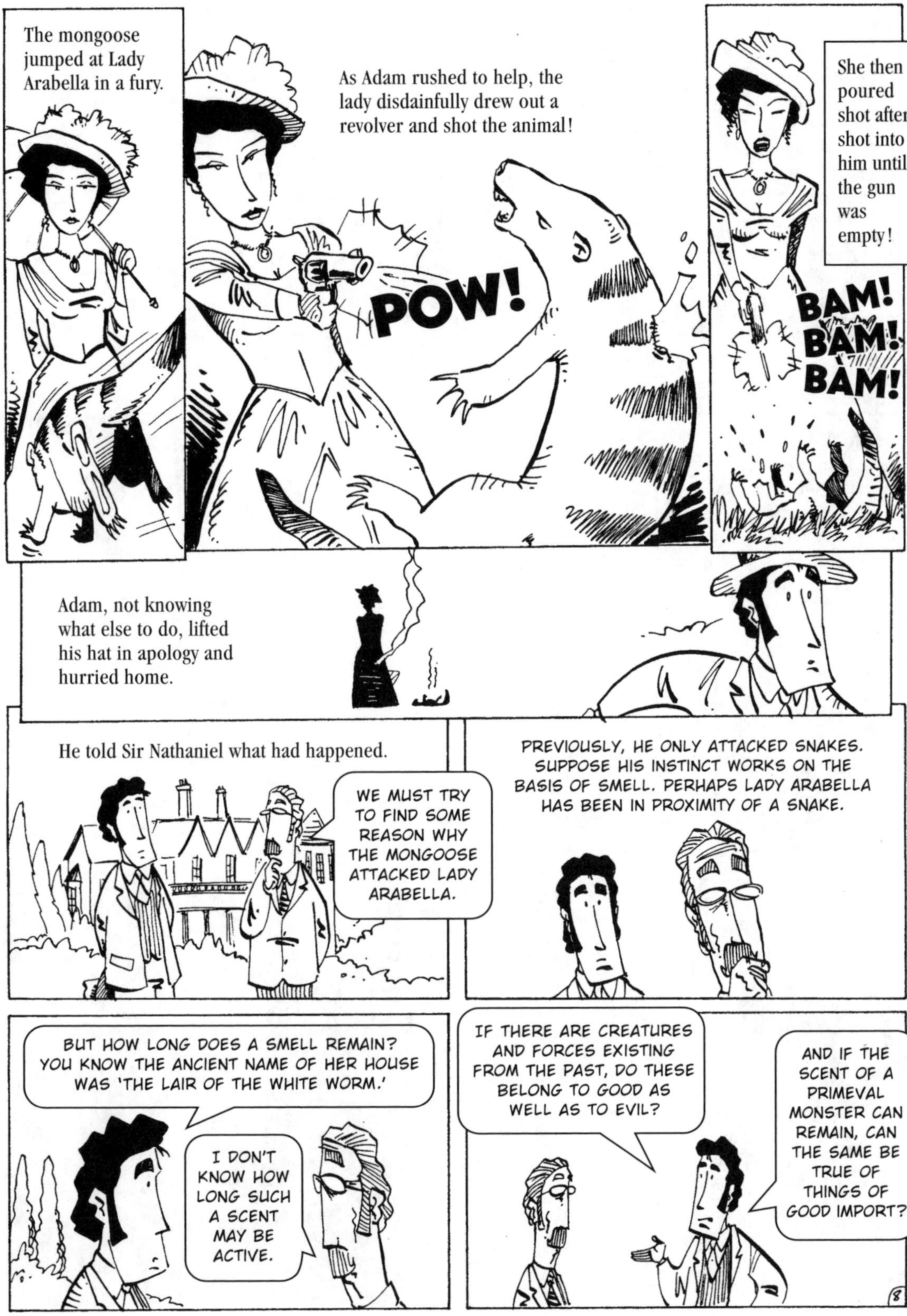
The mongoose jumped at Lady Arabella in a fury.
As Adam rushed to help, the lady disdainfully drew out a revolver and shot the animal!
POW!
She then poured shot after shot into him until the gun was empty!
BAM! BAM! BAM!
Adam, not knowing what else to do, lifted his hat in apology and hurried home.
He told Sir Nathaniel what had happened.
WE MUST TRY TO FIND SOME REASON WHY THE MONGOOSE ATTACKED LADY ARABELLA.
PREVIOUSLY, HE ONLY ATTACKED SNAKES. SUPPOSE HIS INSTINCT WORKS ON THE BASIS OF SMELL. PERHAPS LADY ARABELLA HAS BEEN IN PROXIMITY OF A SNAKE.
BUT HOW LONG DOES A SMELL REMAIN? YOU KNOW THE ANCIENT NAME OF HER HOUSE WAS 'THE LAIR OF THE WHITE WORM.'
I DON'T KNOW HOW LONG SUCH A SCENT MAY BE ACTIVE.
IF THERE ARE CREATURES AND FORCES EXISTING FROM THE PAST, DO THESE BELONG TO GOOD AS WELL AS TO EVIL?
AND IF THE SCENT OF A PRIMEVAL MONSTER CAN REMAIN, CAN THE SAME BE TRUE OF THINGS OF GOOD IMPORT?
8

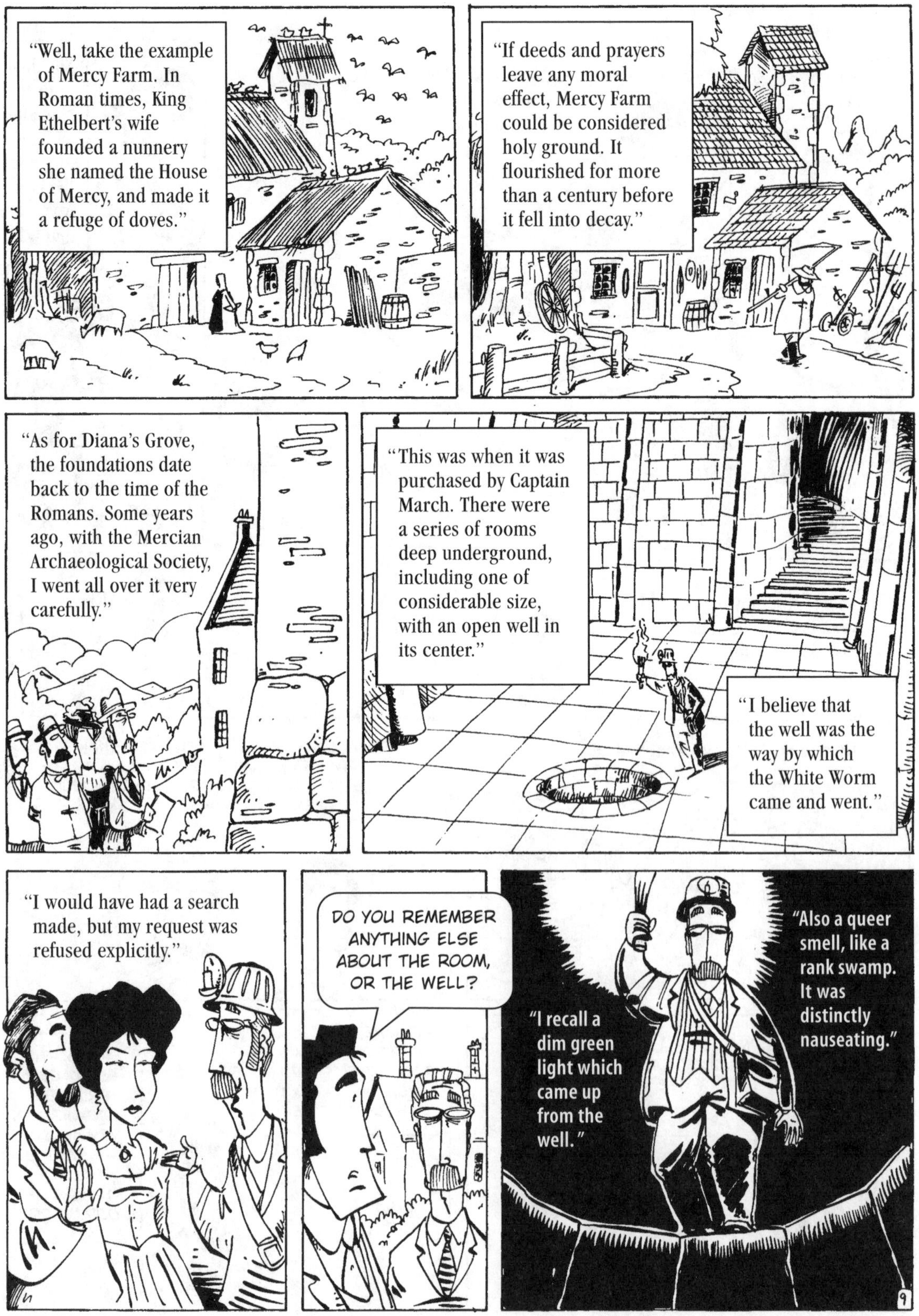
"Well, take the example of Mercy Farm. In Roman times, King Ethelbert's wife founded a nunnery she named the House of Mercy, and made it a refuge of doves."
"If deeds and prayers leave any moral effect, Mercy Farm could be considered holy ground. It flourished for more than a century before it fell into decay."
"As for Diana's Grove, the foundations date back to the time of the Romans. Some years ago, with the Mercian Archaeological Society, I went all over it very carefully."
"This was when it was purchased by Captain March. There were a series of rooms deep underground, including one of considerable size, with an open well in its center."
"I believe that the well was the way by which the White Worm came and went."
"I would have had a search made, but my request was refused explicitly."
DO YOU REMEMBER ANYTHING ELSE ABOUT THE ROOM, OR THE WELL?
"I recall a dim green light which came up from the well."
"Also a queer smell, like a rank swamp. It was distinctly nauseating."

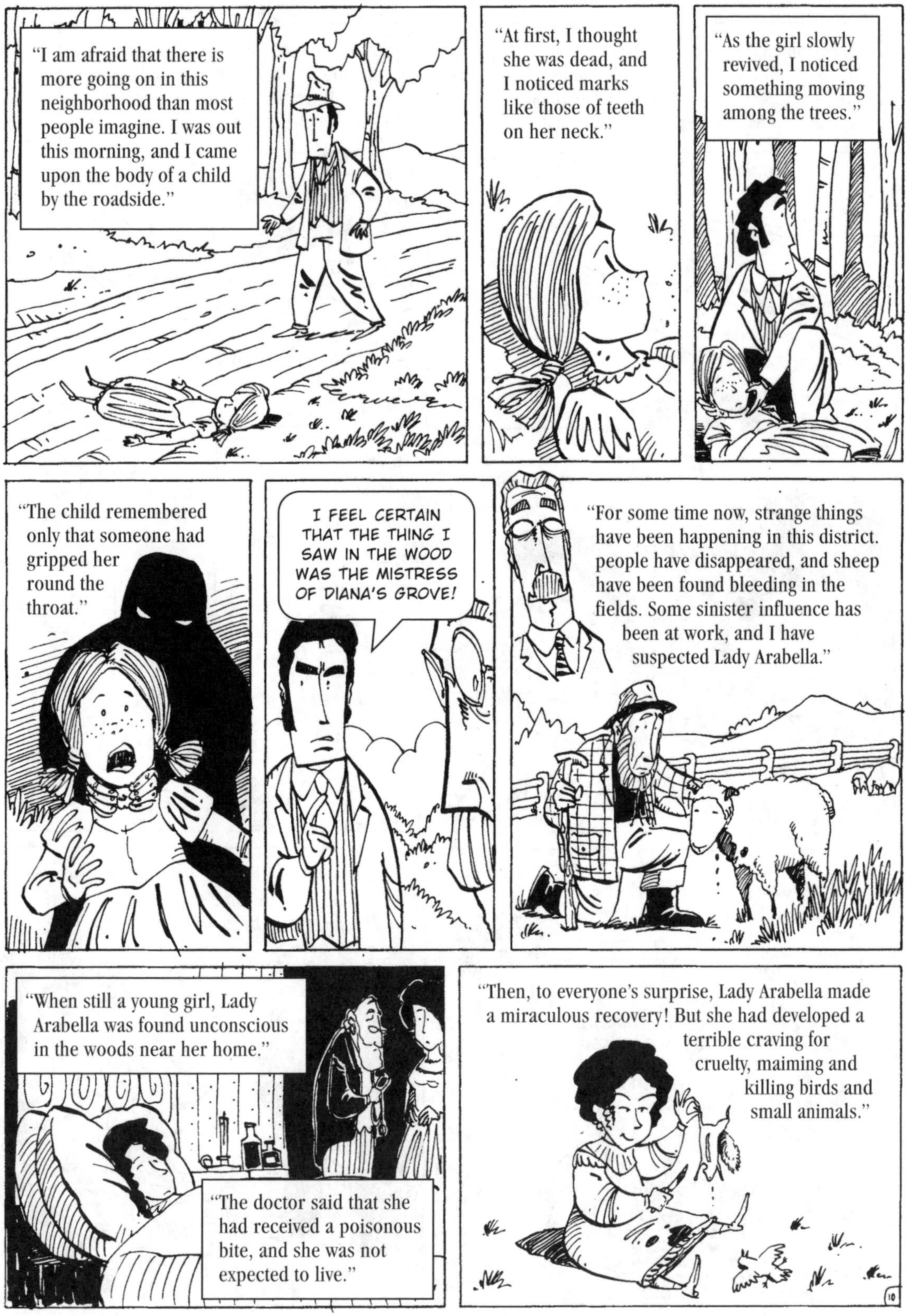
"I am afraid that there is more going on in this neighborhood than most people imagine. I was out this morning, and I came upon the body of a child by the roadside."
"At first, I thought she was dead, and I noticed marks like those of teeth on her neck."
"As the girl slowly revived, I noticed something moving among the trees."
"The child remembered only that someone had gripped her round the throat."
I FEEL CERTAIN THAT THE THING I SAW IN THE WOOD WAS THE MISTRESS OF DIANA'S GROVE!
"For some time now, strange things have been happening in this district. people have disappeared, and sheep have been found bleeding in the fields. Some sinister influence has been at work, and I have suspected Lady Arabella."
"When still a young girl, Lady Arabella was found unconscious in the woods near her home."
"The doctor said that she had received a poisonous bite, and she was not expected to live."
"Then, to everyone's surprise, Lady Arabella made a miraculous recovery! But she had developed a terrible craving for cruelty, maiming and killing birds and small animals."
10

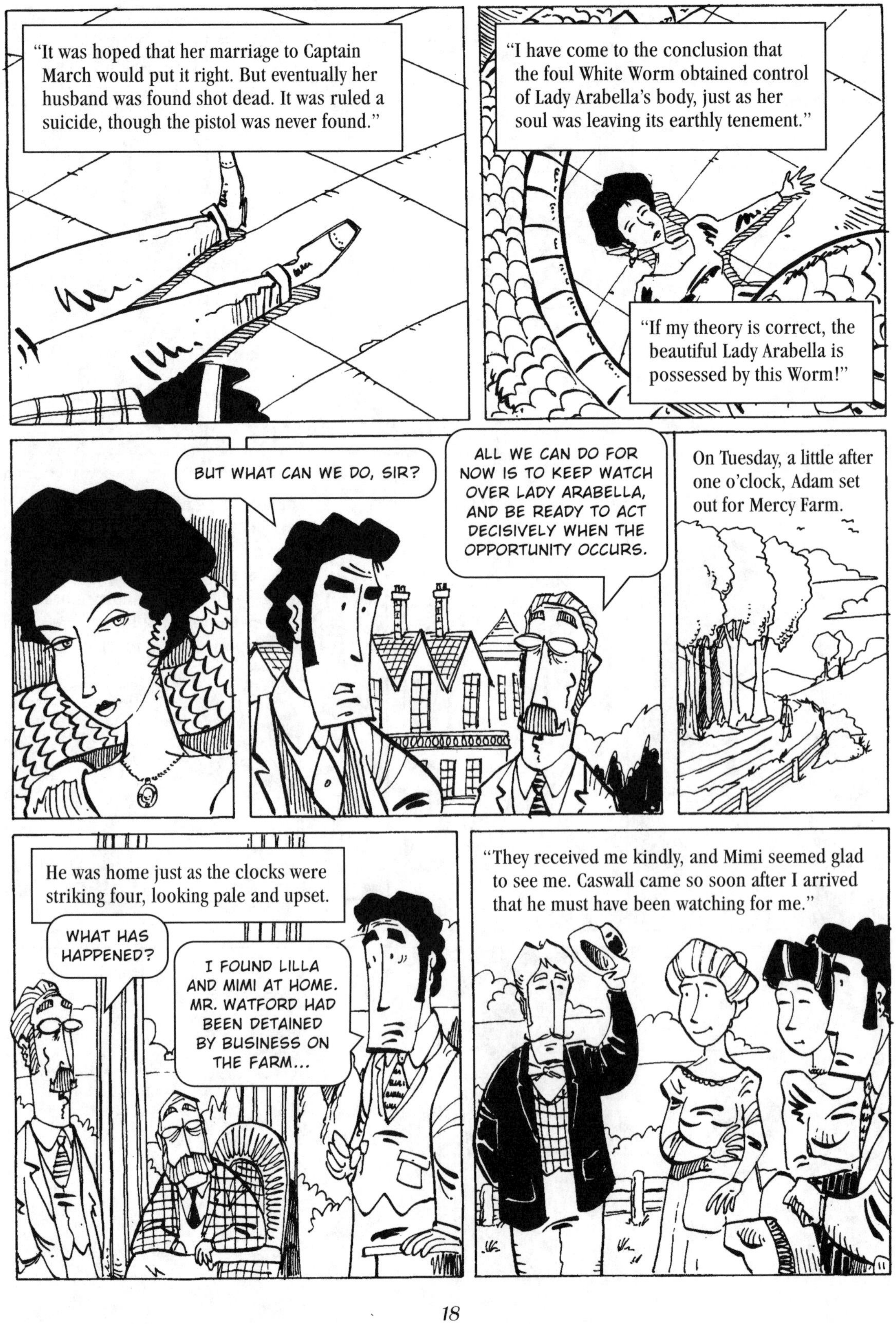
"It was hoped that her marriage to Captain March would put it right. But eventually her husband was found shot dead. It was ruled a suicide, though the pistol was never found."
"I have come to the conclusion that the foul White Worm obtained control of Lady Arabella's body, just as her soul was leaving its earthly tenement."
"If my theory is correct, the beautiful Lady Arabella is possessed by this Worm!"
BUT WHAT CAN WE DO, SIR?
ALL WE CAN DO FOR NOW IS TO KEEP WATCH OVER LADY ARABELLA, AND BE READY TO ACT DECISIVELY WHEN THE OPPORTUNITY OCCURS.
On Tuesday, a little after one o'clock, Adam set out for Mercy Farm.
He was home just as the clocks were striking four, looking pale and upset.
WHAT HAS HAPPENED?
I FOUND LILLA AND MIMI AT HOME. MR. WATFORD HAD BEEN DETAINED BY BUSINESS ON THE FARM...
"They received me kindly, and Mimi seemed glad to see me. Caswall came so soon after I arrived that he must have been watching for me."

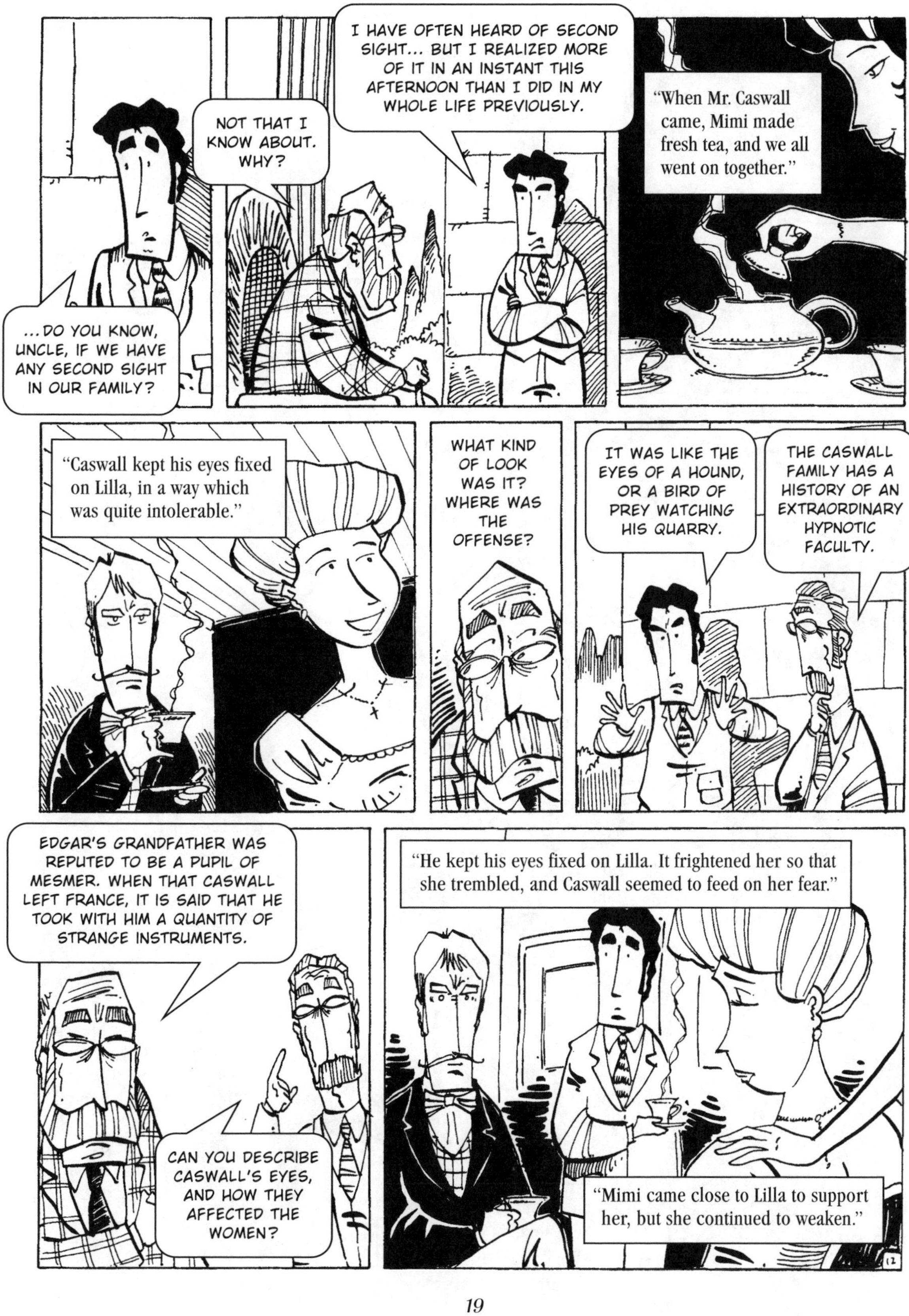
...DO YOU KNOW, UNCLE, IF WE HAVE ANY SECOND SIGHT IN OUR FAMILY?
NOT THAT I KNOW ABOUT. WHY?
I HAVE OFTEN HEARD OF SECOND SIGHT... BUT I REALIZED MORE OF IT IN AN INSTANT THIS AFTERNOON THAN I DID IN MY WHOLE LIFE PREVIOUSLY.
"When Mr. Caswall came, Mimi made fresh tea, and we all went on together."
"Caswall kept his eyes fixed on Lilla, in a way which was quite intolerable."
WHAT KIND OF LOOK WAS IT? WHERE WAS THE OFFENSE?
IT WAS LIKE THE EYES OF A HOUND, OR A BIRD OF PREY WATCHING HIS QUARRY.
THE CASWALL FAMILY HAS A HISTORY OF AN EXTRAORDINARY HYPNOTIC FACULTY.
EDGAR'S GRANDFATHER WAS REPUTED TO BE A PUPIL OF MESMER. WHEN THAT CASWALL LEFT FRANCE, IT IS SAID THAT HE TOOK WITH HIM A QUANTITY OF STRANGE INSTRUMENTS.
CAN YOU DESCRIBE CASWALL'S EYES, AND HOW THEY AFFECTED THE WOMEN?
"He kept his eyes fixed on Lilla. It frightened her so that she trembled, and Caswall seemed to feed on her fear."
"Mimi came close to Lilla to support her, but she continued to weaken."

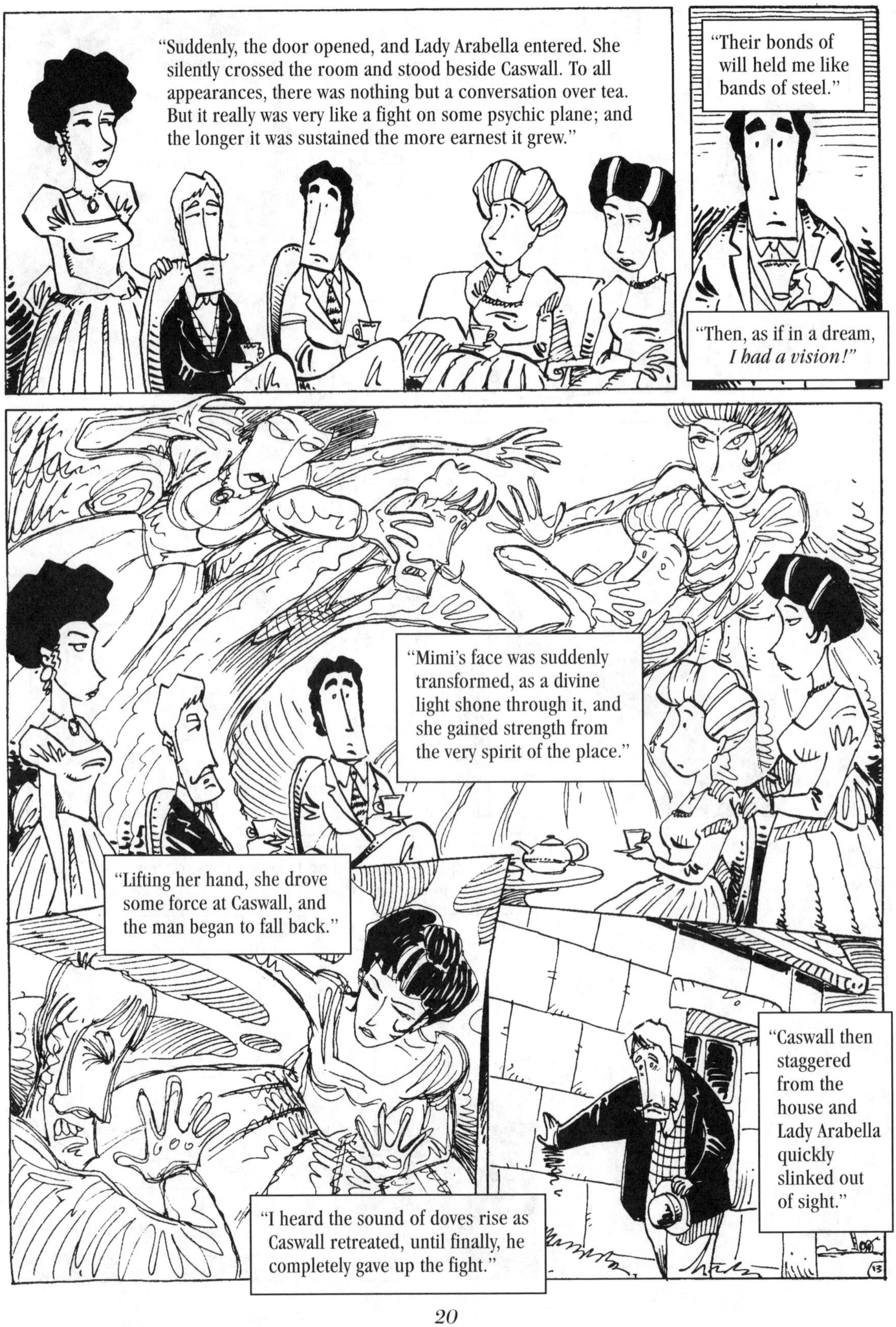
"Suddenly, the door opened, and Lady Arabella entered. She silently crossed the room and stood beside Caswall. To all appearances, there was nothing but a conversation over tea. But it really was very like a fight on some psychic plane; and the longer it was sustained the more earnest it grew."
"Their bonds of will held me like bands of steel."
"Then, as if in a dream, *I had a vision!*"
"Mimi's face was suddenly transformed, as a divine light shone through it, and she gained strength from the very spirit of the place."
"Lifting her hand, she drove some force at Caswall, and the man began to fall back."
"I heard the sound of doves rise as Caswall retreated, until finally, he completely gave up the fight."
"Caswall then staggered from the house and Lady Arabella quickly slinked out of sight."

"All at once my own faculties were restored."

"I saw Lilla sink in a swoon, but Mimi was triumphant."

Meanwhile, the sunlight was being eclipsed by an onrush of doves.

THIS INCIDENT WITH MR. CASWALL IS TERRIBLE NEWS!

I FEAR IT IS ONLY THE BEGINNING.

The next morning, reports were received of an enormous immigration of doves, soon joined by a multitude of other birds.

Edgar Caswall tortured his brain to think of some means of getting rid of the plague of birds.

At last he recalled a solution, utilized by Chinese farmers during their rice harvests...

Mr. Caswall ordered his men to construct an immense kite shaped like a great hawk. The moment it rose into the air, the birds began to disappear. The following morning, no bird was to be seen near Castra Regis.

Caswall became completely absorbed in watching the flight of his kite, often all day long, and into the night.

The neighbors thought he was going mad.

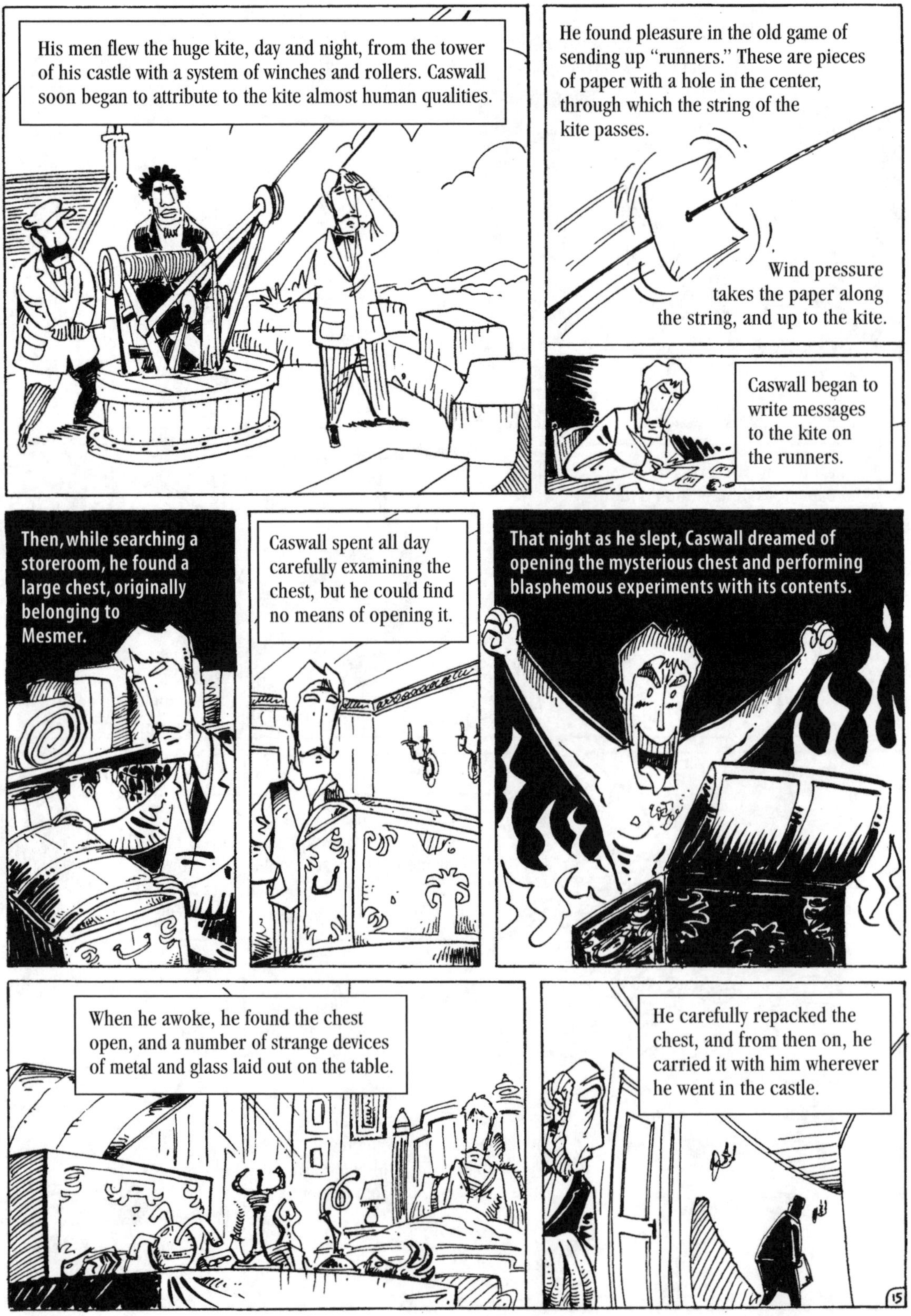
His men flew the huge kite, day and night, from the tower of his castle with a system of winches and rollers. Caswall soon began to attribute to the kite almost human qualities.
He found pleasure in the old game of sending up "runners." These are pieces of paper with a hole in the center, through which the string of the kite passes.
Wind pressure takes the paper along the string, and up to the kite.
Caswall began to write messages to the kite on the runners.
Then, while searching a storeroom, he found a large chest, originally belonging to Mesmer.
Caswall spent all day carefully examining the chest, but he could find no means of opening it.
That night as he slept, Caswall dreamed of opening the mysterious chest and performing blasphemous experiments with its contents.
When he awoke, he found the chest open, and a number of strange devices of metal and glass laid out on the table.
He carefully repacked the chest, and from then on, he carried it with him wherever he went in the castle.
15

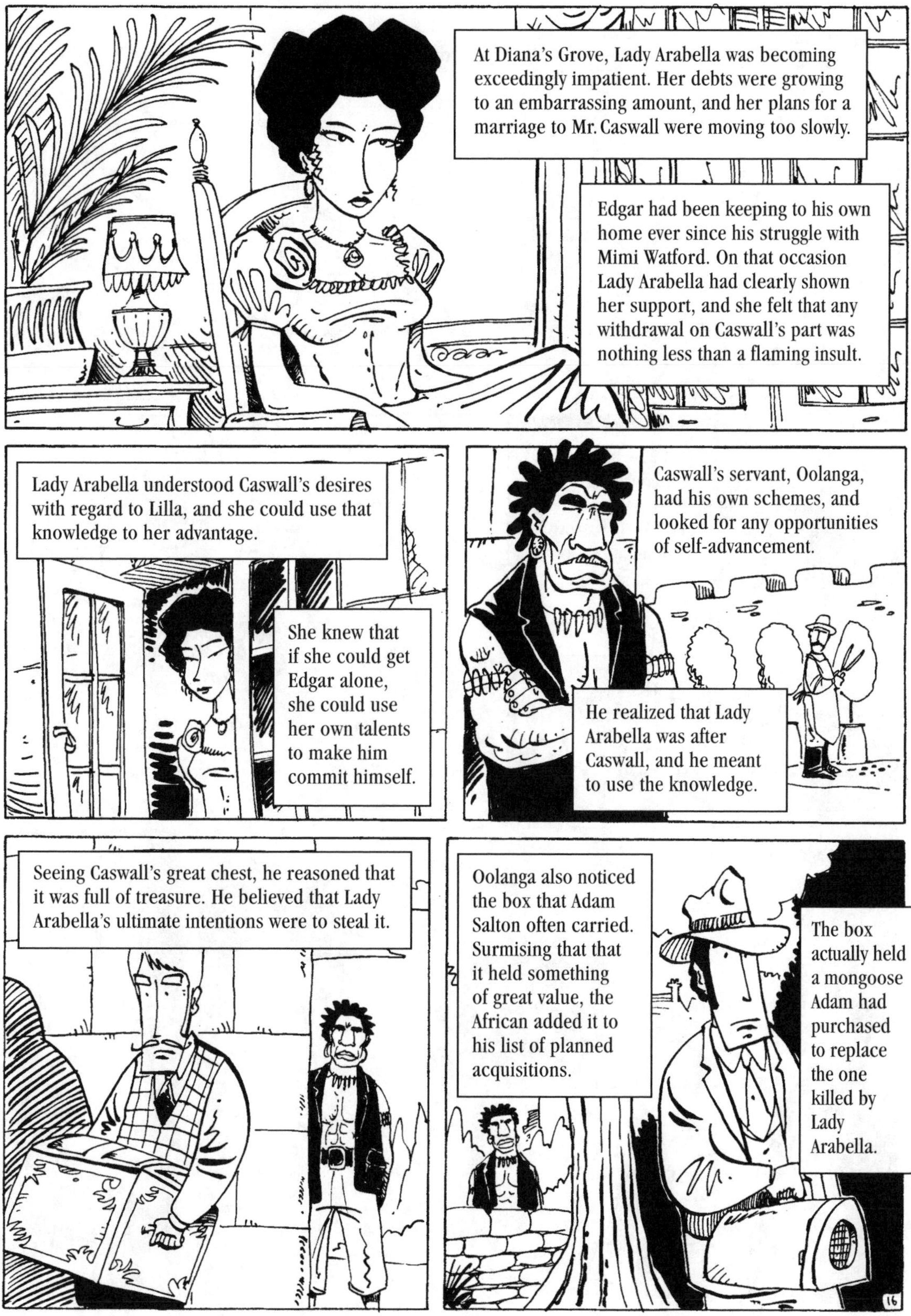
At Diana's Grove, Lady Arabella was becoming exceedingly impatient. Her debts were growing to an embarrassing amount, and her plans for a marriage to Mr. Caswall were moving too slowly.
Edgar had been keeping to his own home ever since his struggle with Mimi Watford. On that occasion Lady Arabella had clearly shown her support, and she felt that any withdrawal on Caswall's part was nothing less than a flaming insult.
Lady Arabella understood Caswall's desires with regard to Lilla, and she could use that knowledge to her advantage.
She knew that if she could get Edgar alone, she could use her own talents to make him commit himself.
Caswall's servant, Oolanga, had his own schemes, and looked for any opportunities of self-advancement.
He realized that Lady Arabella was after Caswall, and he meant to use the knowledge.
Seeing Caswall's great chest, he reasoned that it was full of treasure. He believed that Lady Arabella's ultimate intentions were to steal it.
Oolanga also noticed the box that Adam Salton often carried. Surmising that that it held something of great value, the African added it to his list of planned acquisitions.
The box actually held a mongoose Adam had purchased to replace the one killed by Lady Arabella.
16

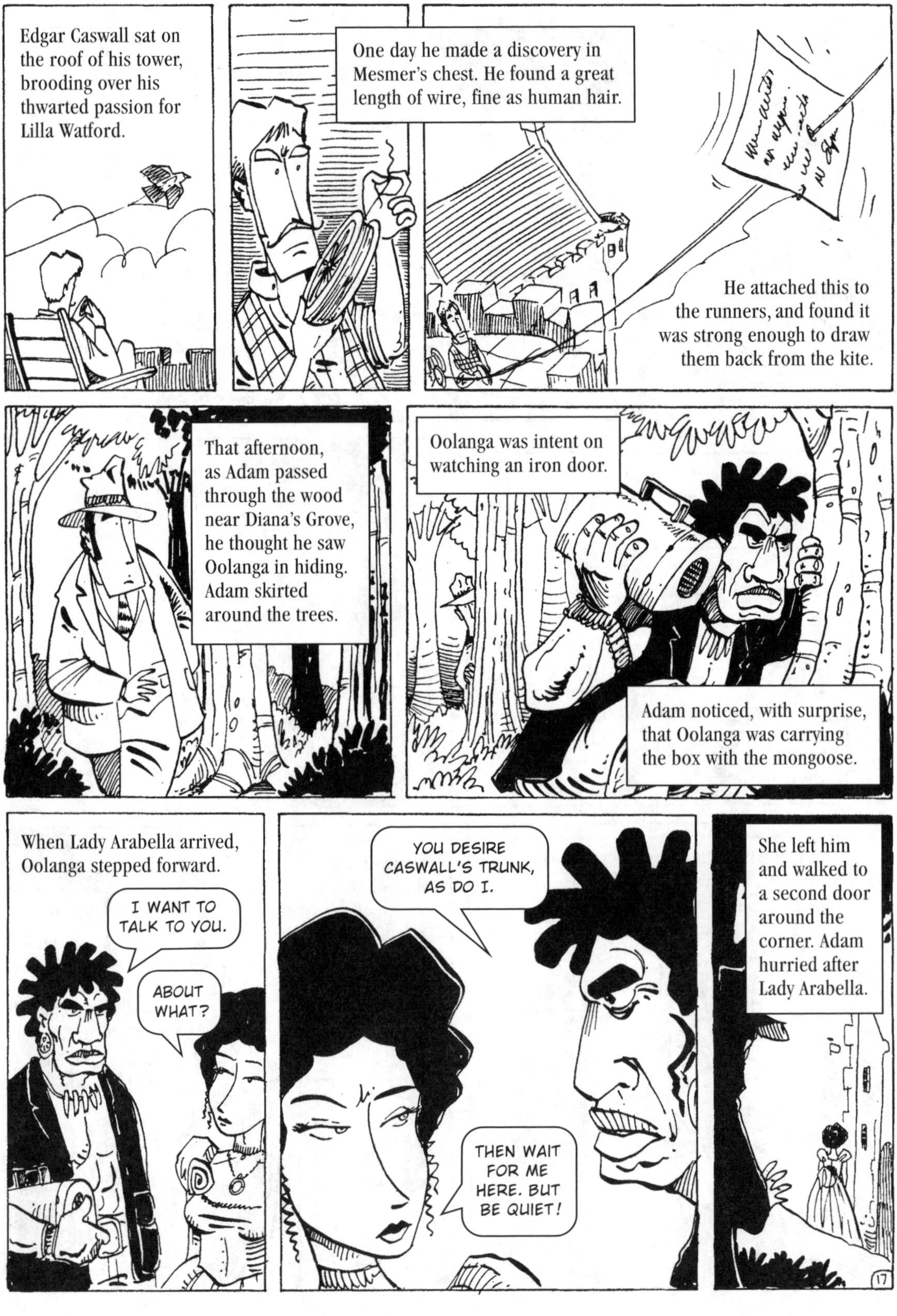
Edgar Caswall sat on the roof of his tower, brooding over his thwarted passion for Lilla Watford.
One day he made a discovery in Mesmer's chest. He found a great length of wire, fine as human hair.
He attached this to the runners, and found it was strong enough to draw them back from the kite.
That afternoon, as Adam passed through the wood near Diana's Grove, he thought he saw Oolanga in hiding. Adam skirted around the trees.
Oolanga was intent on watching an iron door.
Adam noticed, with surprise, that Oolanga was carrying the box with the mongoose.
When Lady Arabella arrived, Oolanga stepped forward.
I WANT TO TALK TO YOU.
ABOUT WHAT?
YOU DESIRE CASWALL'S TRUNK, AS DO I.
THEN WAIT FOR ME HERE. BUT BE QUIET!
She left him and walked to a second door around the corner. Adam hurried after Lady Arabella.

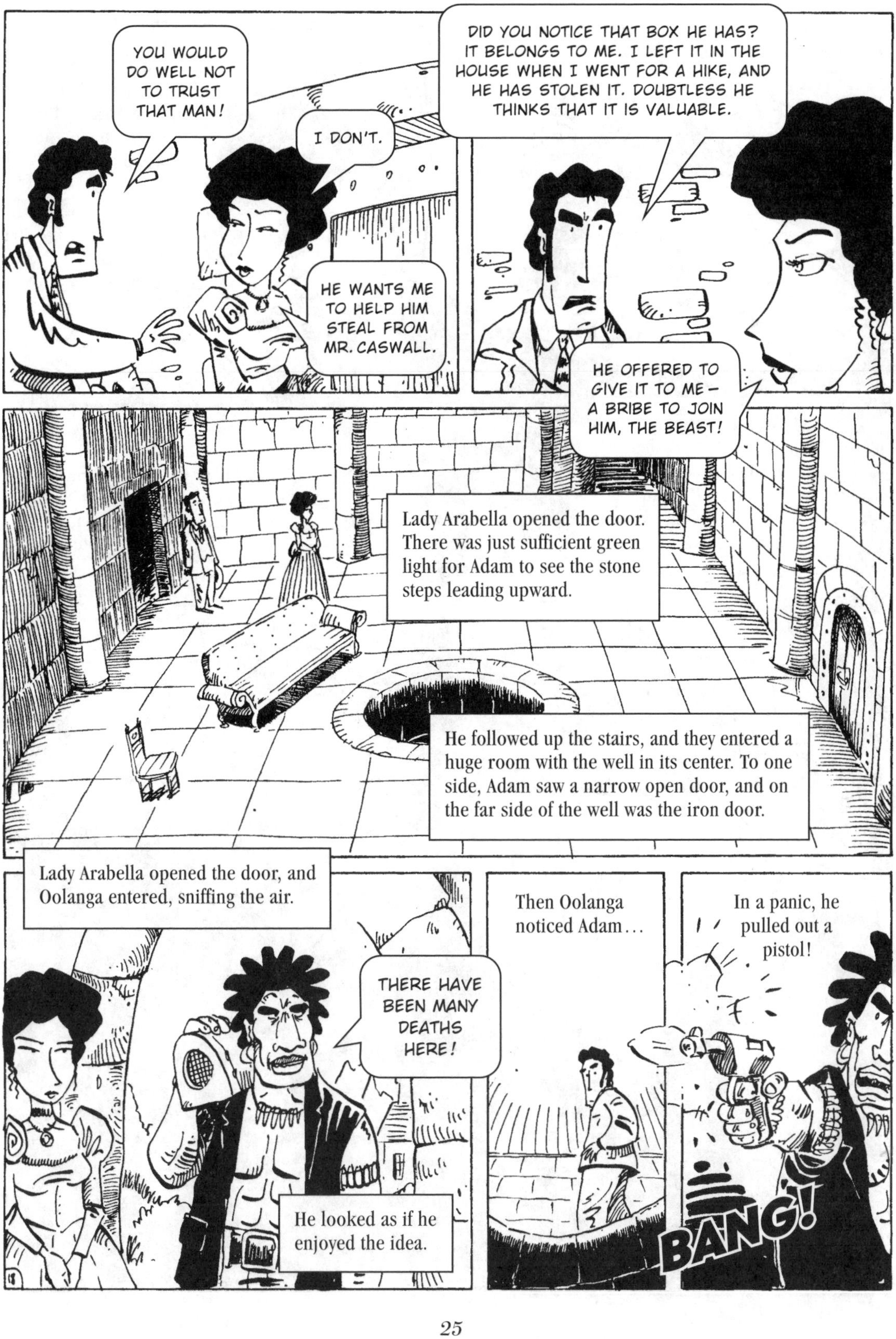
YOU WOULD DO WELL NOT TO TRUST THAT MAN!
I DON'T.
HE WANTS ME TO HELP HIM STEAL FROM MR. CASWALL.
DID YOU NOTICE THAT BOX HE HAS? IT BELONGS TO ME. I LEFT IT IN THE HOUSE WHEN I WENT FOR A HIKE, AND HE HAS STOLEN IT. DOUBTLESS HE THINKS THAT IT IS VALUABLE.
HE OFFERED TO GIVE IT TO ME – A BRIBE TO JOIN HIM, THE BEAST!
Lady Arabella opened the door. There was just sufficient green light for Adam to see the stone steps leading upward.
He followed up the stairs, and they entered a huge room with the well in its center. To one side, Adam saw a narrow open door, and on the far side of the well was the iron door.
Lady Arabella opened the door, and Oolanga entered, sniffing the air.
THERE HAVE BEEN MANY DEATHS HERE!
He looked as if he enjoyed the idea.
Then Oolanga noticed Adam…
In a panic, he pulled out a pistol!
BANG!

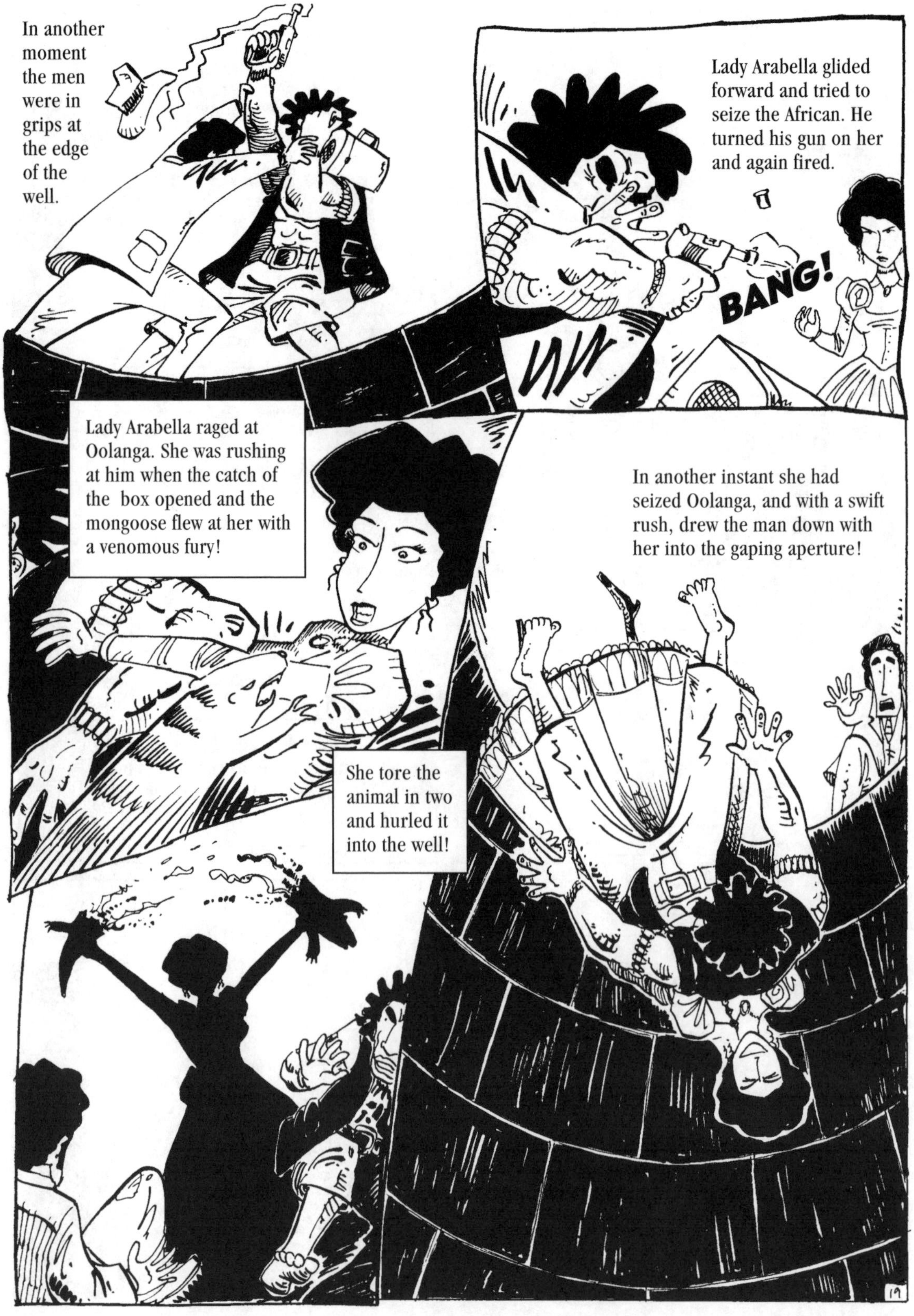
In another moment the men were in grips at the edge of the well.
Lady Arabella glided forward and tried to seize the African. He turned his gun on her and again fired.
BANG!
Lady Arabella raged at Oolanga. She was rushing at him when the catch of the box opened and the mongoose flew at her with a venomous fury!
She tore the animal in two and hurled it into the well!
In another instant she had seized Oolanga, and with a swift rush, drew the man down with her into the gaping aperture!
19

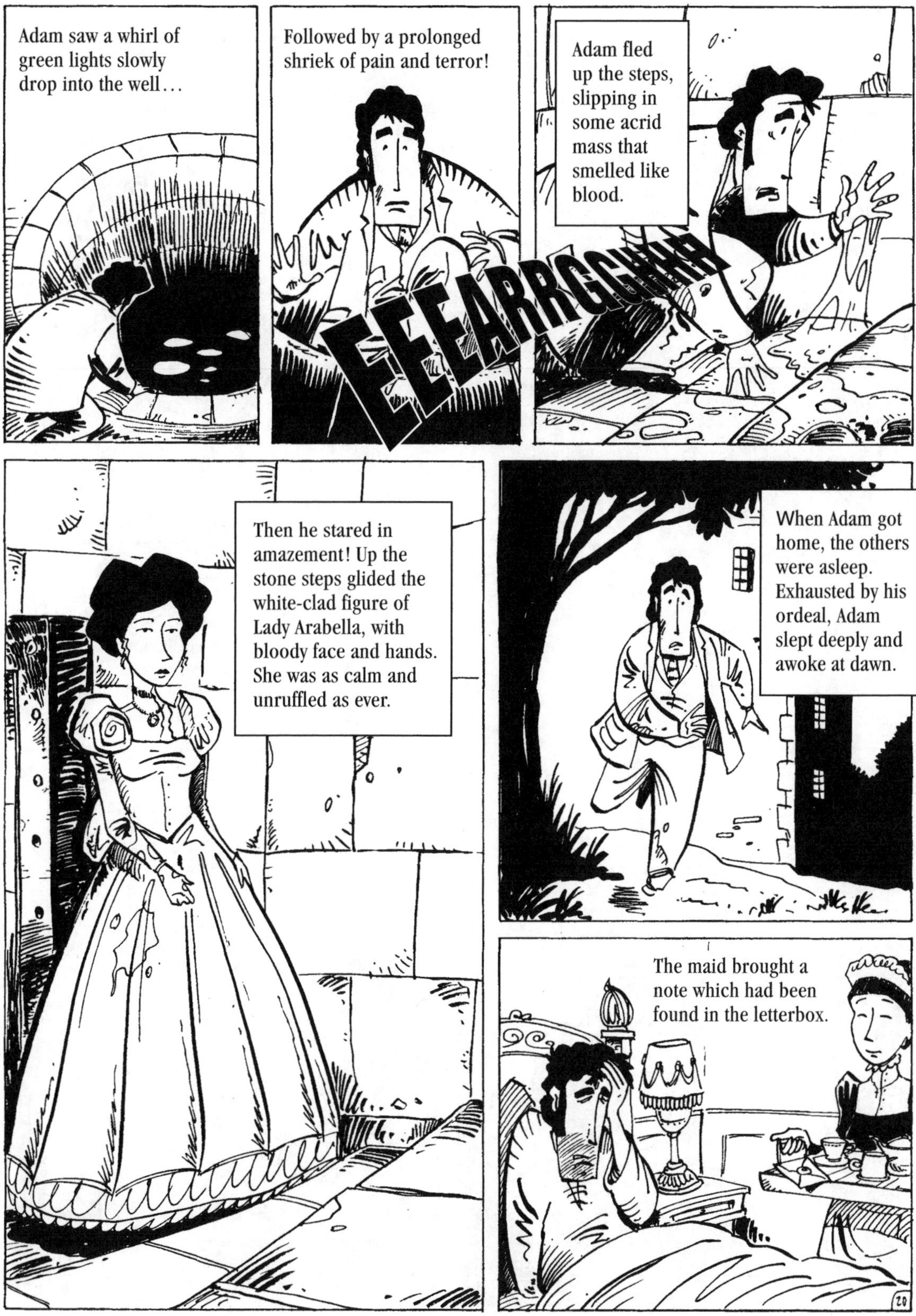
Adam saw a whirl of green lights slowly drop into the well…
Followed by a prolonged shriek of pain and terror!
EEEARRGGHHH
Adam fled up the steps, slipping in some acrid mass that smelled like blood.
Then he stared in amazement! Up the stone steps glided the white-clad figure of Lady Arabella, with bloody face and hands. She was as calm and unruffled as ever.
When Adam got home, the others were asleep. Exhausted by his ordeal, Adam slept deeply and awoke at dawn.
The maid brought a note which had been found in the letterbox.

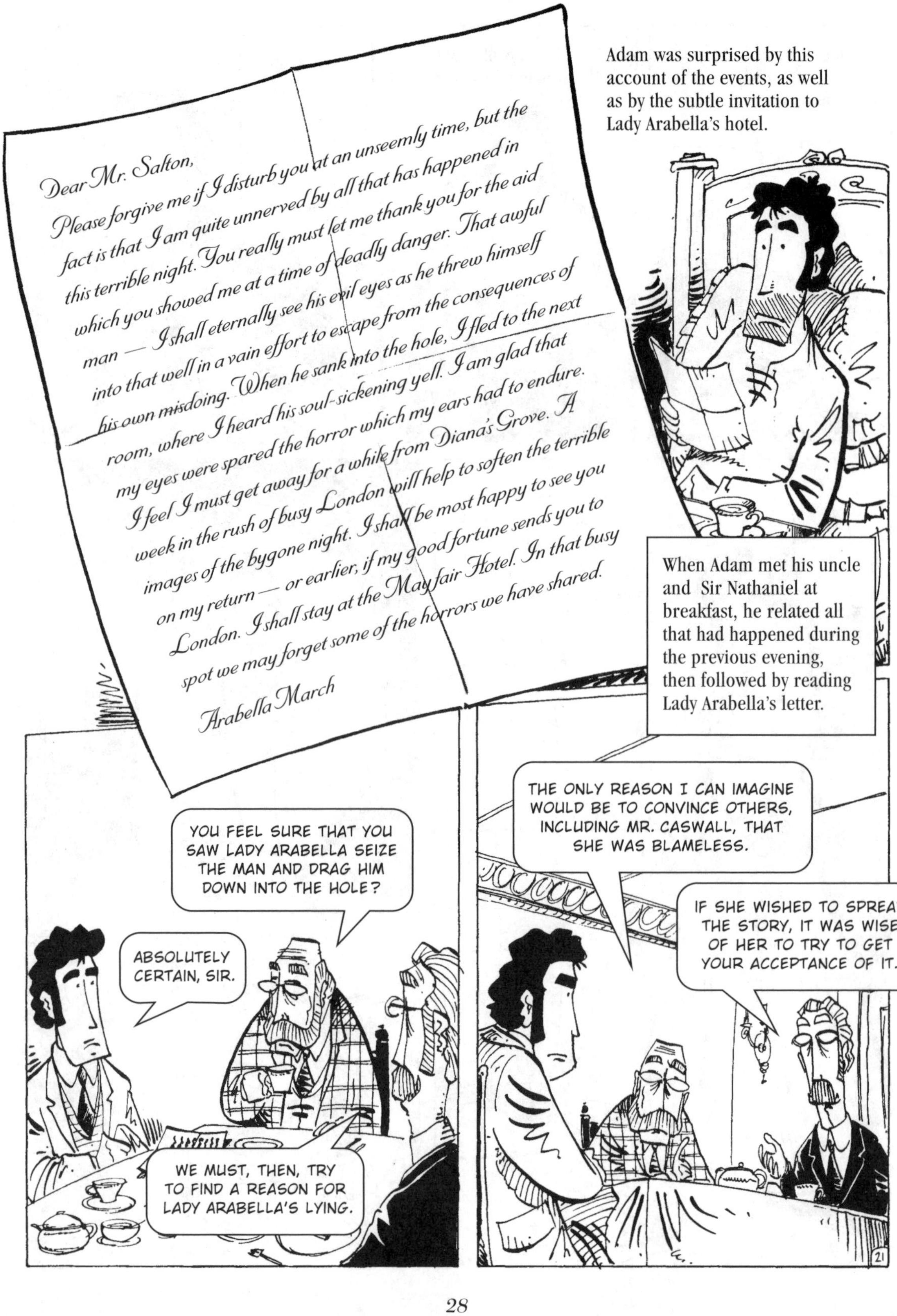
Dear Mr. Salton,
Please forgive me if I disturb you at an unseemly time, but the fact is that I am quite unnerved by all that has happened in this terrible night. You really must let me thank you for the aid which you showed me at a time of deadly danger. That awful man — I shall eternally see his evil eyes as he threw himself into that well in a vain effort to escape from the consequences of his own misdoing. When he sank into the hole, I fled to the next room, where I heard his soul-sickening yell. I am glad that my eyes were spared the horror which my ears had to endure. I feel I must get away for a while from Diana's Grove. A week in the rush of busy London will help to soften the terrible images of the bygone night. I shall be most happy to see you on my return — or earlier, if my good fortune sends you to London. I shall stay at the Mayfair Hotel. In that busy spot we may forget some of the horrors we have shared.
Arabella March
Adam was surprised by this account of the events, as well as by the subtle invitation to Lady Arabella's hotel.
When Adam met his uncle and Sir Nathaniel at breakfast, he related all that had happened during the previous evening, then followed by reading Lady Arabella's letter.
YOU FEEL SURE THAT YOU SAW LADY ARABELLA SEIZE THE MAN AND DRAG HIM DOWN INTO THE HOLE?
ABSOLUTELY CERTAIN, SIR.
WE MUST, THEN, TRY TO FIND A REASON FOR LADY ARABELLA'S LYING.
THE ONLY REASON I CAN IMAGINE WOULD BE TO CONVINCE OTHERS, INCLUDING MR. CASWALL, THAT SHE WAS BLAMELESS.
IF SHE WISHED TO SPREAD THE STORY, IT WAS WISE OF HER TO TRY TO GET YOUR ACCEPTANCE OF IT.
21

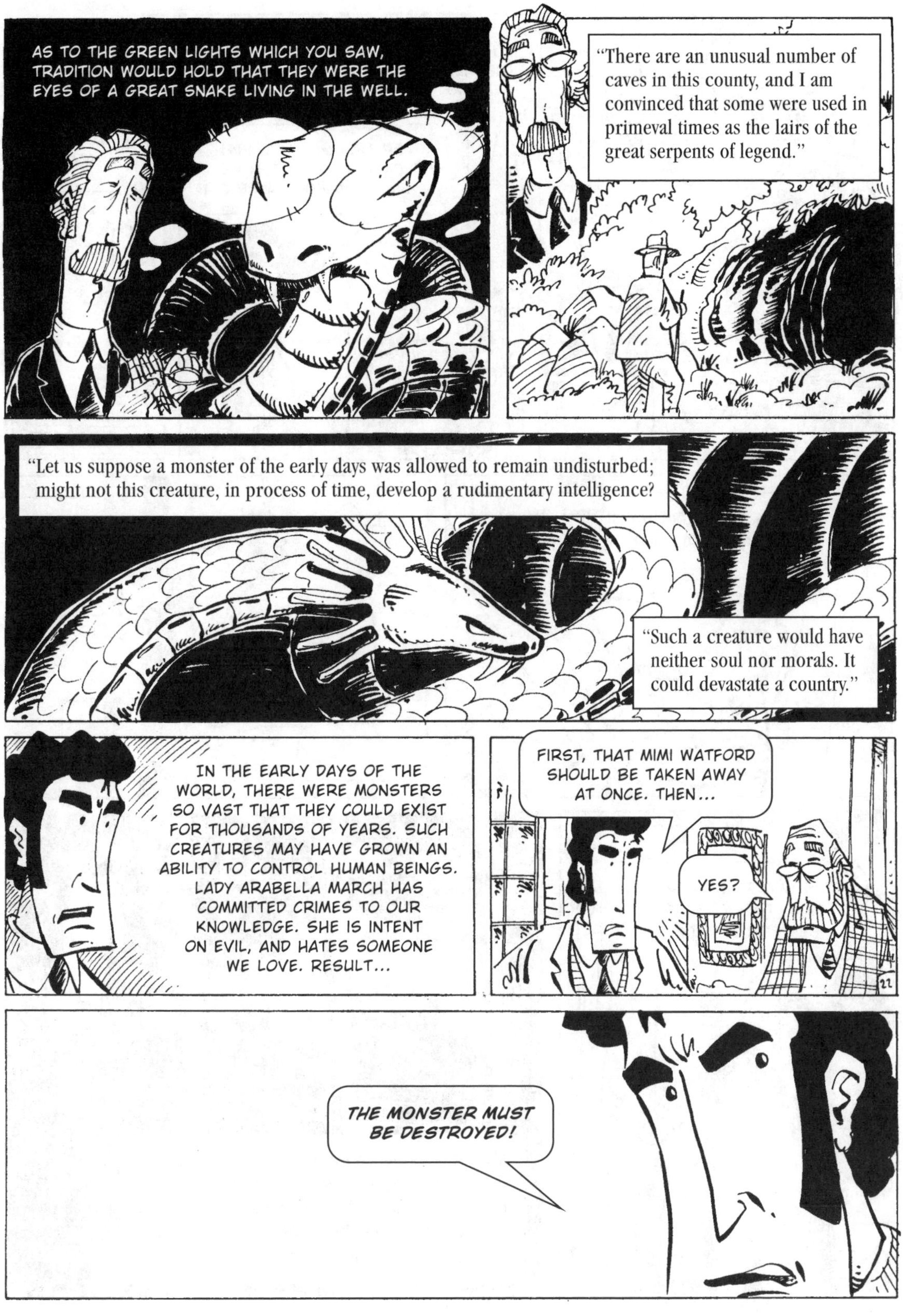
AS TO THE GREEN LIGHTS WHICH YOU SAW, TRADITION WOULD HOLD THAT THEY WERE THE EYES OF A GREAT SNAKE LIVING IN THE WELL.
"There are an unusual number of caves in this county, and I am convinced that some were used in primeval times as the lairs of the great serpents of legend."
"Let us suppose a monster of the early days was allowed to remain undisturbed; might not this creature, in process of time, develop a rudimentary intelligence?
"Such a creature would have neither soul nor morals. It could devastate a country."
IN THE EARLY DAYS OF THE WORLD, THERE WERE MONSTERS SO VAST THAT THEY COULD EXIST FOR THOUSANDS OF YEARS. SUCH CREATURES MAY HAVE GROWN AN ABILITY TO CONTROL HUMAN BEINGS. LADY ARABELLA MARCH HAS COMMITTED CRIMES TO OUR KNOWLEDGE. SHE IS INTENT ON EVIL, AND HATES SOMEONE WE LOVE. RESULT...
FIRST, THAT MIMI WATFORD SHOULD BE TAKEN AWAY AT ONCE. THEN...
YES?
THE MONSTER MUST BE DESTROYED!

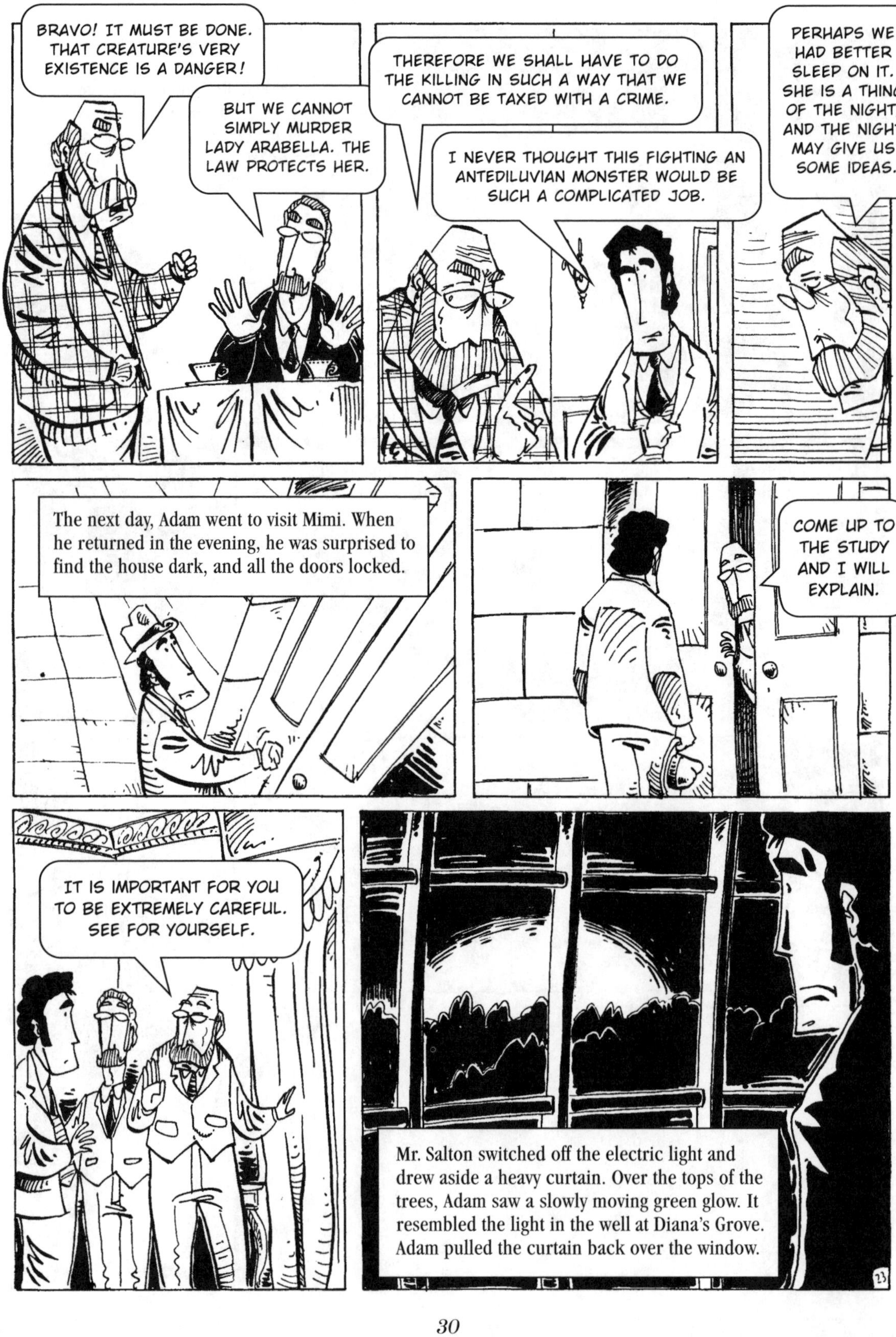
BRAVO! IT MUST BE DONE. THAT CREATURE'S VERY EXISTENCE IS A DANGER!
BUT WE CANNOT SIMPLY MURDER LADY ARABELLA. THE LAW PROTECTS HER.
THEREFORE WE SHALL HAVE TO DO THE KILLING IN SUCH A WAY THAT WE CANNOT BE TAXED WITH A CRIME.
I NEVER THOUGHT THIS FIGHTING AN ANTEDILUVIAN MONSTER WOULD BE SUCH A COMPLICATED JOB.
PERHAPS WE HAD BETTER SLEEP ON IT. SHE IS A THING OF THE NIGHT, AND THE NIGHT MAY GIVE US SOME IDEAS.
The next day, Adam went to visit Mimi. When he returned in the evening, he was surprised to find the house dark, and all the doors locked.
COME UP TO THE STUDY AND I WILL EXPLAIN.
IT IS IMPORTANT FOR YOU TO BE EXTREMELY CAREFUL. SEE FOR YOURSELF.
Mr. Salton switched off the electric light and drew aside a heavy curtain. Over the tops of the trees, Adam saw a slowly moving green glow. It resembled the light in the well at Diana's Grove. Adam pulled the curtain back over the window.
23

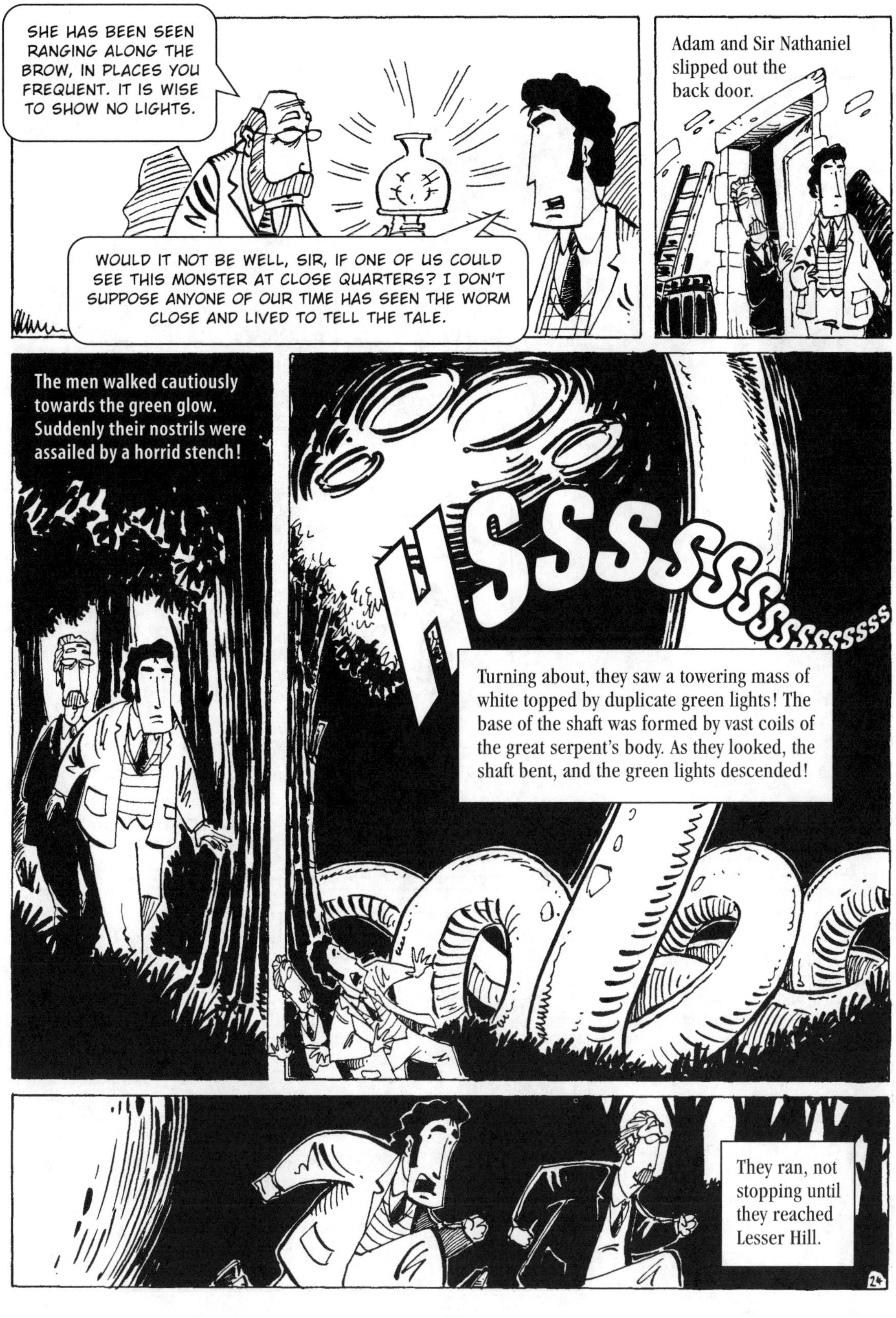
SHE HAS BEEN SEEN RANGING ALONG THE BROW, IN PLACES YOU FREQUENT. IT IS WISE TO SHOW NO LIGHTS.
WOULD IT NOT BE WELL, SIR, IF ONE OF US COULD SEE THIS MONSTER AT CLOSE QUARTERS? I DON'T SUPPOSE ANYONE OF OUR TIME HAS SEEN THE WORM CLOSE AND LIVED TO TELL THE TALE.
Adam and Sir Nathaniel slipped out the back door.
The men walked cautiously towards the green glow. Suddenly their nostrils were assailed by a horrid stench!
HSSSSSSSSSSSSSSS
Turning about, they saw a towering mass of white topped by duplicate green lights! The base of the shaft was formed by vast coils of the great serpent's body. As they looked, the shaft bent, and the green lights descended!
They ran, not stopping until they reached Lesser Hill.

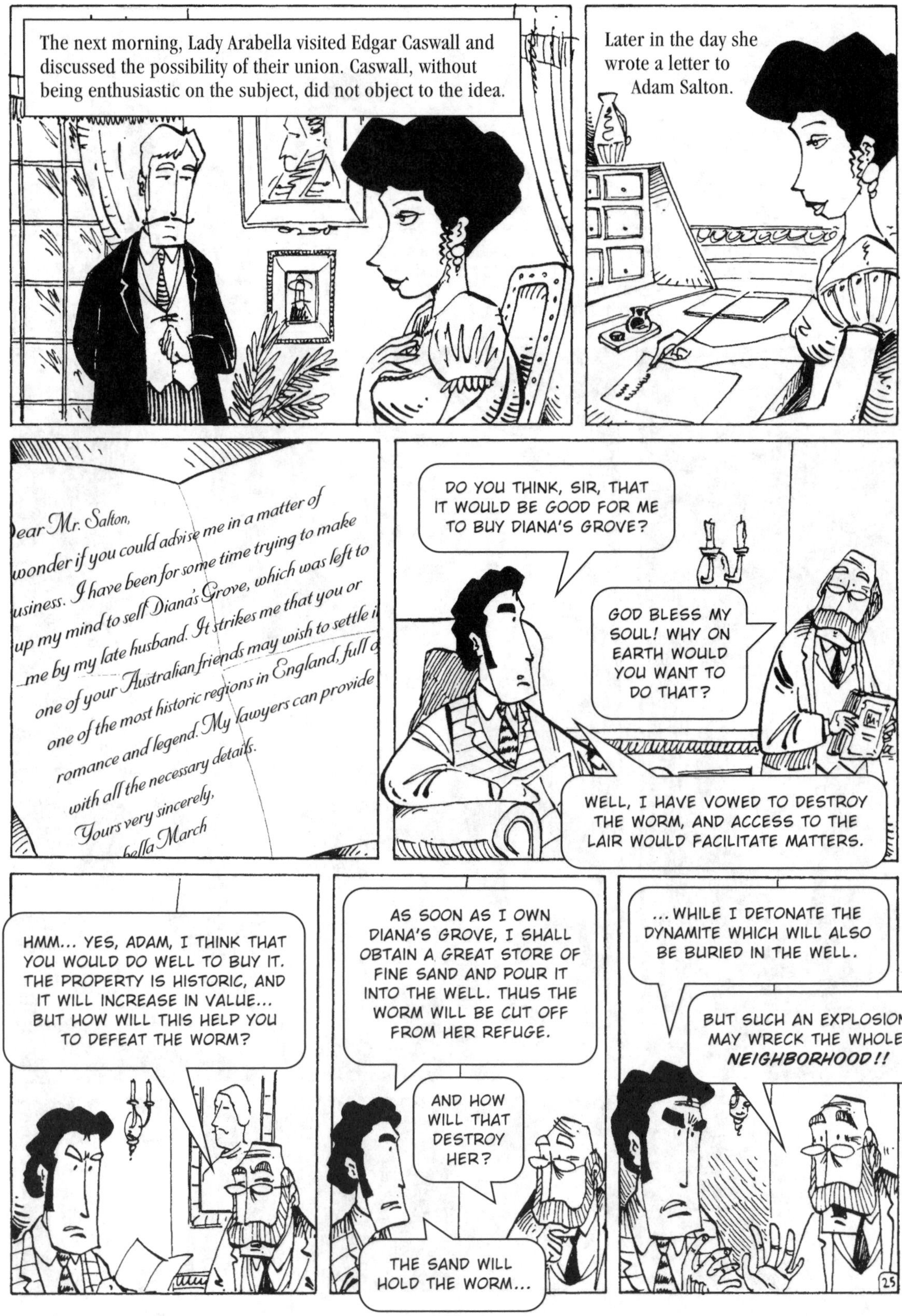
The next morning, Lady Arabella visited Edgar Caswall and discussed the possibility of their union. Caswall, without being enthusiastic on the subject, did not object to the idea.
Later in the day she wrote a letter to Adam Salton.
ear Mr. Salton,
wonder if you could advise me in a matter of
usiness. I have been for some time trying to make
up my mind to sell Diana's Grove, which was left to
me by my late husband. It strikes me that you or
one of your Australian friends may wish to settle i
one of the most historic regions in England, full o
romance and legend. My lawyers can provide
with all the necessary details.
Yours very sincerely,
bella March
DO YOU THINK, SIR, THAT IT WOULD BE GOOD FOR ME TO BUY DIANA'S GROVE?
GOD BLESS MY SOUL! WHY ON EARTH WOULD YOU WANT TO DO THAT?
WELL, I HAVE VOWED TO DESTROY THE WORM, AND ACCESS TO THE LAIR WOULD FACILITATE MATTERS.
HMM... YES, ADAM, I THINK THAT YOU WOULD DO WELL TO BUY IT. THE PROPERTY IS HISTORIC, AND IT WILL INCREASE IN VALUE... BUT HOW WILL THIS HELP YOU TO DEFEAT THE WORM?
AS SOON AS I OWN DIANA'S GROVE, I SHALL OBTAIN A GREAT STORE OF FINE SAND AND POUR IT INTO THE WELL. THUS THE WORM WILL BE CUT OFF FROM HER REFUGE.
AND HOW WILL THAT DESTROY HER?
THE SAND WILL HOLD THE WORM...
...WHILE I DETONATE THE DYNAMITE WHICH WILL ALSO BE BURIED IN THE WELL.
BUT SUCH AN EXPLOSION MAY WRECK THE WHOLE ***NEIGHBORHOOD!!***
25

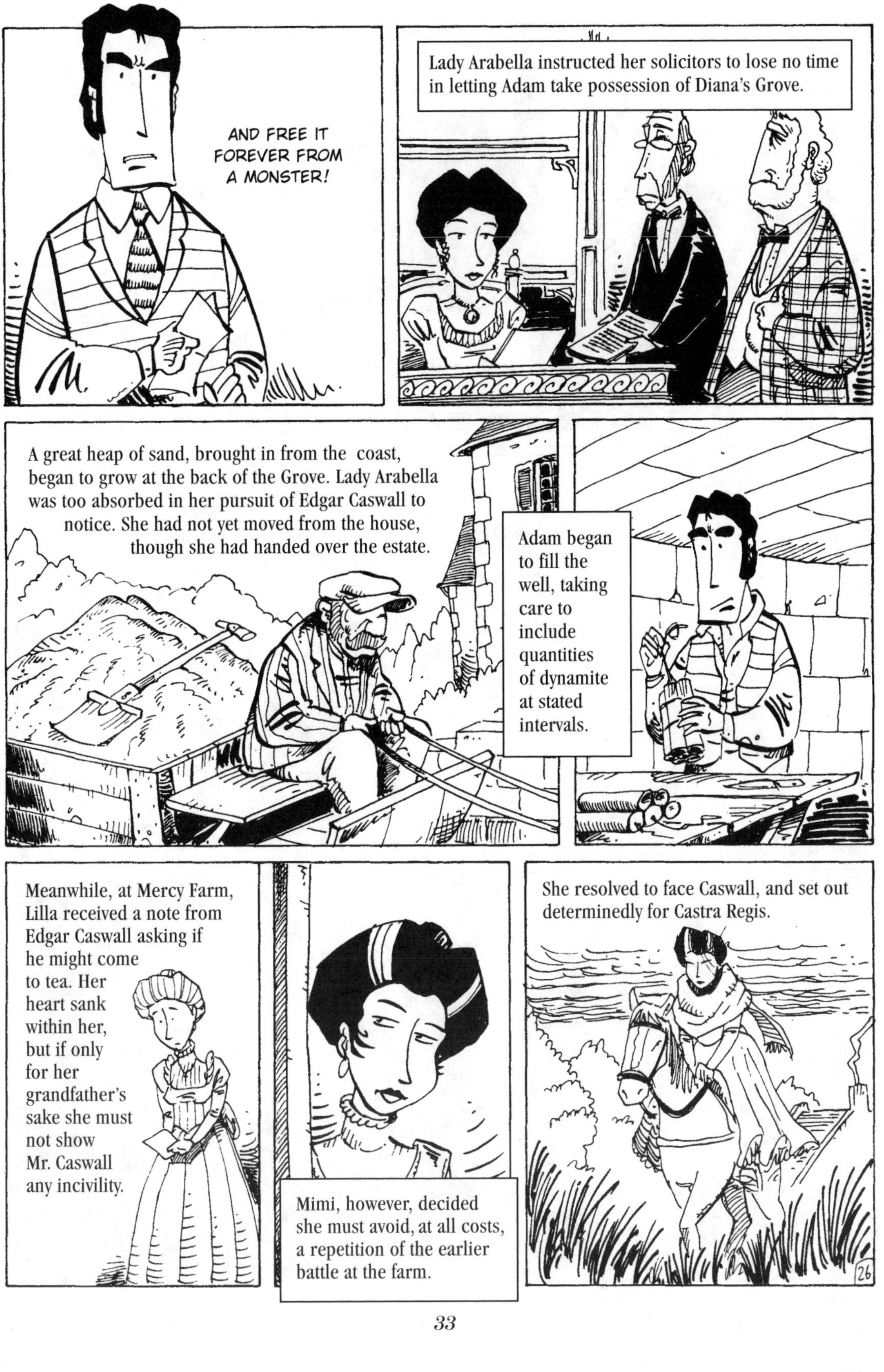
AND FREE IT FOREVER FROM A MONSTER!
Lady Arabella instructed her solicitors to lose no time in letting Adam take possession of Diana's Grove.
A great heap of sand, brought in from the coast, began to grow at the back of the Grove. Lady Arabella was too absorbed in her pursuit of Edgar Caswall to notice. She had not yet moved from the house, though she had handed over the estate.
Adam began to fill the well, taking care to include quantities of dynamite at stated intervals.
Meanwhile, at Mercy Farm, Lilla received a note from Edgar Caswall asking if he might come to tea. Her heart sank within her, but if only for her grandfather's sake she must not show Mr. Caswall any incivility.
Mimi, however, decided she must avoid, at all costs, a repetition of the earlier battle at the farm.
She resolved to face Caswall, and set out determinedly for Castra Regis.
26

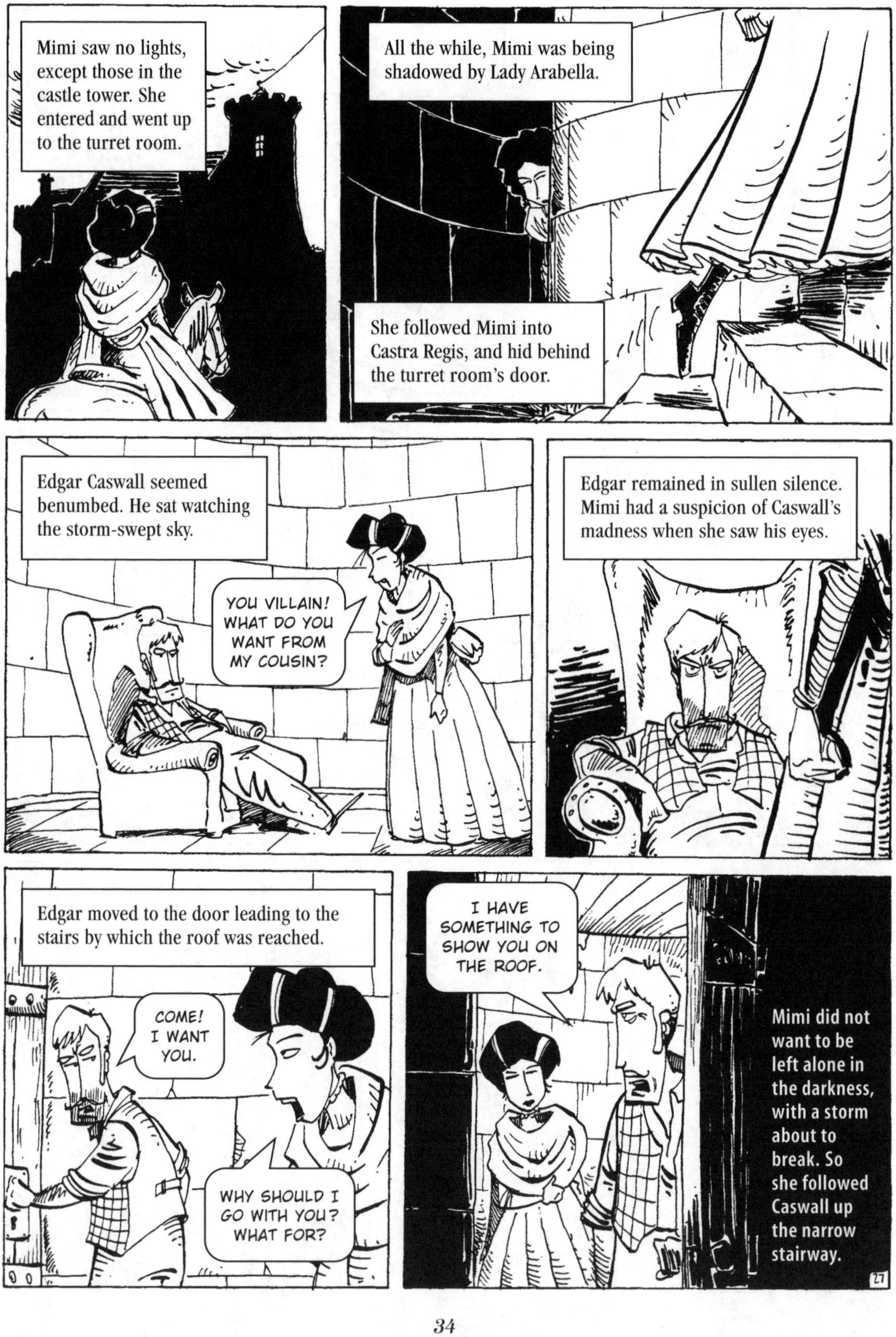
Mimi saw no lights, except those in the castle tower. She entered and went up to the turret room.
All the while, Mimi was being shadowed by Lady Arabella.
She followed Mimi into Castra Regis, and hid behind the turret room's door.
Edgar Caswall seemed benumbed. He sat watching the storm-swept sky.
YOU VILLAIN! WHAT DO YOU WANT FROM MY COUSIN?
Edgar remained in sullen silence. Mimi had a suspicion of Caswall's madness when she saw his eyes.
Edgar moved to the door leading to the stairs by which the roof was reached.
COME! I WANT YOU.
WHY SHOULD I GO WITH YOU? WHAT FOR?
I HAVE SOMETHING TO SHOW YOU ON THE ROOF.
Mimi did not want to be left alone in the darkness, with a storm about to break. So she followed Caswall up the narrow stairway.
27

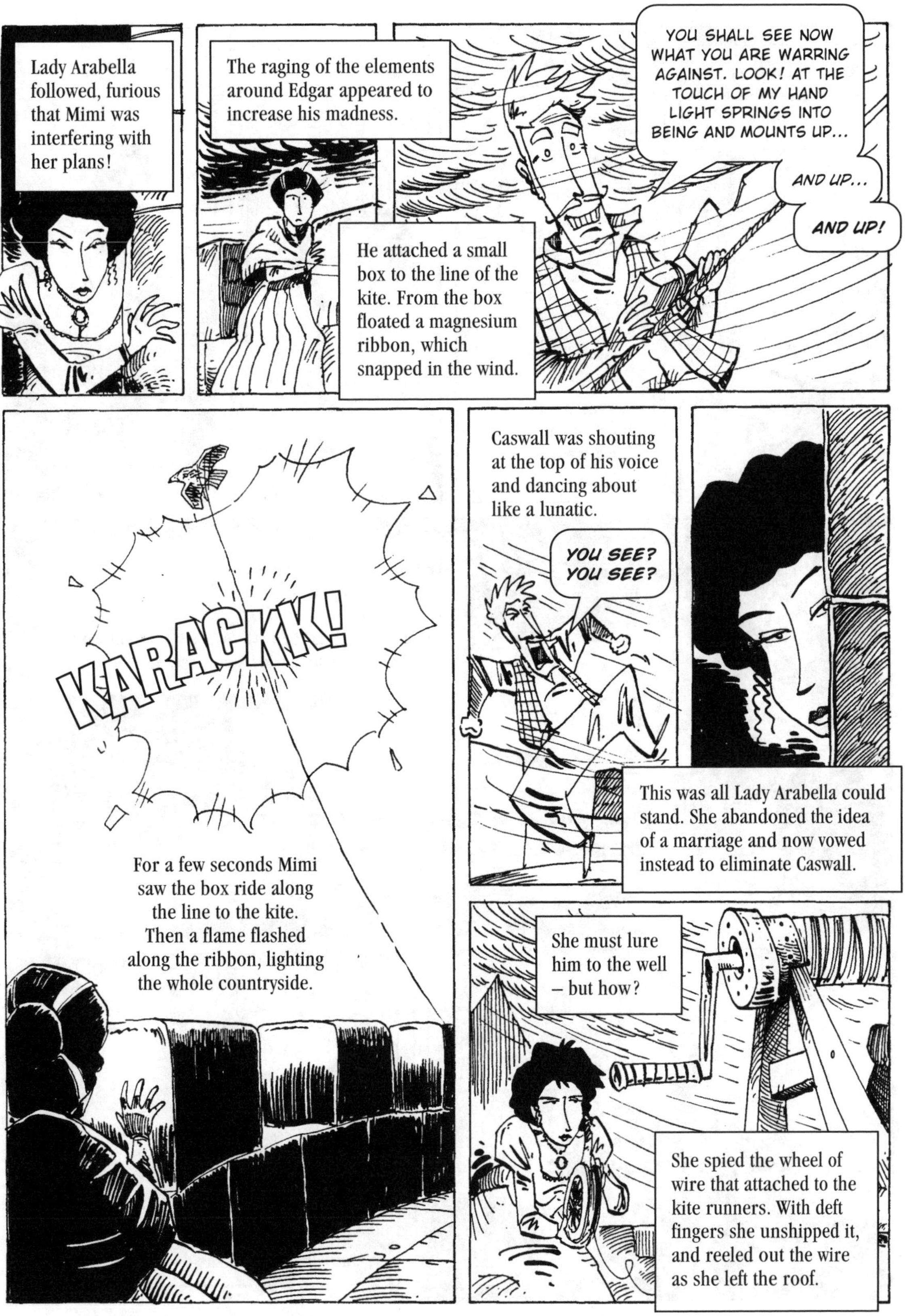
Lady Arabella followed, furious that Mimi was interfering with her plans!
The raging of the elements around Edgar appeared to increase his madness.
He attached a small box to the line of the kite. From the box floated a magnesium ribbon, which snapped in the wind.
YOU SHALL SEE NOW WHAT YOU ARE WARRING AGAINST. LOOK! AT THE TOUCH OF MY HAND LIGHT SPRINGS INTO BEING AND MOUNTS UP...
AND UP...
AND UP!
KARACKK!
For a few seconds Mimi saw the box ride along the line to the kite. Then a flame flashed along the ribbon, lighting the whole countryside.
Caswall was shouting at the top of his voice and dancing about like a lunatic.
YOU SEE? YOU SEE?
This was all Lady Arabella could stand. She abandoned the idea of a marriage and now vowed instead to eliminate Caswall.
She must lure him to the well – but how?
She spied the wheel of wire that attached to the kite runners. With deft fingers she unshipped it, and reeled out the wire as she left the roof.

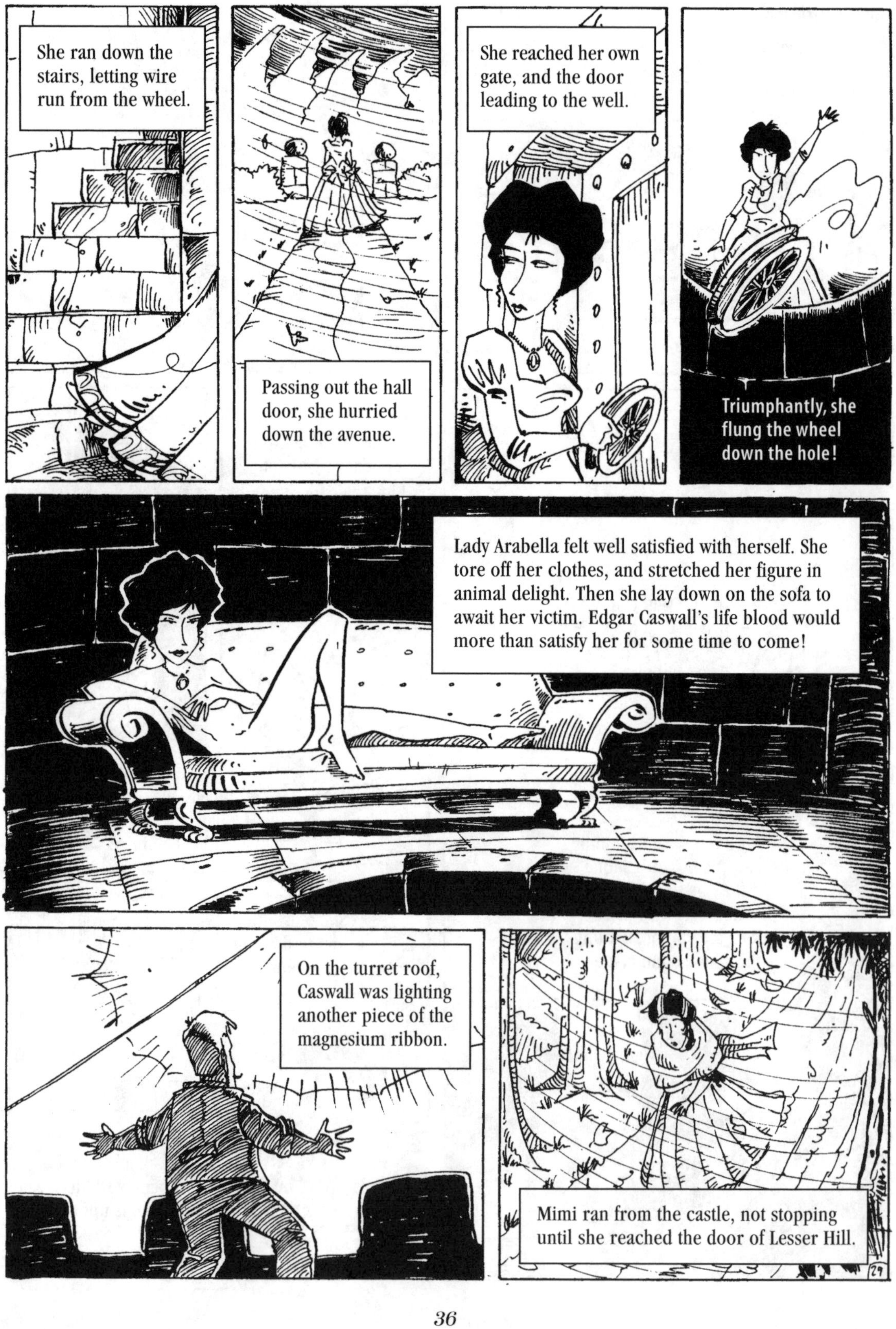
She ran down the stairs, letting wire run from the wheel.
Passing out the hall door, she hurried down the avenue.
She reached her own gate, and the door leading to the well.
Triumphantly, she flung the wheel down the hole!
Lady Arabella felt well satisfied with herself. She tore off her clothes, and stretched her figure in animal delight. Then she lay down on the sofa to await her victim. Edgar Caswall's life blood would more than satisfy her for some time to come!
On the turret roof, Caswall was lighting another piece of the magnesium ribbon.
Mimi ran from the castle, not stopping until she reached the door of Lesser Hill.

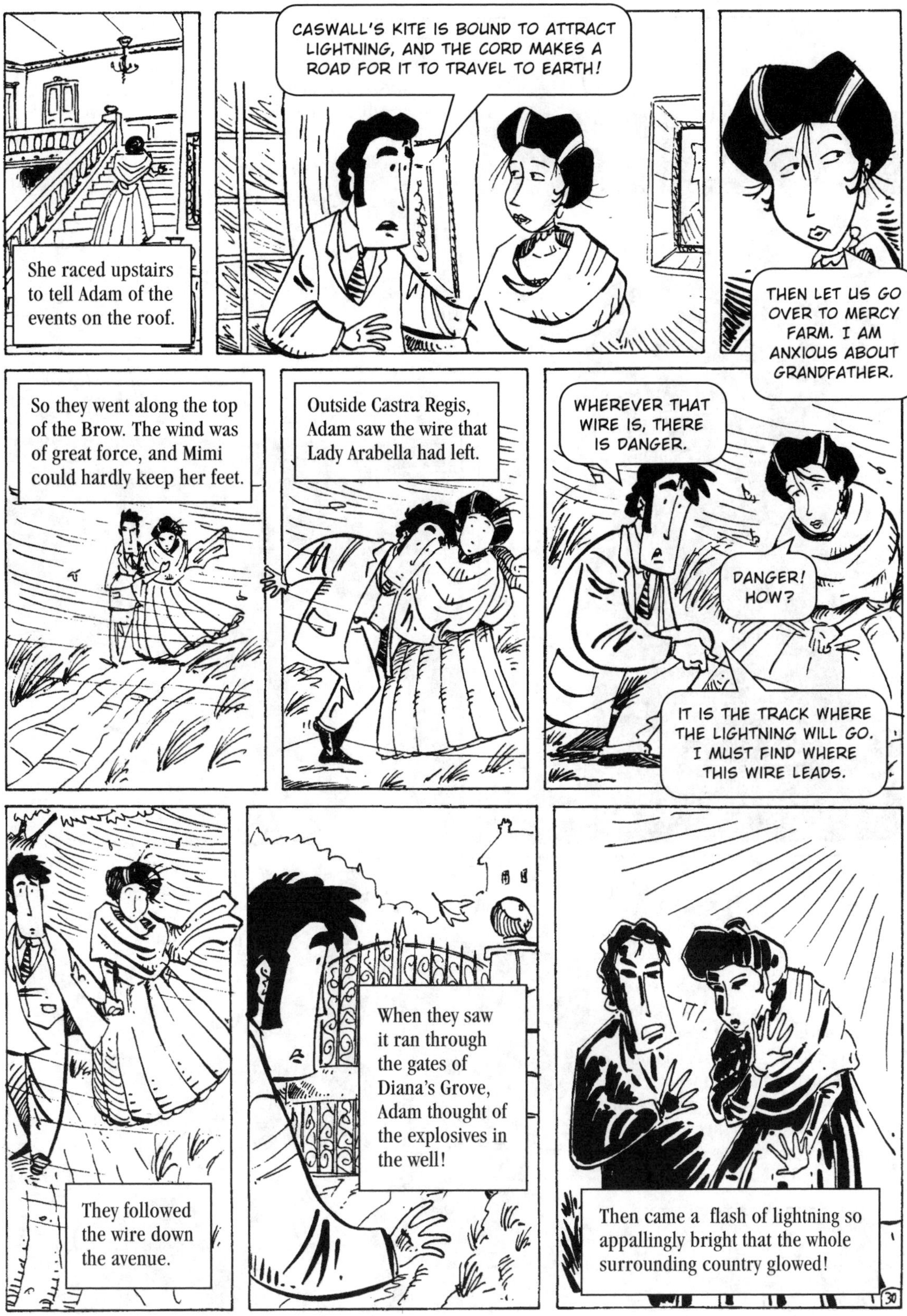
She raced upstairs to tell Adam of the events on the roof.
CASWALL'S KITE IS BOUND TO ATTRACT LIGHTNING, AND THE CORD MAKES A ROAD FOR IT TO TRAVEL TO EARTH!
THEN LET US GO OVER TO MERCY FARM. I AM ANXIOUS ABOUT GRANDFATHER.
So they went along the top of the Brow. The wind was of great force, and Mimi could hardly keep her feet.
Outside Castra Regis, Adam saw the wire that Lady Arabella had left.
WHEREVER THAT WIRE IS, THERE IS DANGER.
DANGER! HOW?
IT IS THE TRACK WHERE THE LIGHTNING WILL GO. I MUST FIND WHERE THIS WIRE LEADS.
They followed the wire down the avenue.
When they saw it ran through the gates of Diana's Grove, Adam thought of the explosives in the well!
Then came a flash of lightning so appallingly bright that the whole surrounding country glowed!
30

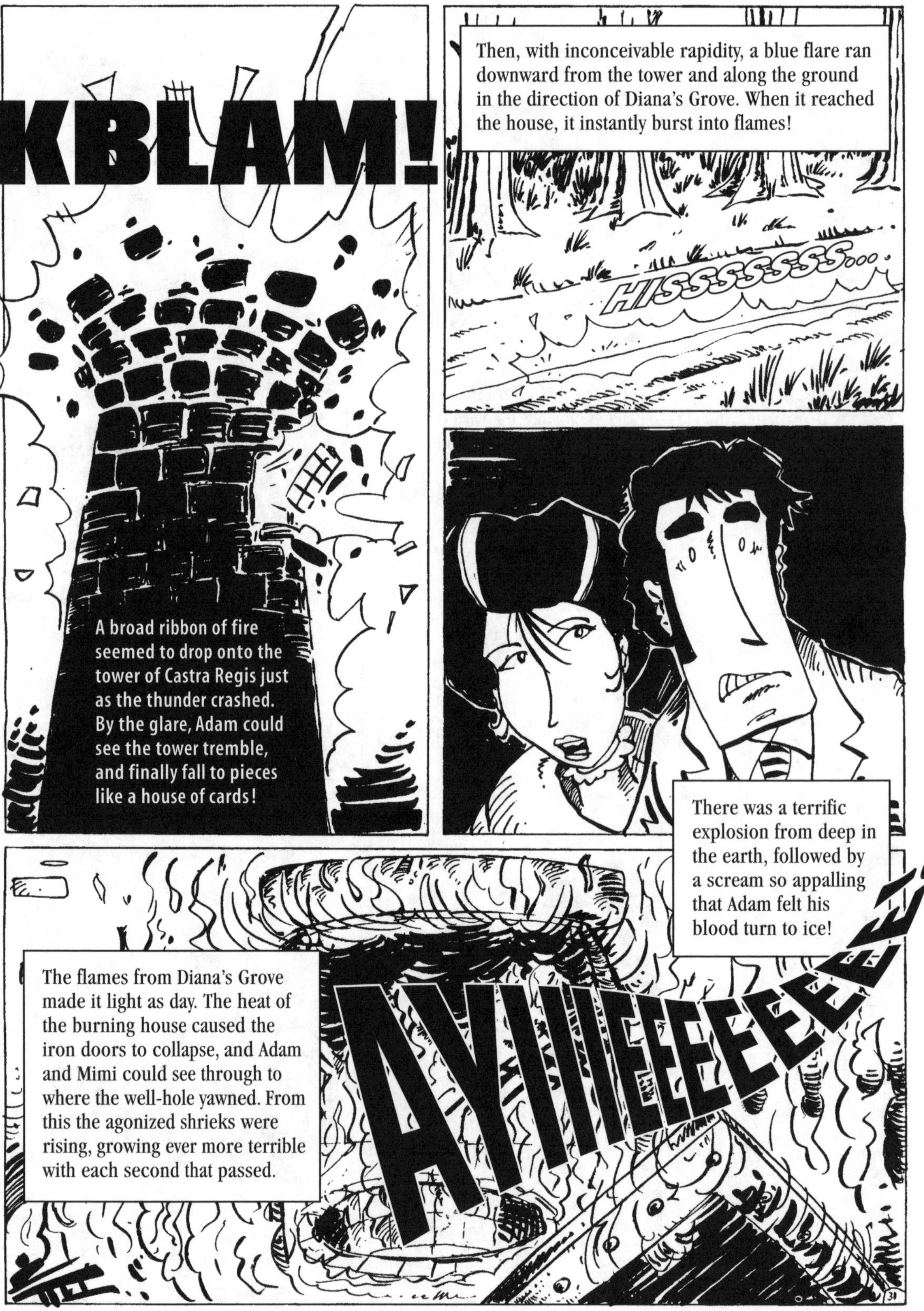
KBLAM!
A broad ribbon of fire seemed to drop onto the tower of Castra Regis just as the thunder crashed. By the glare, Adam could see the tower tremble, and finally fall to pieces like a house of cards!
Then, with inconceivable rapidity, a blue flare ran downward from the tower and along the ground in the direction of Diana's Grove. When it reached the house, it instantly burst into flames!
HISSSSSSSSooo
There was a terrific explosion from deep in the earth, followed by a scream so appalling that Adam felt his blood turn to ice!
The flames from Diana's Grove made it light as day. The heat of the burning house caused the iron doors to collapse, and Adam and Mimi could see through to where the well-hole yawned. From this the agonized shrieks were rising, growing ever more terrible with each second that passed.
AYIIIEEEEEEEE!

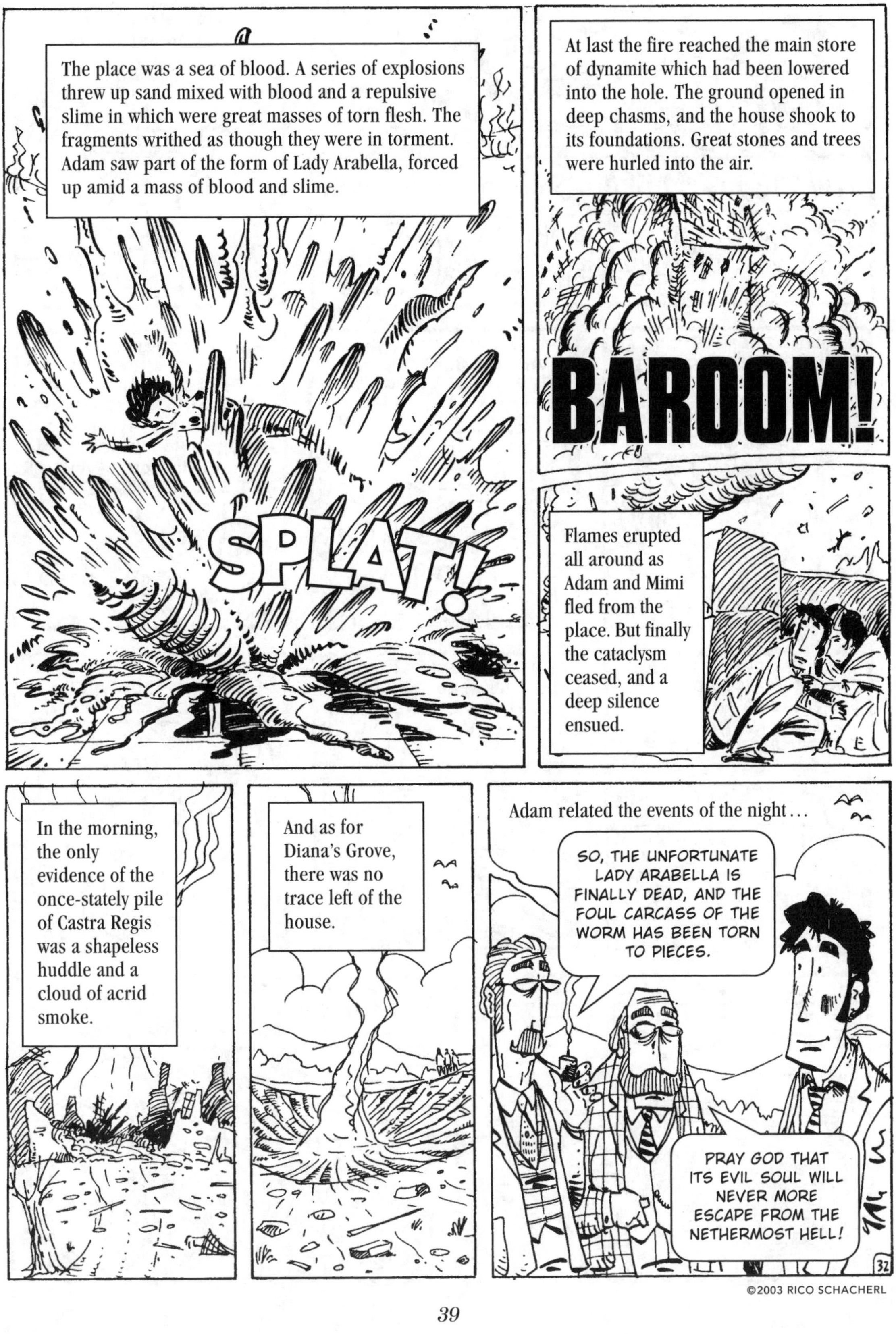
The place was a sea of blood. A series of explosions threw up sand mixed with blood and a repulsive slime in which were great masses of torn flesh. The fragments writhed as though they were in torment. Adam saw part of the form of Lady Arabella, forced up amid a mass of blood and slime.
SPLAT!
At last the fire reached the main store of dynamite which had been lowered into the hole. The ground opened in deep chasms, and the house shook to its foundations. Great stones and trees were hurled into the air.
BAROOM!
Flames erupted all around as Adam and Mimi fled from the place. But finally the cataclysm ceased, and a deep silence ensued.
In the morning, the only evidence of the once-stately pile of Castra Regis was a shapeless huddle and a cloud of acrid smoke.
And as for Diana's Grove, there was no trace left of the house.
Adam related the events of the night…
SO, THE UNFORTUNATE LADY ARABELLA IS FINALLY DEAD, AND THE FOUL CARCASS OF THE WORM HAS BEEN TORN TO PIECES.
PRAY GOD THAT ITS EVIL SOUL WILL NEVER MORE ESCAPE FROM THE NETHERMOST HELL!
32

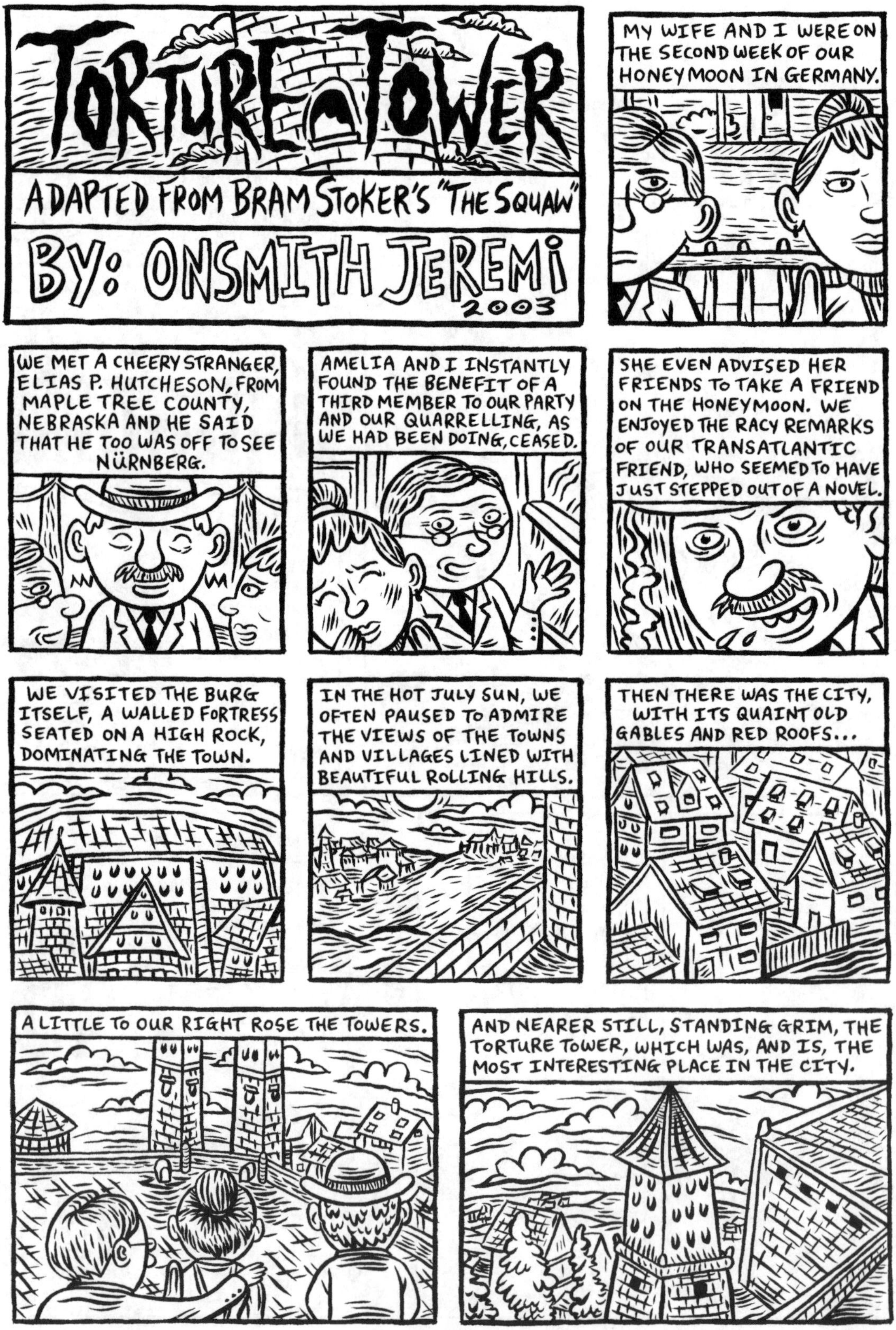
TORTURE TOWER
ADAPTED FROM BRAM STOKER'S "THE SQUAW"
BY: ONSMITH JEREMI
2003
MY WIFE AND I WERE ON THE SECOND WEEK OF OUR HONEYMOON IN GERMANY.
WE MET A CHEERY STRANGER, ELIAS P. HUTCHESON, FROM MAPLE TREE COUNTY, NEBRASKA AND HE SAID THAT HE TOO WAS OFF TO SEE NÜRNBERG.
AMELIA AND I INSTANTLY FOUND THE BENEFIT OF A THIRD MEMBER TO OUR PARTY AND OUR QUARRELLING, AS WE HAD BEEN DOING, CEASED.
SHE EVEN ADVISED HER FRIENDS TO TAKE A FRIEND ON THE HONEYMOON. WE ENJOYED THE RACY REMARKS OF OUR TRANSATLANTIC FRIEND, WHO SEEMED TO HAVE JUST STEPPED OUT OF A NOVEL.
WE VISITED THE BURG ITSELF, A WALLED FORTRESS SEATED ON A HIGH ROCK, DOMINATING THE TOWN.
IN THE HOT JULY SUN, WE OFTEN PAUSED TO ADMIRE THE VIEWS OF THE TOWNS AND VILLAGES LINED WITH BEAUTIFUL ROLLING HILLS.
THEN THERE WAS THE CITY, WITH ITS QUAINT OLD GABLES AND RED ROOFS...
A LITTLE TO OUR RIGHT ROSE THE TOWERS.
AND NEARER STILL, STANDING GRIM, THE TORTURE TOWER, WHICH WAS, AND IS, THE MOST INTERESTING PLACE IN THE CITY.

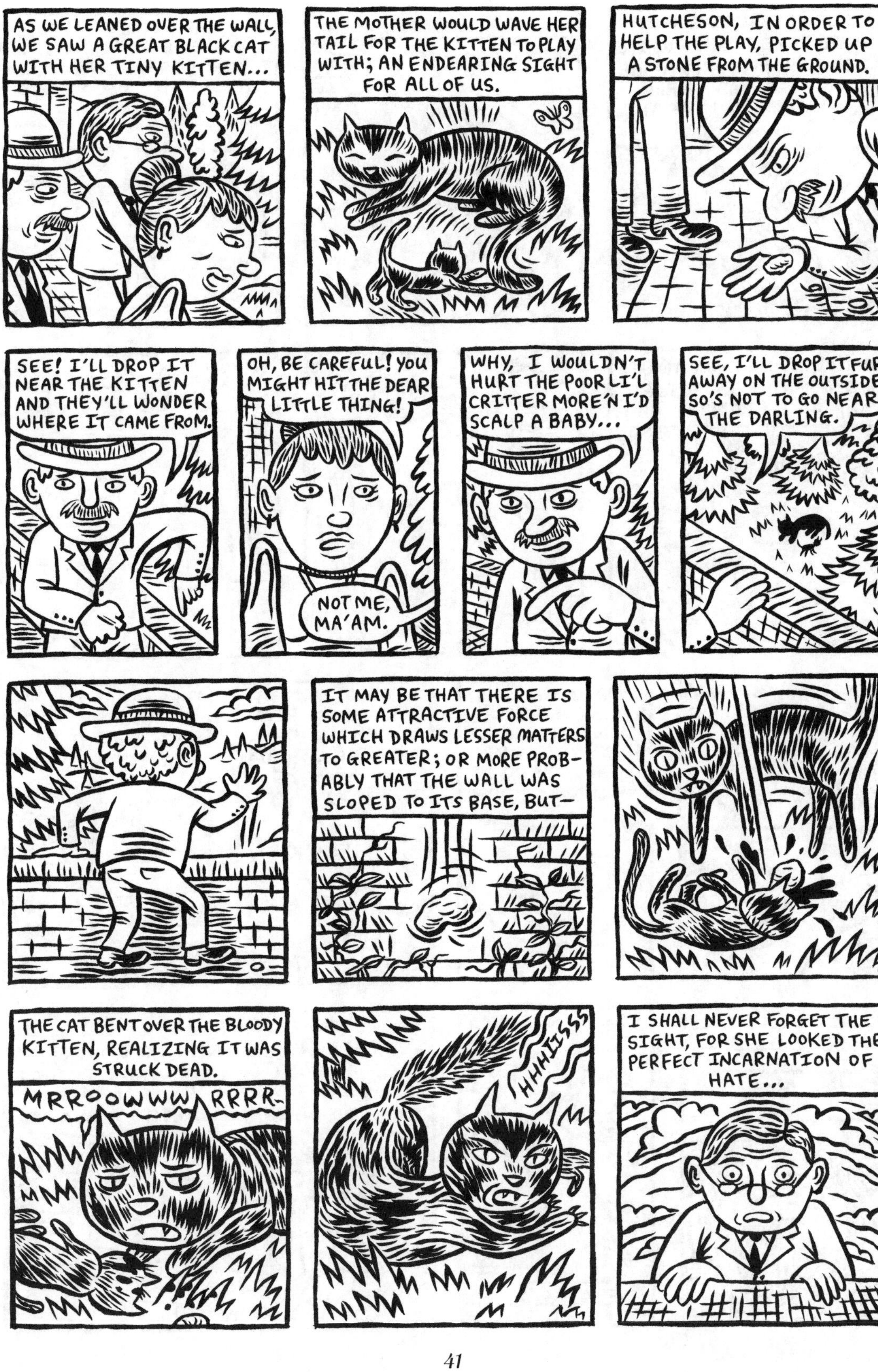
AS WE LEANED OVER THE WALL, WE SAW A GREAT BLACK CAT WITH HER TINY KITTEN...
THE MOTHER WOULD WAVE HER TAIL FOR THE KITTEN TO PLAY WITH; AN ENDEARING SIGHT FOR ALL OF US.
HUTCHESON, IN ORDER TO HELP THE PLAY, PICKED UP A STONE FROM THE GROUND.
SEE! I'LL DROP IT NEAR THE KITTEN AND THEY'LL WONDER WHERE IT CAME FROM.
OH, BE CAREFUL! YOU MIGHT HIT THE DEAR LITTLE THING!
NOT ME, MA'AM.
WHY, I WOULDN'T HURT THE POOR LI'L CRITTER MORE'N I'D SCALP A BABY...
SEE, I'LL DROP IT FUR AWAY ON THE OUTSIDE SO'S NOT TO GO NEAR THE DARLING.
IT MAY BE THAT THERE IS SOME ATTRACTIVE FORCE WHICH DRAWS LESSER MATTERS TO GREATER; OR MORE PROBABLY THAT THE WALL WAS SLOPED TO ITS BASE, BUT—
THE CAT BENT OVER THE BLOODY KITTEN, REALIZING IT WAS STRUCK DEAD.
MRROOWWW RRRR-
HHHIISSS
I SHALL NEVER FORGET THE SIGHT, FOR SHE LOOKED THE PERFECT INCARNATION OF HATE...

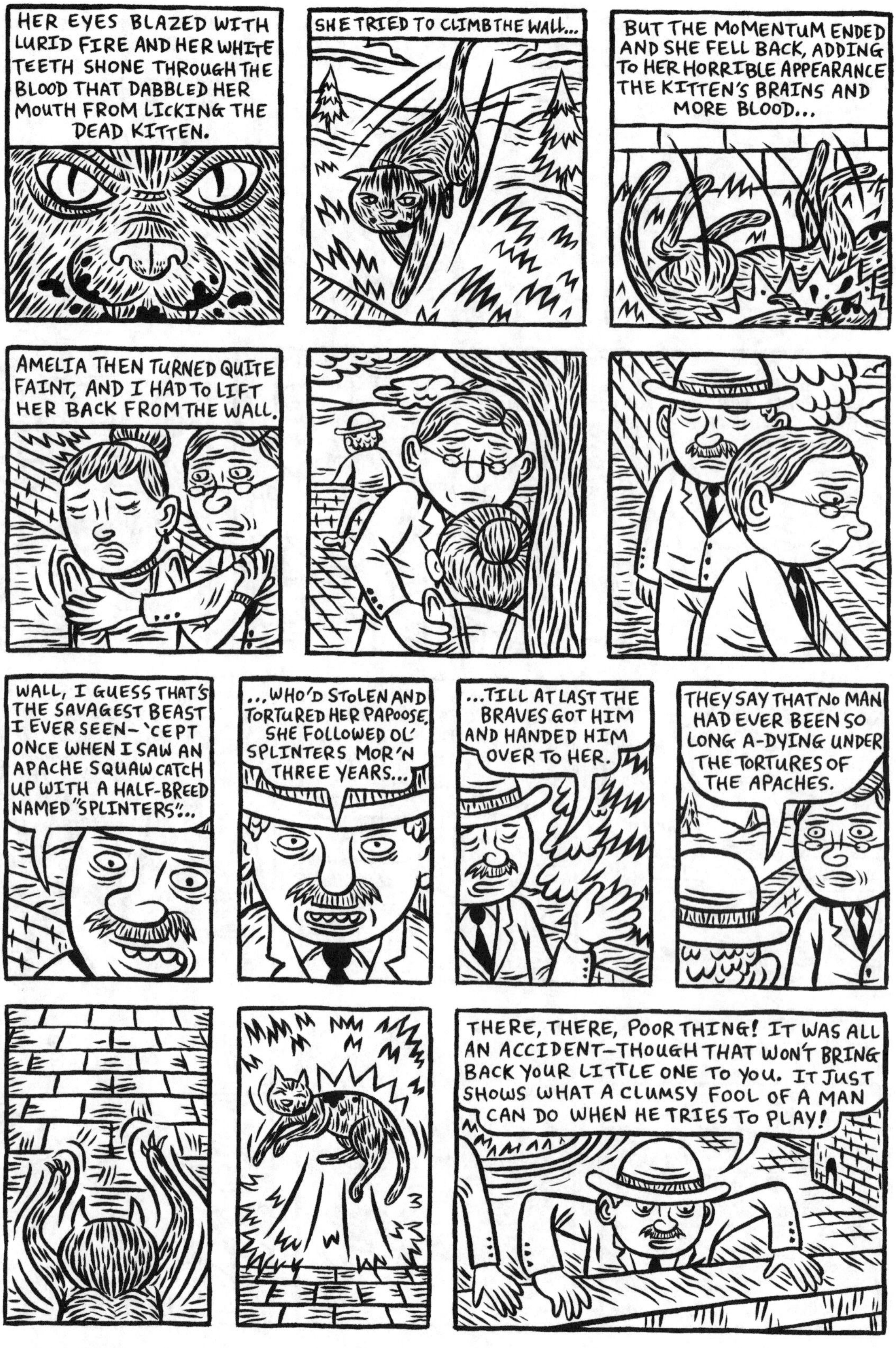
HER EYES BLAZED WITH LURID FIRE AND HER WHITE TEETH SHONE THROUGH THE BLOOD THAT DABBLED HER MOUTH FROM LICKING THE DEAD KITTEN.
SHE TRIED TO CLIMB THE WALL...
BUT THE MOMENTUM ENDED AND SHE FELL BACK, ADDING TO HER HORRIBLE APPEARANCE THE KITTEN'S BRAINS AND MORE BLOOD...
AMELIA THEN TURNED QUITE FAINT, AND I HAD TO LIFT HER BACK FROM THE WALL.
WALL, I GUESS THAT'S THE SAVAGEST BEAST I EVER SEEN– 'CEPT ONCE WHEN I SAW AN APACHE SQUAW CATCH UP WITH A HALF-BREED NAMED "SPLINTERS"...
...WHO'D STOLEN AND TORTURED HER PAPOOSE. SHE FOLLOWED OL' SPLINTERS MOR'N THREE YEARS...
...TILL AT LAST THE BRAVES GOT HIM AND HANDED HIM OVER TO HER.
THEY SAY THAT NO MAN HAD EVER BEEN SO LONG A-DYING UNDER THE TORTURES OF THE APACHES.
THERE, THERE, POOR THING! IT WAS ALL AN ACCIDENT–THOUGH THAT WON'T BRING BACK YOUR LITTLE ONE TO YOU. IT JUST SHOWS WHAT A CLUMSY FOOL OF A MAN CAN DO WHEN HE TRIES TO PLAY!

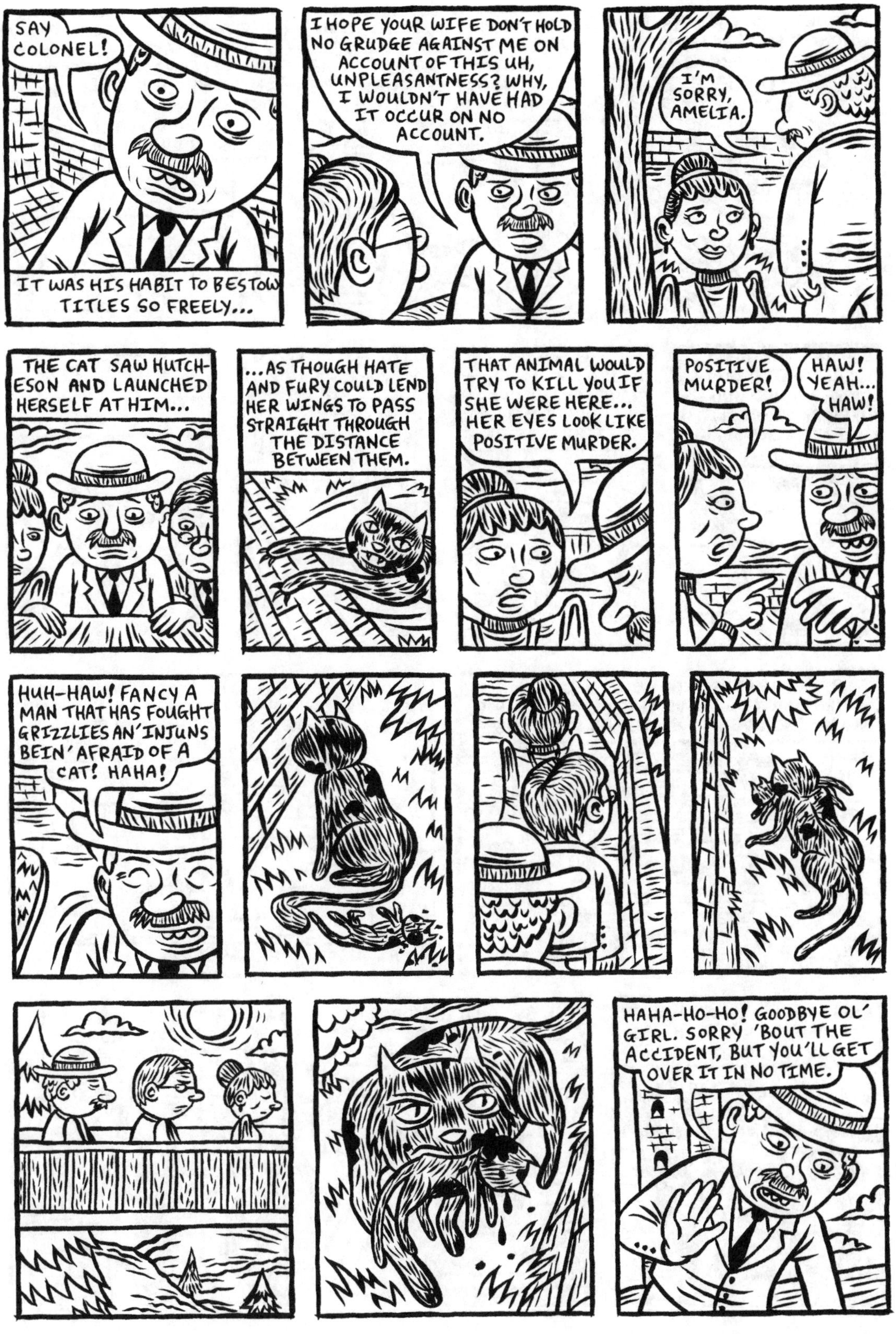
SAY COLONEL!
IT WAS HIS HABIT TO BESTOW TITLES SO FREELY...
I HOPE YOUR WIFE DON'T HOLD NO GRUDGE AGAINST ME ON ACCOUNT OF THIS UH, UNPLEASANTNESS? WHY, I WOULDN'T HAVE HAD IT OCCUR ON NO ACCOUNT.
I'M SORRY, AMELIA.
THE CAT SAW HUTCHESON AND LAUNCHED HERSELF AT HIM...
...AS THOUGH HATE AND FURY COULD LEND HER WINGS TO PASS STRAIGHT THROUGH THE DISTANCE BETWEEN THEM.
THAT ANIMAL WOULD TRY TO KILL YOU IF SHE WERE HERE... HER EYES LOOK LIKE POSITIVE MURDER.
POSITIVE MURDER!
HAW! YEAH... HAW!
HUH-HAW! FANCY A MAN THAT HAS FOUGHT GRIZZLIES AN' INJUNS BEIN' AFRAID OF A CAT! HAHA!
HAHA-HO-HO! GOODBYE OL' GIRL. SORRY 'BOUT THE ACCIDENT, BUT YOU'LL GET OVER IT IN NO TIME.

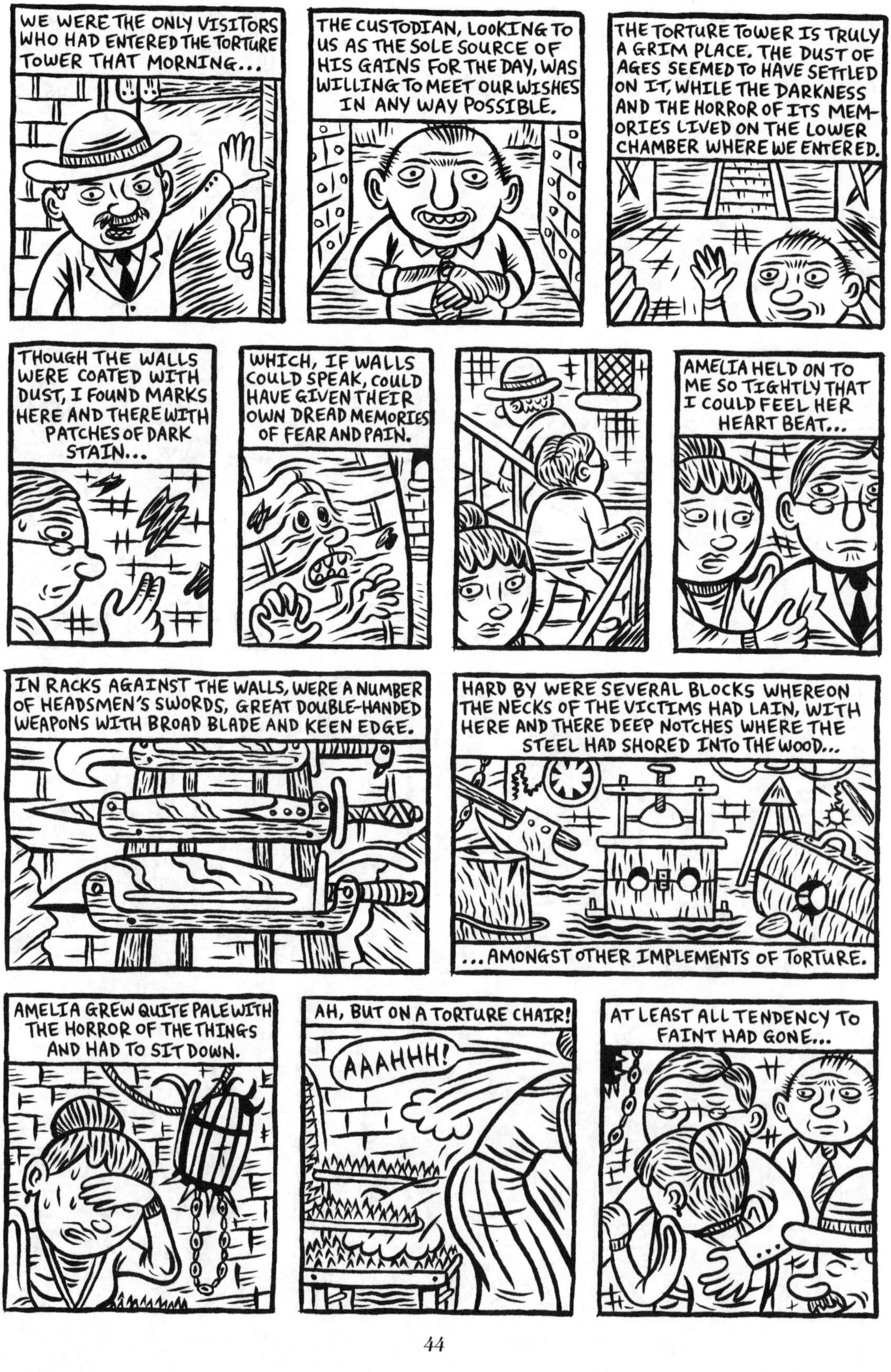
WE WERE THE ONLY VISITORS WHO HAD ENTERED THE TORTURE TOWER THAT MORNING...
THE CUSTODIAN, LOOKING TO US AS THE SOLE SOURCE OF HIS GAINS FOR THE DAY, WAS WILLING TO MEET OUR WISHES IN ANY WAY POSSIBLE.
THE TORTURE TOWER IS TRULY A GRIM PLACE. THE DUST OF AGES SEEMED TO HAVE SETTLED ON IT, WHILE THE DARKNESS AND THE HORROR OF ITS MEMORIES LIVED ON THE LOWER CHAMBER WHERE WE ENTERED.
THOUGH THE WALLS WERE COATED WITH DUST, I FOUND MARKS HERE AND THERE WITH PATCHES OF DARK STAIN...
WHICH, IF WALLS COULD SPEAK, COULD HAVE GIVEN THEIR OWN DREAD MEMORIES OF FEAR AND PAIN.
AMELIA HELD ON TO ME SO TIGHTLY THAT I COULD FEEL HER HEART BEAT...
IN RACKS AGAINST THE WALLS, WERE A NUMBER OF HEADSMEN'S SWORDS, GREAT DOUBLE-HANDED WEAPONS WITH BROAD BLADE AND KEEN EDGE.
HARD BY WERE SEVERAL BLOCKS WHEREON THE NECKS OF THE VICTIMS HAD LAIN, WITH HERE AND THERE DEEP NOTCHES WHERE THE STEEL HAD SHORED INTO THE WOOD...
...AMONGST OTHER IMPLEMENTS OF TORTURE.
AMELIA GREW QUITE PALE WITH THE HORROR OF THE THINGS AND HAD TO SIT DOWN.
AH, BUT ON A TORTURE CHAIR!
AAAHHH!
AT LEAST ALL TENDENCY TO FAINT HAD GONE...

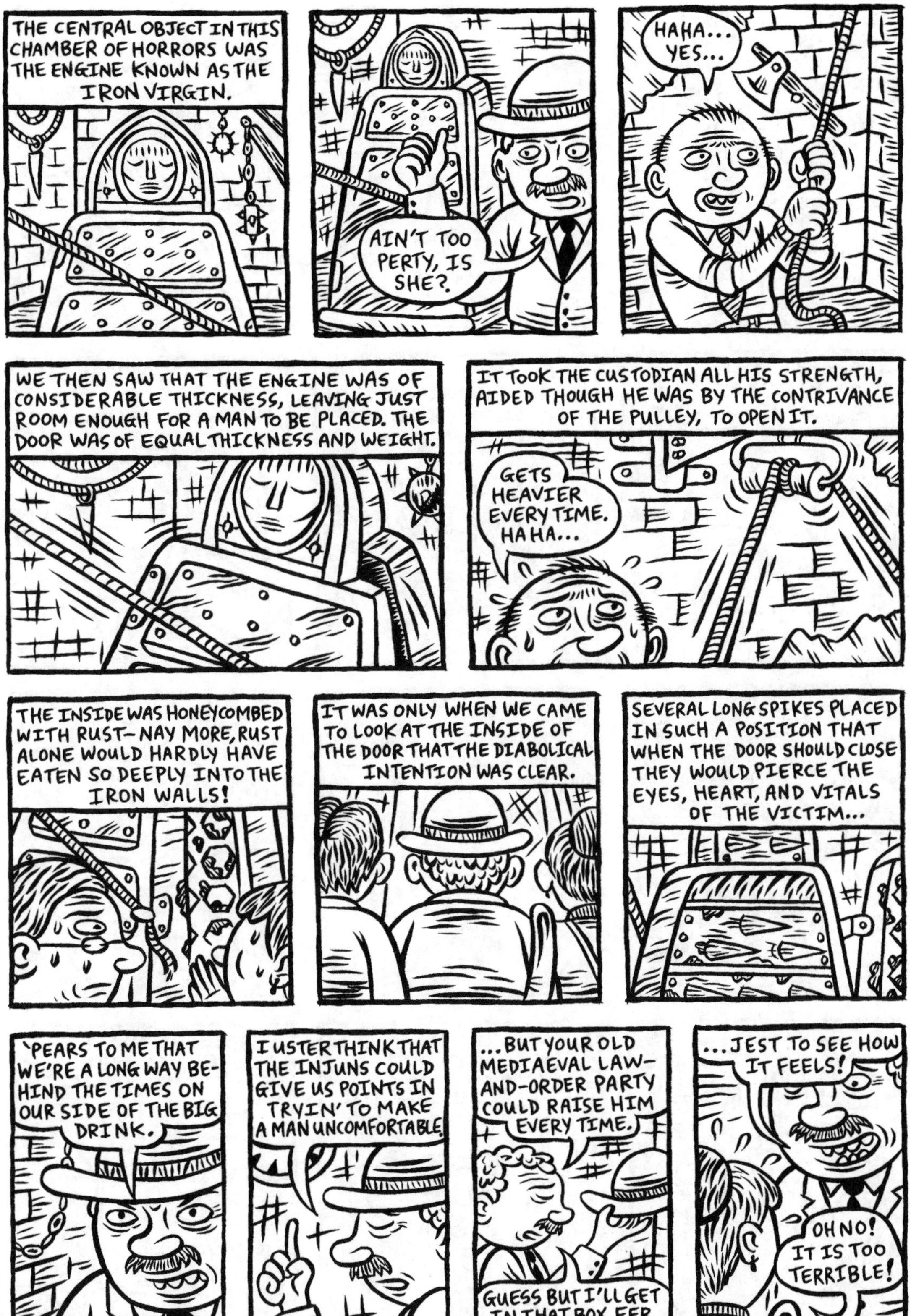
THE CENTRAL OBJECT IN THIS CHAMBER OF HORRORS WAS THE ENGINE KNOWN AS THE IRON VIRGIN.
AIN'T TOO PERTY, IS SHE?
HAHA... YES...
WE THEN SAW THAT THE ENGINE WAS OF CONSIDERABLE THICKNESS, LEAVING JUST ROOM ENOUGH FOR A MAN TO BE PLACED. THE DOOR WAS OF EQUAL THICKNESS AND WEIGHT.
IT TOOK THE CUSTODIAN ALL HIS STRENGTH, AIDED THOUGH HE WAS BY THE CONTRIVANCE OF THE PULLEY, TO OPEN IT.
GETS HEAVIER EVERY TIME. HA HA...
THE INSIDE WAS HONEYCOMBED WITH RUST– NAY MORE, RUST ALONE WOULD HARDLY HAVE EATEN SO DEEPLY INTO THE IRON WALLS!
IT WAS ONLY WHEN WE CAME TO LOOK AT THE INSIDE OF THE DOOR THAT THE DIABOLICAL INTENTION WAS CLEAR.
SEVERAL LONG SPIKES PLACED IN SUCH A POSITION THAT WHEN THE DOOR SHOULD CLOSE THEY WOULD PIERCE THE EYES, HEART, AND VITALS OF THE VICTIM...
'PEARS TO ME THAT WE'RE A LONG WAY BEHIND THE TIMES ON OUR SIDE OF THE BIG DRINK.
I USTER THINK THAT THE INJUNS COULD GIVE US POINTS IN TRYIN' TO MAKE A MAN UNCOMFORTABLE.
...BUT YOUR OLD MEDIAEVAL LAW-AND-ORDER PARTY COULD RAISE HIM EVERY TIME.
GUESS BUT I'LL GET IN THAT BOX FER A MINUTE...
...JEST TO SEE HOW IT FEELS!
OH NO! IT IS TOO TERRIBLE!

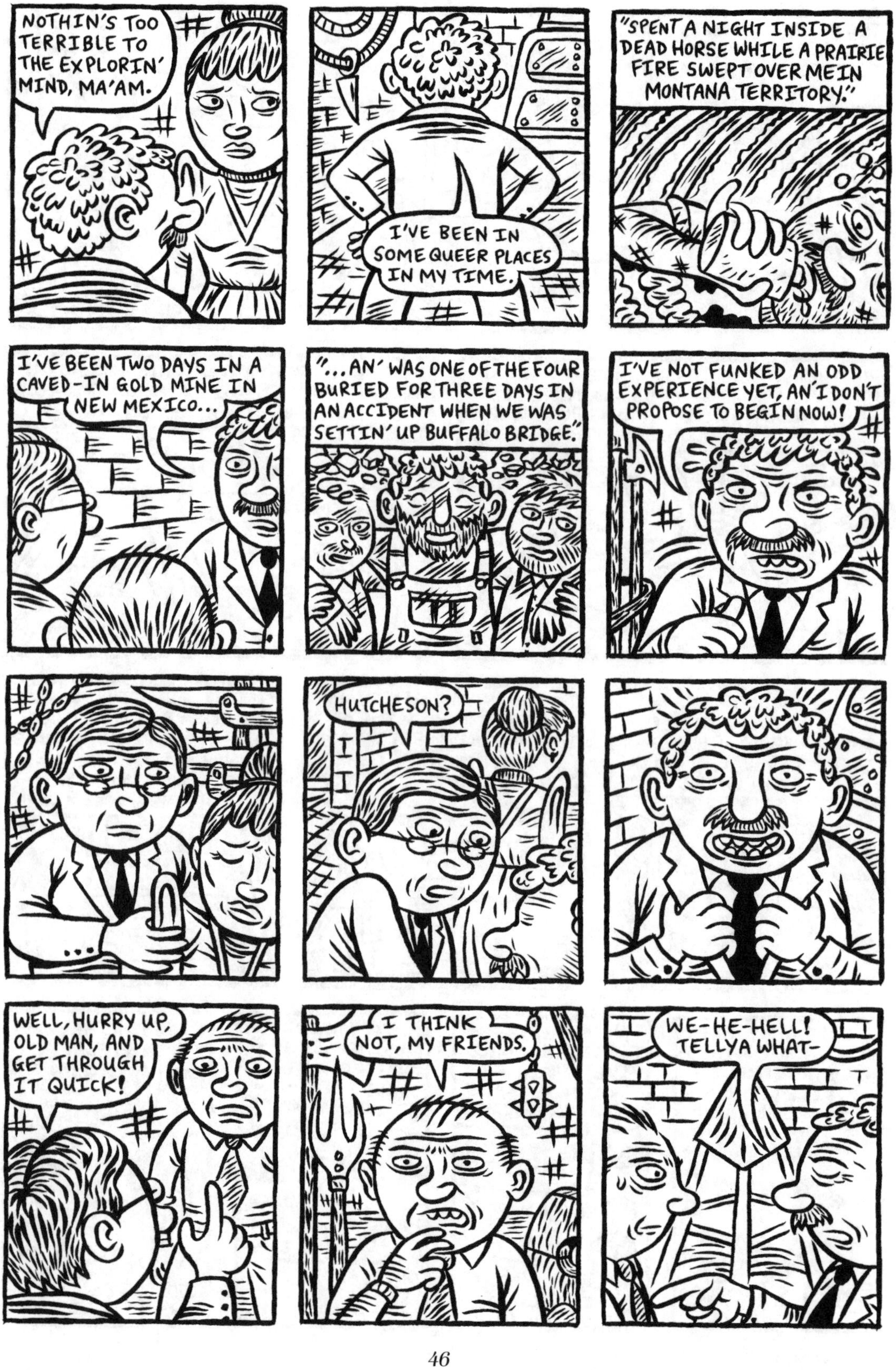
NOTHIN'S TOO TERRIBLE TO THE EXPLORIN' MIND, MA'AM.
I'VE BEEN IN SOME QUEER PLACES IN MY TIME.
"SPENT A NIGHT INSIDE A DEAD HORSE WHILE A PRAIRIE FIRE SWEPT OVER ME IN MONTANA TERRITORY."
I'VE BEEN TWO DAYS IN A CAVED-IN GOLD MINE IN NEW MEXICO...
"...AN' WAS ONE OF THE FOUR BURIED FOR THREE DAYS IN AN ACCIDENT WHEN WE WAS SETTIN' UP BUFFALO BRIDGE."
I'VE NOT FUNKED AN ODD EXPERIENCE YET, AN' I DON'T PROPOSE TO BEGIN NOW!
HUTCHESON?
WELL, HURRY UP, OLD MAN, AND GET THROUGH IT QUICK!
I THINK NOT, MY FRIENDS.
WE-HE-HELL! TELLYA WHAT-

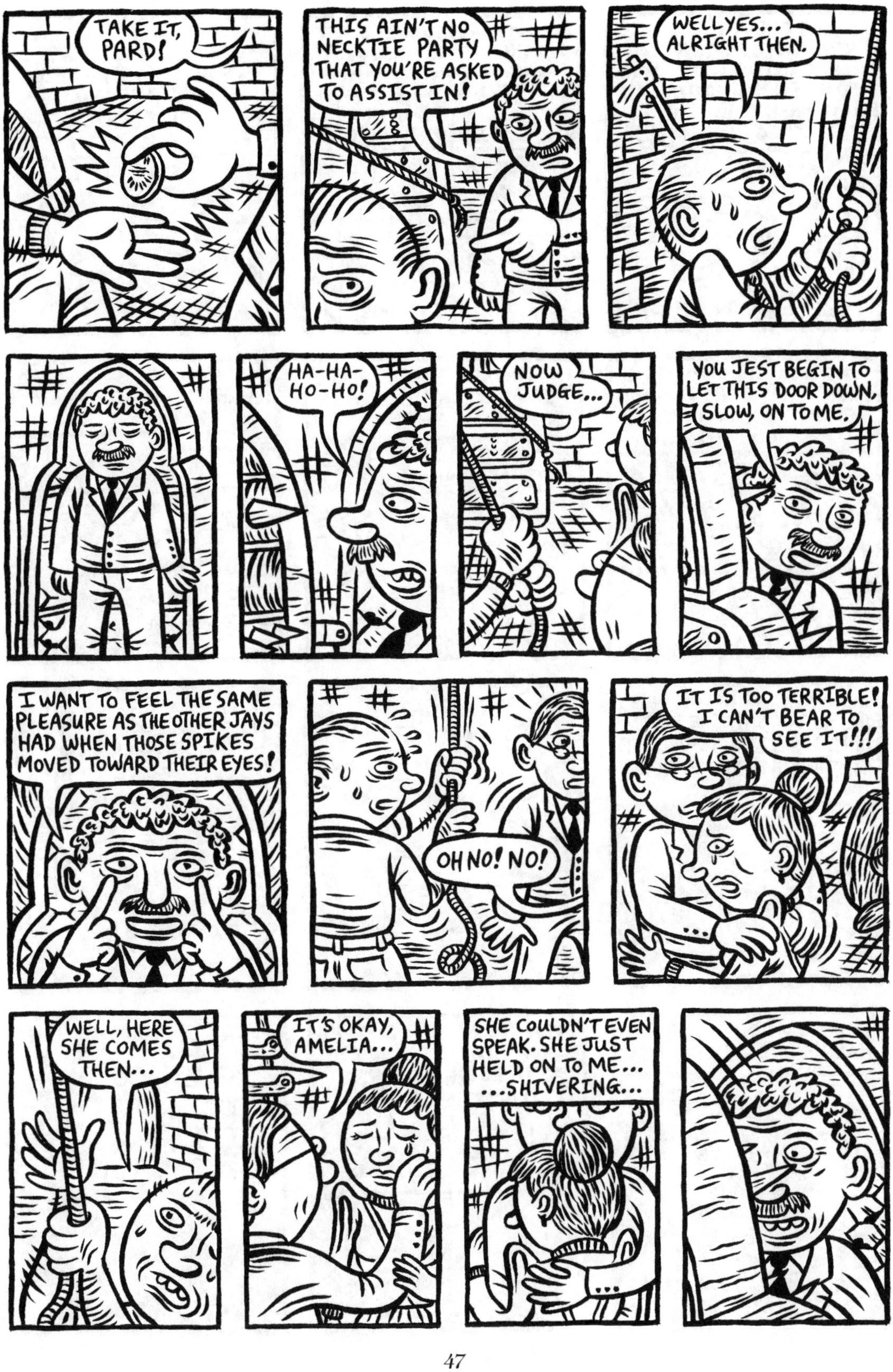
TAKE IT, PARD!
THIS AIN'T NO NECKTIE PARTY THAT YOU'RE ASKED TO ASSIST IN!
WELL YES... ALRIGHT THEN.
HA-HA-HO-HO!
NOW JUDGE...
YOU JEST BEGIN TO LET THIS DOOR DOWN, SLOW, ON TO ME.
I WANT TO FEEL THE SAME PLEASURE AS THE OTHER JAYS HAD WHEN THOSE SPIKES MOVED TOWARD THEIR EYES!
OH NO! NO!
IT IS TOO TERRIBLE! I CAN'T BEAR TO SEE IT!!!
WELL, HERE SHE COMES THEN...
IT'S OKAY, AMELIA...
SHE COULDN'T EVEN SPEAK. SHE JUST HELD ON TO ME... ...SHIVERING...

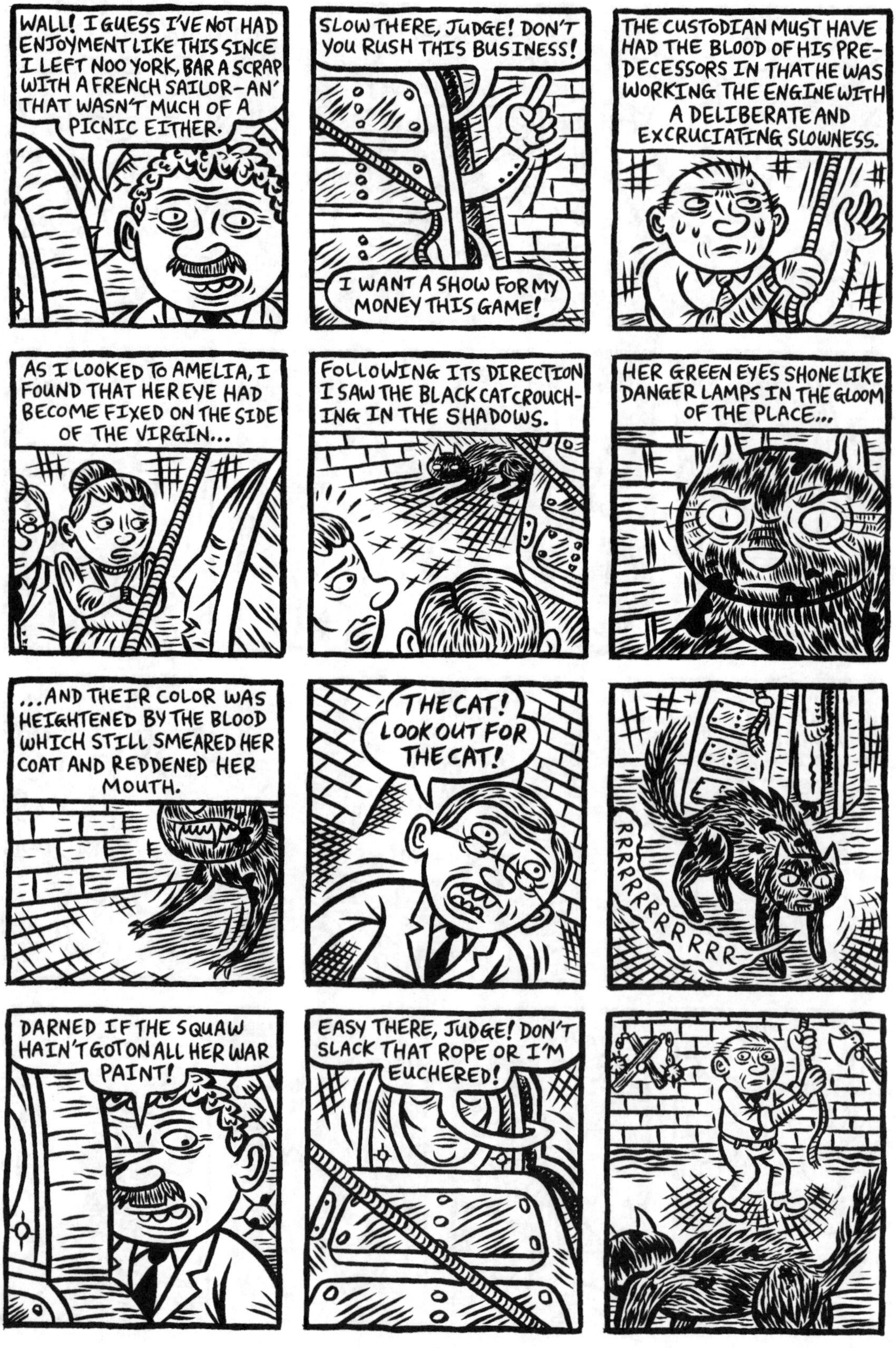
WALL! I GUESS I'VE NOT HAD ENJOYMENT LIKE THIS SINCE I LEFT NOO YORK, BAR A SCRAP WITH A FRENCH SAILOR—AN' THAT WASN'T MUCH OF A PICNIC EITHER.
SLOW THERE, JUDGE! DON'T YOU RUSH THIS BUSINESS!
I WANT A SHOW FOR MY MONEY THIS GAME!
THE CUSTODIAN MUST HAVE HAD THE BLOOD OF HIS PREDECESSORS IN THAT HE WAS WORKING THE ENGINE WITH A DELIBERATE AND EXCRUCIATING SLOWNESS.
AS I LOOKED TO AMELIA, I FOUND THAT HER EYE HAD BECOME FIXED ON THE SIDE OF THE VIRGIN...
FOLLOWING ITS DIRECTION I SAW THE BLACK CAT CROUCHING IN THE SHADOWS.
HER GREEN EYES SHONE LIKE DANGER LAMPS IN THE GLOOM OF THE PLACE...
...AND THEIR COLOR WAS HEIGHTENED BY THE BLOOD WHICH STILL SMEARED HER COAT AND REDDENED HER MOUTH.
THE CAT! LOOK OUT FOR THE CAT!
RRRRRRRRRRRRRR—
DARNED IF THE SQUAW HAIN'T GOT ON ALL HER WAR PAINT!
EASY THERE, JUDGE! DON'T SLACK THAT ROPE OR I'M EUCHERED!

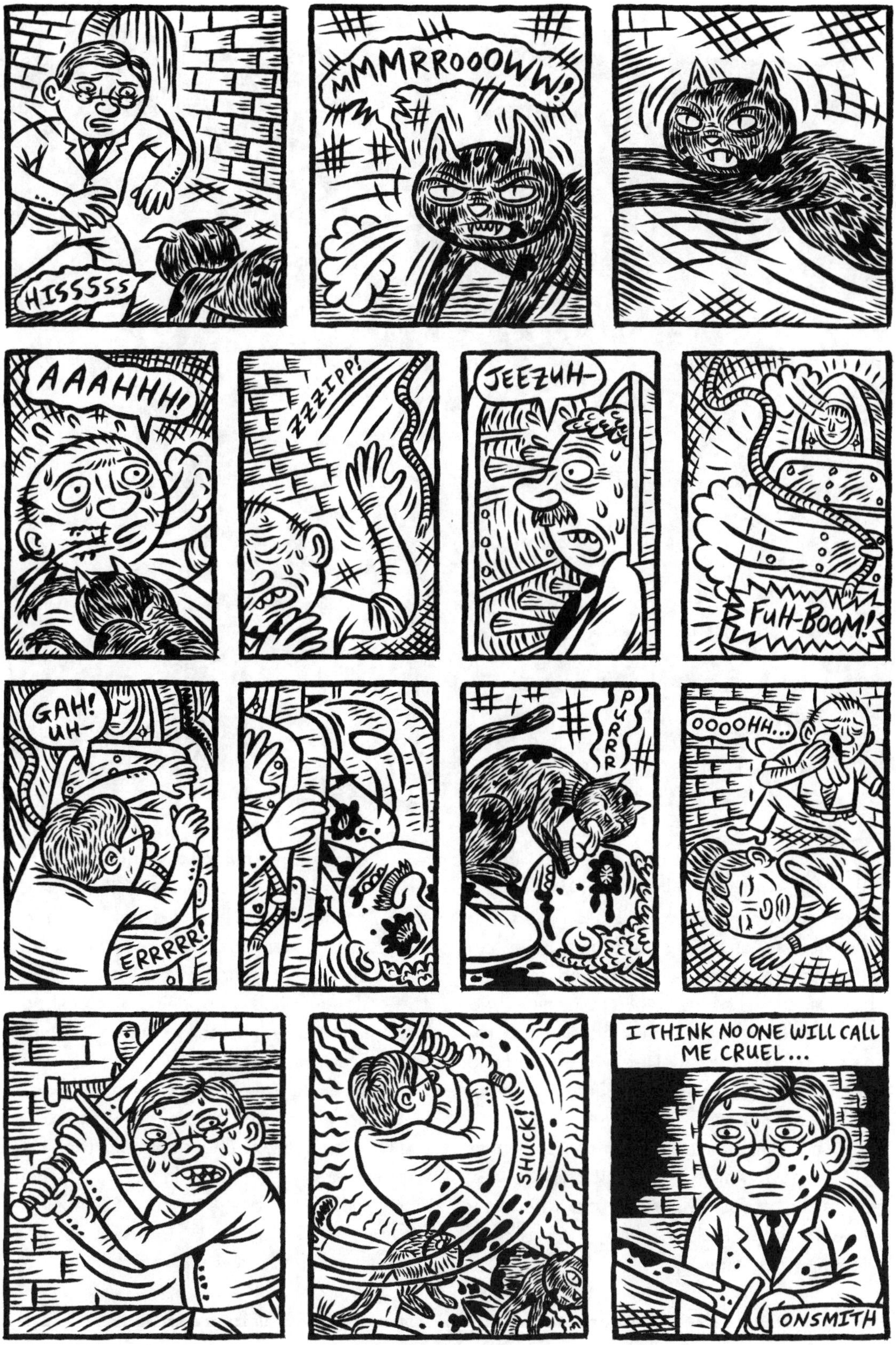
HISSSSS
MMMRROOOWW!
AAAHHH!
ZZZIPP!
JEEZUH-
FUH-BOOM!
GAH! UH-
ERRRRR!
PURRR
OOOOHH...
SHUCK!
I THINK NO ONE WILL CALL ME CRUEL...
ONSMITH

The Wondrous Child

Far away on the edge of a great creek that stretched inland from the endless sea, there lay a peaceful village. The lord of this village was a very good man, who had three children, Sibold and May, and one baby boy just come home who had no name as yet.

Sibold had just reached his eighth birthday, and May was six. They were very fond of each other, as brother and sister should be, and always played together.

The children had certain secret haunts that nobody knew of except themselves. There they would tell each other what they thought about, and what they would like to do when they grew up.

Their favorite place was under a great weeping willow. This was a mighty tree, many hundreds of years old, whose long branches fell down so thickly that one could hardly see into the hollow that lay within. The children found an opening and pushed the branches aside so they could enter and play in the beautiful bower.

Around the great tree were many beds of beautiful flowers; asters, pansies, tulips and huge sunflowers abounded. But their favorites were the poppies. In the moss from which the willow rose, they grew to an enormous size; so high that Sibold could not reach the scarlet flowers.

story by **Bram Stoker**, *edited by Tom Pomplun, illustrated by* **Evert Geradts**

One day after breakfast, Sibold and May took their lunch with them, and went out to spend the day wandering in the woods.

Sibold and May sat in the sunlight and talked of their new baby brother. They wondered where he came from, and Sibold said that he must have come over the sea, and been laid in the parsley-bed by the angels, so that nurse might find him there and bring him to comfort their poor sick mother.

After a while they got tired of sitting in the sun; so they wandered hand in hand until they reached the great willow and the bed of poppies. They each gathered an armful of flowers, then entered the bower to eat their lunch. When they finished, they felt very tired, so they lay down together and went to sleep with the poppies all around them.

After a time they were not asleep. It did not seem to be any later in the day, but to be the early morning. Neither of them felt the least sleepy.

"Come down to the creek," said Sibold, "and let us get out my boat."

May arose, and they left the bower. They went down to the creek, and there they found Sibold's little boat with its white sails set.

"Let's get in," said Sibold.

"But it is too small," said May.

"Let us try," said her brother. He took hold of the cord that tied the boat to the bank, and pulled it in. As the boat drew nearer, it got bigger and bigger, and when it touched the bank, they saw that it was just large enough to hold them both.

They got in and Sibold untied the boat. The white sails swelled, and they began to move away from the shore.

The sun shone very brightly. The water was as blue as the sky, and the shore was varied. Each moment showed something new and beautiful.

Now it was a jutting rock all covered with trailing plants whose flowers almost touched the water.

Now it was a beach, where the white sand glittered and glistened in the light.

Then there were places where great lilacs made the air sweet with the breath of their pink and white blossoms.

There were also great coconut trees up whose stems monkeys ran to gather the coconuts that they threw down below.

The children liked all these places, but presently they come to a spot where there was a patch of emerald grass shaded by giant trees and surrounded by flowers.

When they saw this place they cried out, "Oh, how beautiful! Let us stop here."

The boat seemed to understand their wishes, for it turned and drifted in gently to the shore. The moment the children got out, the sails folded themselves, and the anchor jumped overboard.

Sibold and May took each other's hands, and they explored the place together. Presently May said, in a whisper: "Oh, Sibold, this place is so nice, I wonder if there is any parsley here."

"Why do you want parsley?" he asked.

"Because if there was a nice bed of parsley we might be able to find a baby — and oh, Sibold, I do so want a baby."

So the children went searching; and soon, sure enough, they found the biggest parsley plant they had ever seen.

Then May heard a queer kind of sound — a very soft laugh — like a smile set to music. She pointed and said, "Look, look!"

Sibold ran forward, and lifted up the leaf of an enormous parsley plant; and there — joy of joys! — was the dearest little baby that ever was seen.

May lifted the baby up, and began to rock him, and sing, while Sibold looked on complacently. However, after a while he got impatient, and said, "Look here, you know, I found that baby; he belongs to me."

"I heard him first," said May. "He is mine."

"He is mine," said Sibold.

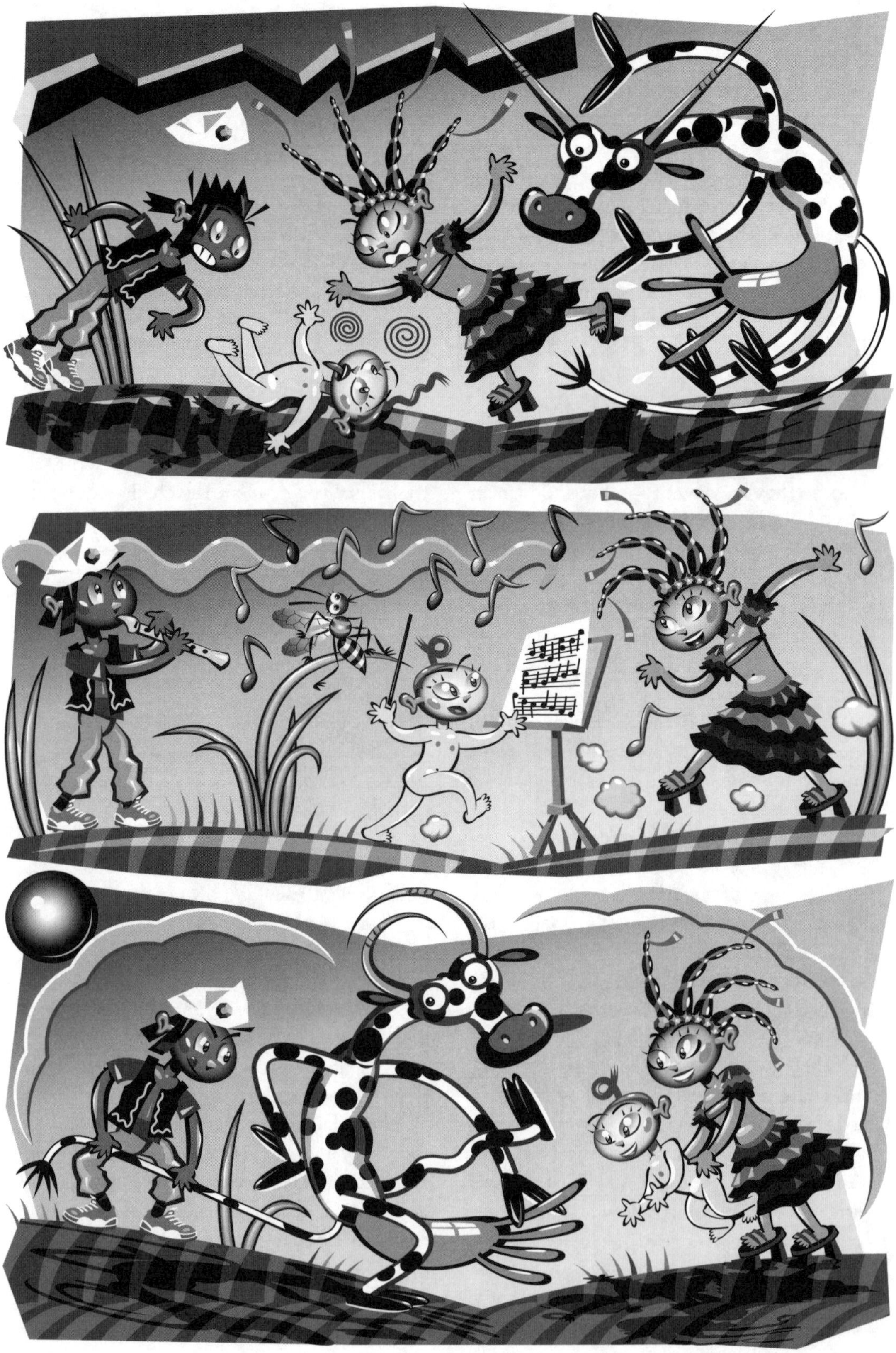

"He is mine," said May; and both began to get angry.

Suddenly they heard a low groan. Both children looked down in alarm, and saw that the poor baby was dead.

They were horrorstruck, and each begged the other's forgiveness, and promised that never again would they argue. When they had done this, the child opened its eyes, looked at them gravely, and said, "Now never quarrel again. If you get angry, I shall be dead and gone."

"Indeed, Ba," said May, "I shall never be angry again."

Said Sibold, "I assure you, sir, that under no provocation shall I be guilty of the malfeasance of anger."

"How pretty he speaks," said May. Then for a while they were all quiet.

Presently the baby turned its eyes up to May, and said, "Please, Little Mother, will you sing to me?"

"What would you like, Ba?" said May.

"Oh, anything that comes handy. I prefer something simple — as, for instance, any little tune beginning with a chromatic scale in consecutive fifths and octaves, pianissimo — rallentando — accellerando — crescendo — up to an inharmonic change on the dominant of the diminished flat ninth."

"Oh, please, Ba," said May, "I do not know anything about that yet. I am only in scales."

"Very well, dear," said the child, kissing her, "anything you please, only let it come straight from your heart."

Then May sang something very sweet and pretty. She did not know the words, and she did not know the tune, and she had only a vague sort of idea what it was all about; but it was very pretty.

When she finished, the Child said, "Chlap, Chlap, M-chlap!"

"What does he mean?" she asked Sibold, in distress, for she saw that the Baby wanted something.

Just then a big cow put its head over the bushes, and said, "Moo-oo-oo."

The beautiful child clapped his hands, and May said, "Oh, I know. He wants to be fed."

The cow walked in, and Sibold said, "I suppose I had better milk him."

"Please do, dear," said May, and she began cuddling the baby again, and telling him that he would soon be fed now.

While she was thus engaged, she was sitting with her back to Sibold; but then the baby began to laugh so much that May turned around to see what he was looking at. There was Sibold trying to milk the cow by pumping its tail.

The cow did not seem to mind him, but went on grazing. "Oh, I say," said Sibold, "do hurry up now, and give us some milk; the Ba wants some."

The cow answered, "Don't blame me. It is your own fault. Try some other way."

All at once, without knowing how it came to pass, May found herself pouring milk out of a watering can all over the baby, who lay on the ground. He was laughing like mad; and when the can was all emptied, he said, "Thank you. I never enjoyed dinner so much in my life."

"This is a very queer baby!" said May, in a whisper.

"Very," said Sibold.

While they were talking there came a dreadful sound among the trees, far away at first, but getting nearer every moment. May hugged the child and said to him, "Do not fear, dear Ba. We will not let it touch you."

At that moment a great angry tiger bounded over the bushes and stood glaring at them out of green flaming eyes.

May looked on with terror, then she saw that the tiger was eyeing not her nor Sibold, but the baby. This made her more frightened than ever, and she clasped him closer. As she looked, however, she saw that the tiger's eyes got less and less angry, until at last they were as tame as those of her own favorite tabby.

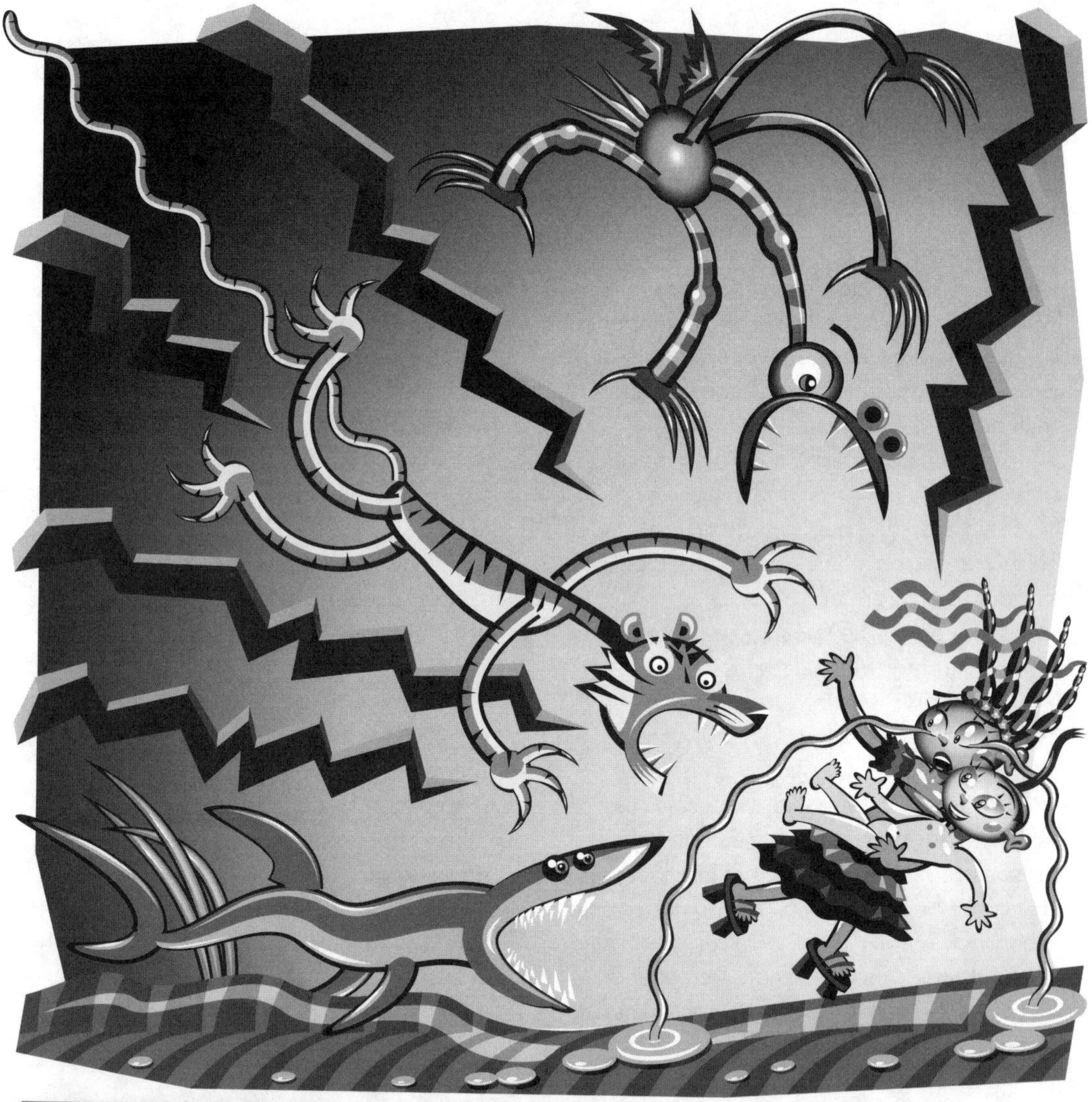

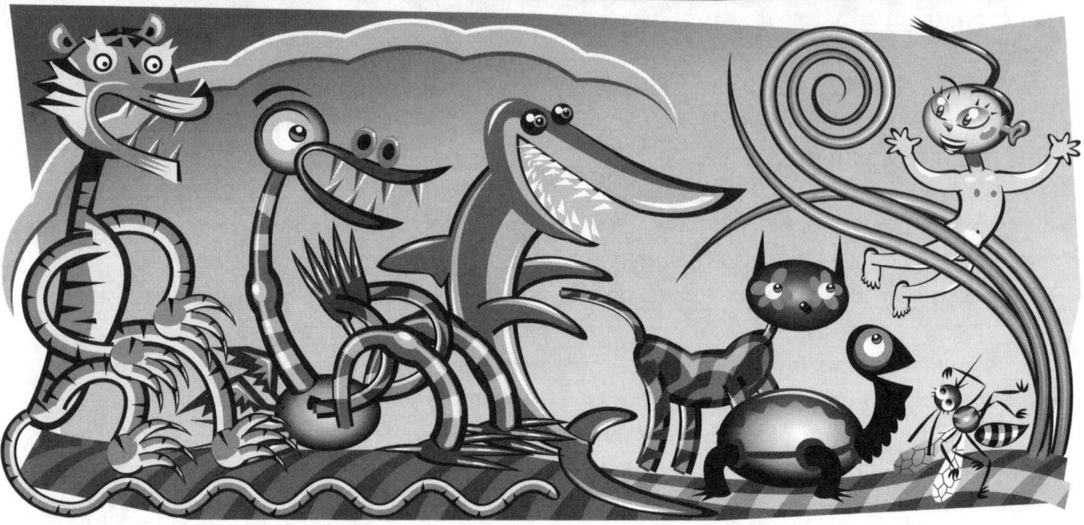

Then the tiger began to purr. It came and crouched before the wondrous child, and licked his little fat hands with its rough tongue. The tiger then lay down, purring, and watched over the child as if on guard.

Presently there came another loud sound. Great wings flapped like thunder, and the air was darkened by a mighty bird of prey that made a shadow over the land.

As the bird swooped down, the tiger rose as though about to spring to meet it.

But when the bird saw the child it hung in mid-air with its huge head drooped in submission. Then it alit in the glade and guarded alongside the tiger.

Again there was a terrible sound, this time out to sea, as if some giant thing was lashing the water.

Looking around, the children saw a huge shark rise out of the sea and come up on land. The shark was jumping along, with its tail beating about and its great teeth grinding together.

When it saw the baby, the shark also made submission, and then kept guard. It swam back and forth along the shore like a sentry.

May and Sibold looked in wonder at the beautiful child, before whom these monsters made obeisance. May whispered into Sibold's ear, "I think the Ba is an angel!"

Sibold looked at the baby in awe as he answered quietly, "I think so, too. What are we to do?"

"I do not know," said May; "I hope he will not be angry with us for calling him 'Ba.'"

While they were talking, all sorts of animals and birds and fishes were coming into the glade. A lion and a lamb came first, and these two bowed to the child, and then went and lay down together. Then came a hawk and a pigeon; and then a dog and a cat; and then a hare and a tortoise; and a sparrow and a worm; and many others, until all the glade was full of living things all at peace with one another.

May said to the child, "Oh, dear Ba, I do so wish they would always continue happy and at peace like this."

The child put his little arms around her neck and kissed her, and said, very low and very sweetly, words that all her life long she never forgot: "Be always loving and sweet, dear child, and even the angels will know your thoughts and will listen to your words."

The beautiful child then spoke to all, and his words seemed full of sound but very soft, like the echo of distant thunder coming over far waters.

"Know, dear children, there shall be peace between all living things when the children of men are for one hour in perfect harmony with each other. Strive, each and all of you, that it may be so."

Then the wondrous child seemed to float out of May's arms and to move down toward the sea. All the living things instantly hurried to make a great double line between which he passed.

May and Sibold followed him hand in hand. He waited as the boat came close; the anchor climbed on board; the white sails ran aloft, and a fresh breeze began to blow towards home.

The wondrous child moved on to the prow, and Sibold and May went on board. Waving goodbye to all the peaceful animals, they sat hand in hand as the boat moved along swiftly and gently. The shore faded into a dim mist as they swept along.

Presently they saw their own creek, and the great willow towering on the shore.

The boat came to land. The child, floating in the air, moved towards the willow bower as Sibold and May followed.

When the leafy curtain fell behind them, the wondrous child got dimmer and dimmer; until at last, waving his tiny hands, he seemed to melt away into the air.

Sibold and May sat for a long time, thinking. Then both feeling tired, they lay down to sleep, with the poppies all around them.

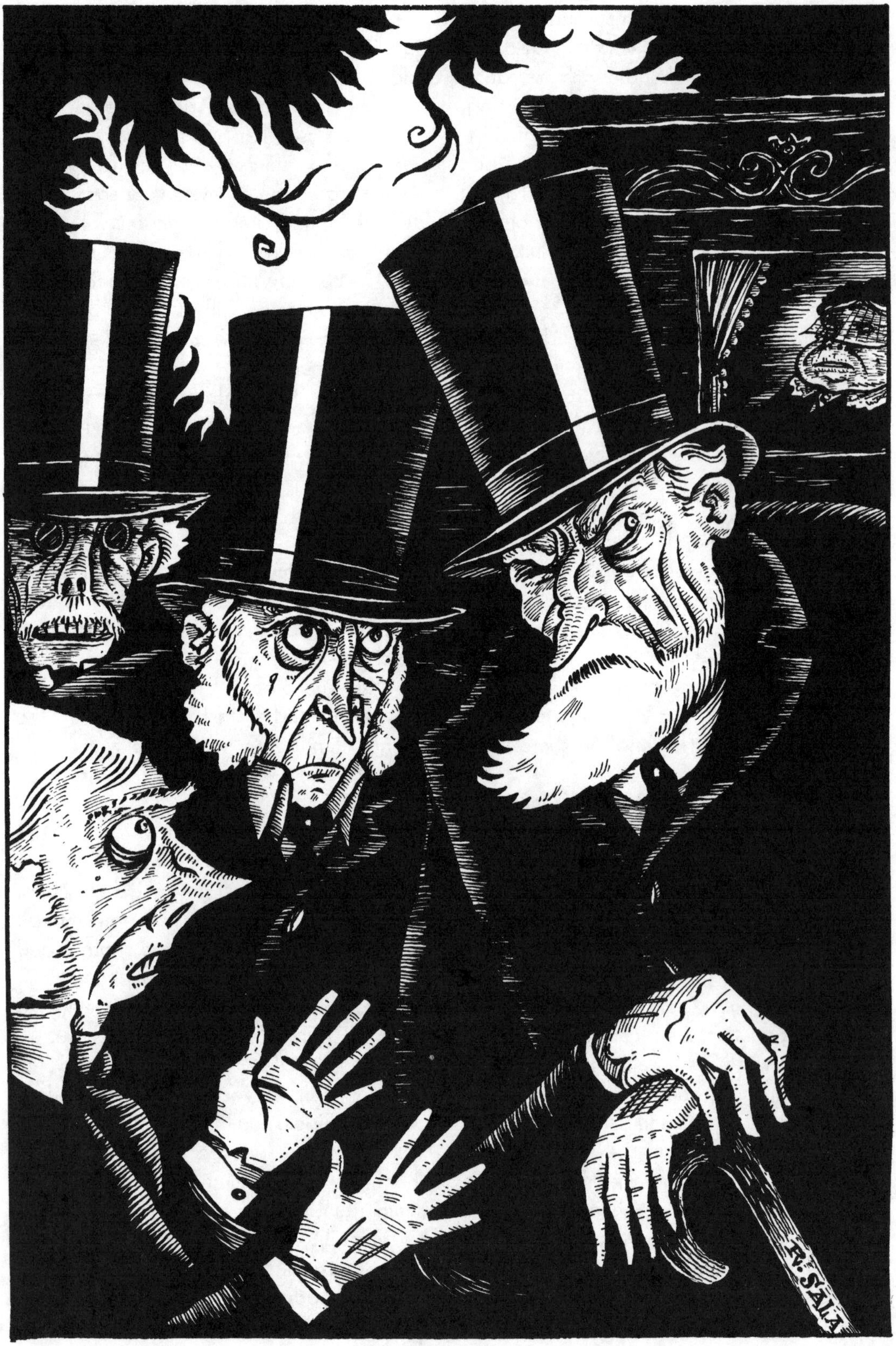
R. SALA

ILLUSTRATION ©2003 RICHARD SALA

THE FUNERAL PARTY

a very short story by **BRAM STOKER**
illustrated by **RICHARD SALA**

THE FUNERAL was taking place in Dublin of a young married woman whose death had been as sudden as it had been mysterious. Her beauty had been the object of much public gossip, the more so because her husband was a man of advancing years.

On the appointed day for her interment, the undertaker, after the wont of his craft, was early at the home of the deceased arranging the whole funeral party according to the local rules of mortuary etiquette.

With due solemnity and lowered voice he spoke to the widower, "You, sir, will of course go in the carriage with the mother of the deceased."

"What! Me go in the carriage with my mother-in-law? Not likely!" the man replied with surprising emphasis.

"Oh, sir, but I assure you it is necessary. The rule is an inviolable one, established by precedents beyond all cavil!" exclaimed the horrified undertaker.

But the widower was obdurate. "I won't go in that carriage — and that's flat."

"Oh, but my good sir. Remember the gravity of the occasion — the publicity — the — the — possibility — of scandal!" The voice of the man in black faded into a gasp.

But still the widower stuck to his resolution, and the undertaker went away to discuss the matter with some of his intimate friends who were awaiting instructions as to their duties for the funeral service. After some discussion, these men then approached the chief mourner and began to remonstrate with him.

"You really must, old chap, it is a necessity," said one.

"Etiquette demands it," insisted another.

"I'll not! Go with my mother-in-law? I'll rot first!" the husband again insisted.

"But look here, old chap."

"I'll not, I tell you! I'll go in any other carriage that you wish — but not that one."

Finally, one of the circle of undertaker's men who had been silent all the while spoke up.

"Well, of course, if you won't, you won't," he said. "But remember it beforehand that afterwards when it will be thrown up against you, it'll be construed into an affront to the poor girl that has gone. You loved her, Jack, we all know that."

This argument at last prevailed. The widower signalled to the undertaker and began to pull on his black gloves. But as he moved towards the carriage in which his mother-in-law already sat, a stone-faced woman all in black, he turned to his friends and said in a low voice: "I'm only doing it because you say I ought to — and for the girl that's gone. But you will spoil my day!"

DRACULA'S VOYAGE
an excerpt from ~ DRACULA ~
—by— BRAM STOKER

ADAPTED BY JOHN W. PIERARD

CUTTING FROM **THE DAILY GRAPH**, 8 AUGUST, FROM A CORRESPONDENT – WHITBY.

ONE OF THE GREATEST AND SUDDENEST STORMS ON RECORD HAS JUST BEEN EXPERIENCED HERE WITH RESULTS BOTH STRANGE AND UNIQUE...

THE ATTENTION OF THE GREAT BODY OF HOLIDAY-MAKERS WAS CALLED TO A SUDDEN SHOW OF 'MARE'S TAILS,' HIGH IN THE SKY TO THE NORTHWEST...

GRAND MASSES OF SPLENDIDLY COLORED CLOUDS... MYRIADS OF EVERY SUNSET HUE...

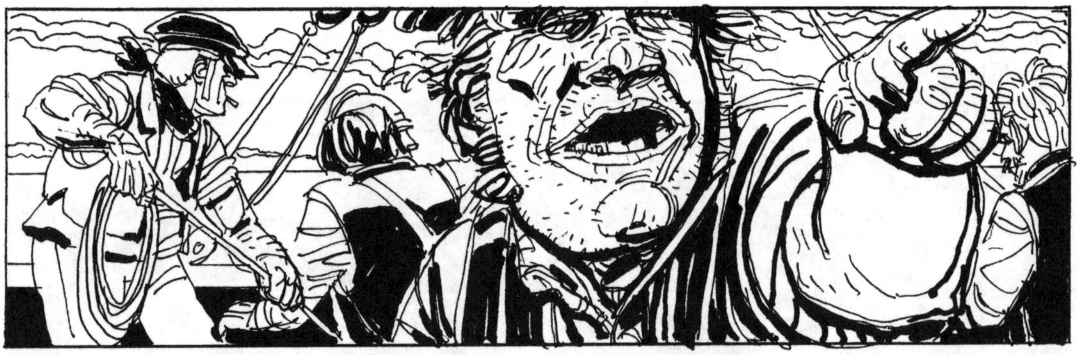

ONE OLD FISHERMAN FORETOLD IN AN EMPHATIC MANNER THE COMING OF A SUDDEN STORM...

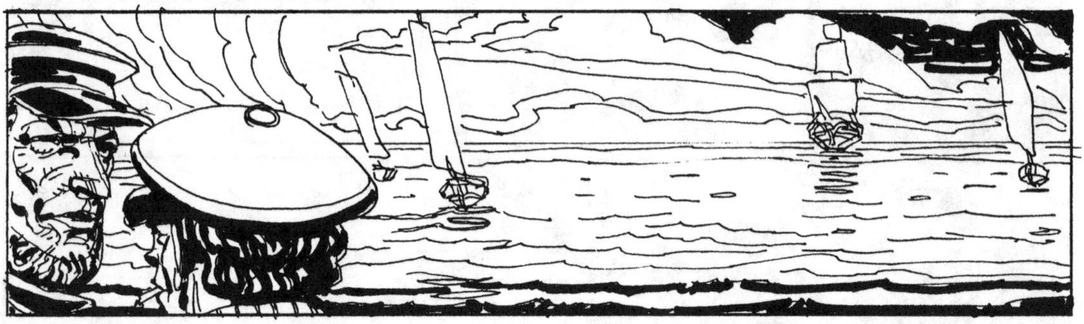

MORE THAN ONE CAPTAIN MADE UP HIS MIND TO REMAIN IN HARBOR...

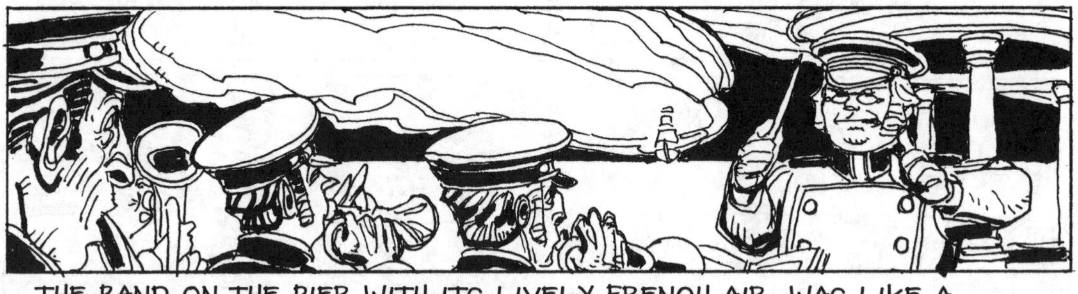

THE BAND ON THE PIER WITH ITS LIVELY FRENCH AIR, WAS LIKE A DISCORD IN THE HARMONY OF NATURE'S SILENCE...

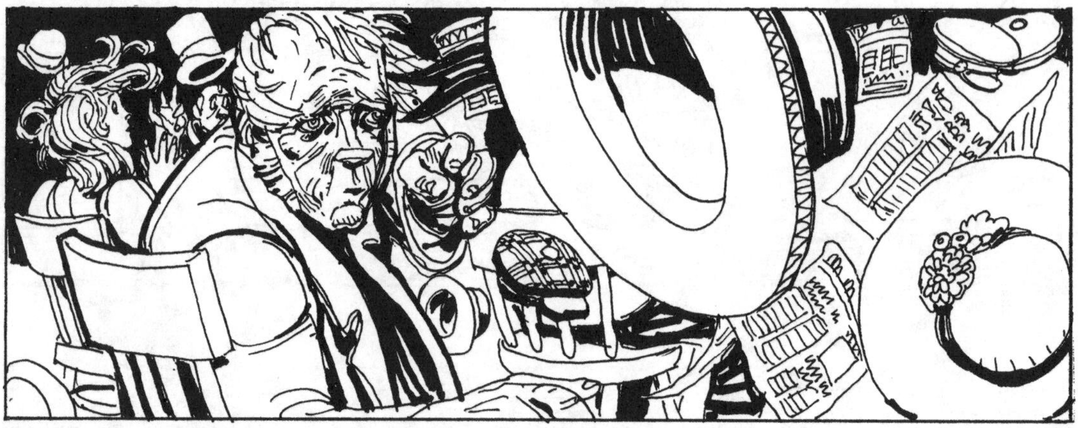

WITHOUT WARNING, THE TEMPEST BROKE.

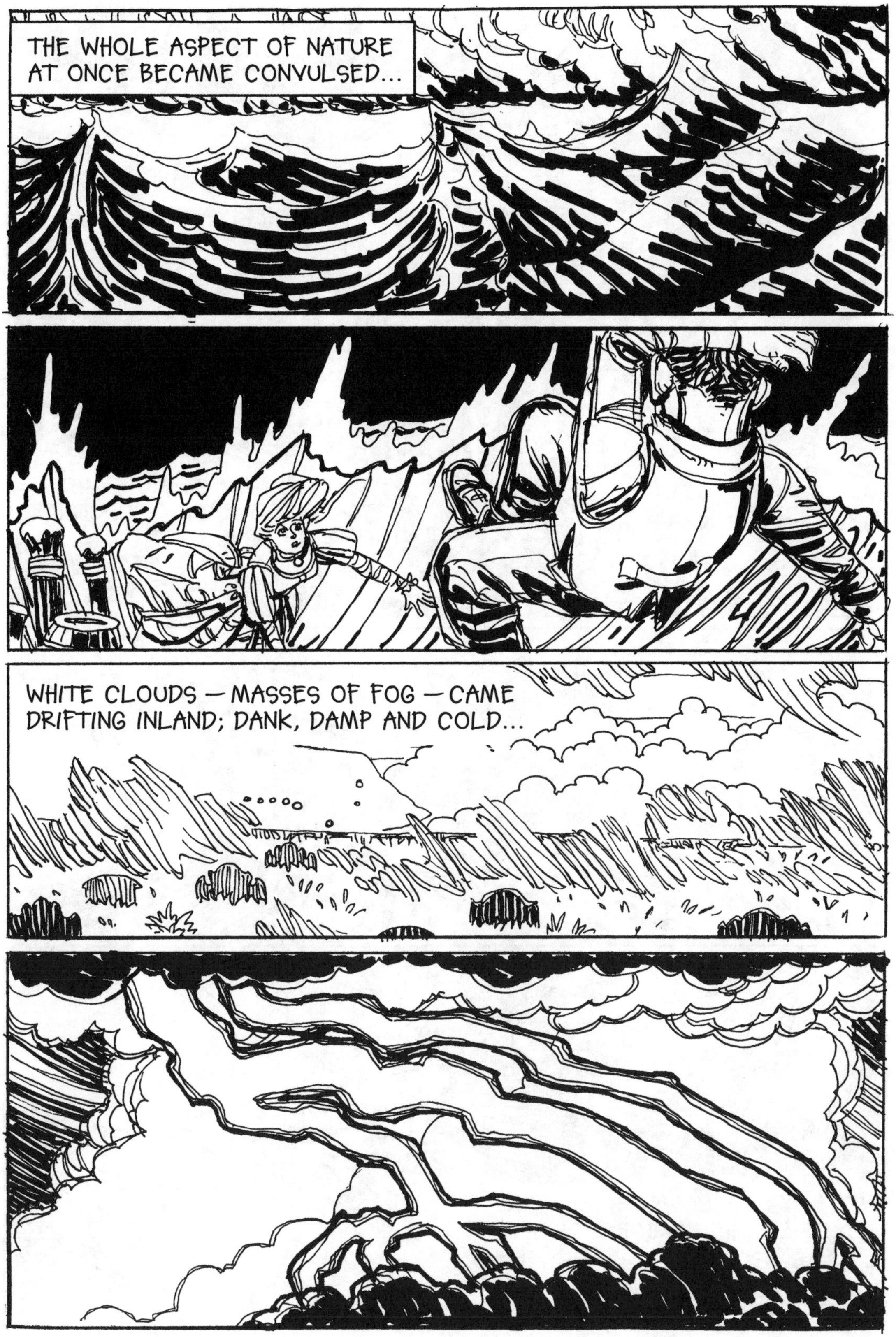
THE WHOLE ASPECT OF NATURE AT ONCE BECAME CONVULSED...
WHITE CLOUDS — MASSES OF FOG — CAME DRIFTING INLAND; DANK, DAMP AND COLD...

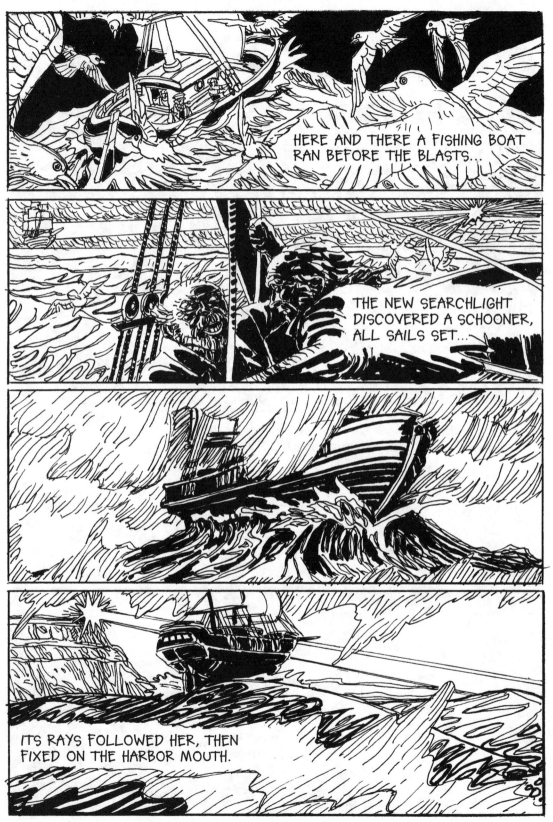

HERE AND THERE A FISHING BOAT RAN BEFORE THE BLASTS...

THE NEW SEARCHLIGHT DISCOVERED A SCHOONER, ALL SAILS SET...

ITS RAYS FOLLOWED HER, THEN FIXED ON THE HARBOR MOUTH.

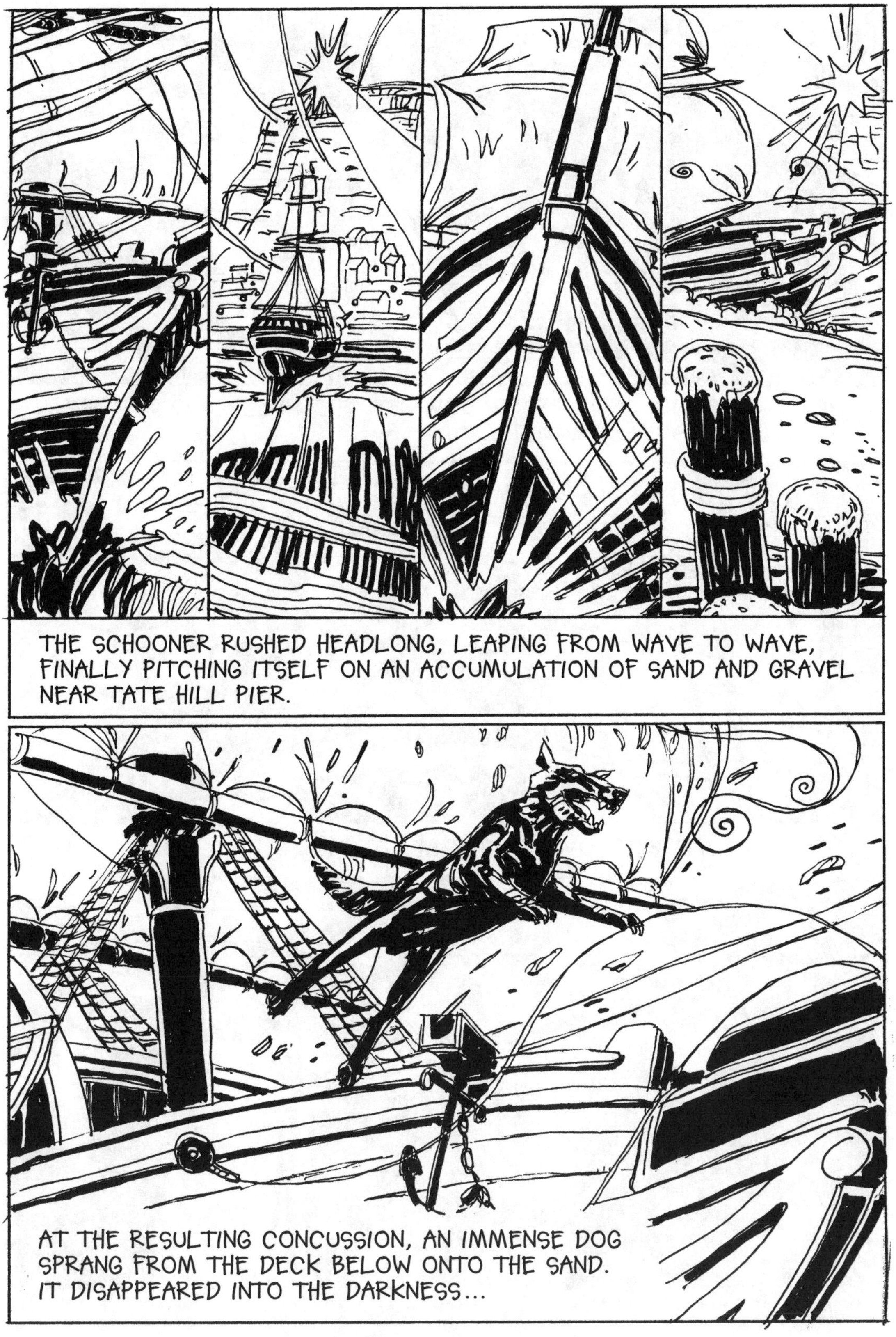
THE SCHOONER RUSHED HEADLONG, LEAPING FROM WAVE TO WAVE, FINALLY PITCHING ITSELF ON AN ACCUMULATION OF SAND AND GRAVEL NEAR TATE HILL PIER.
AT THE RESULTING CONCUSSION, AN IMMENSE DOG SPRANG FROM THE DECK BELOW ONTO THE SAND. IT DISAPPEARED INTO THE DARKNESS...

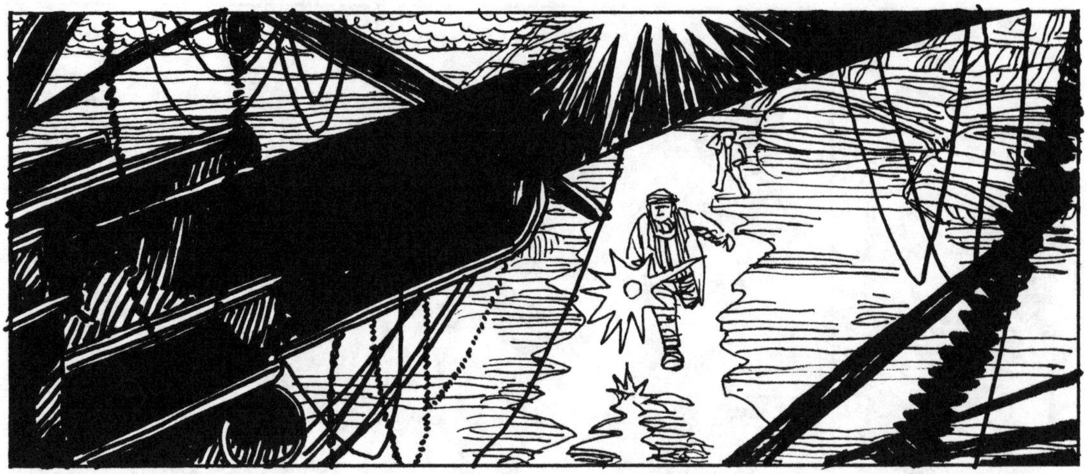

THE COAST GUARD ON DUTY RAN DOWN TO THE WRECK AND WAS THE FIRST TO CLIMB ON BOARD...

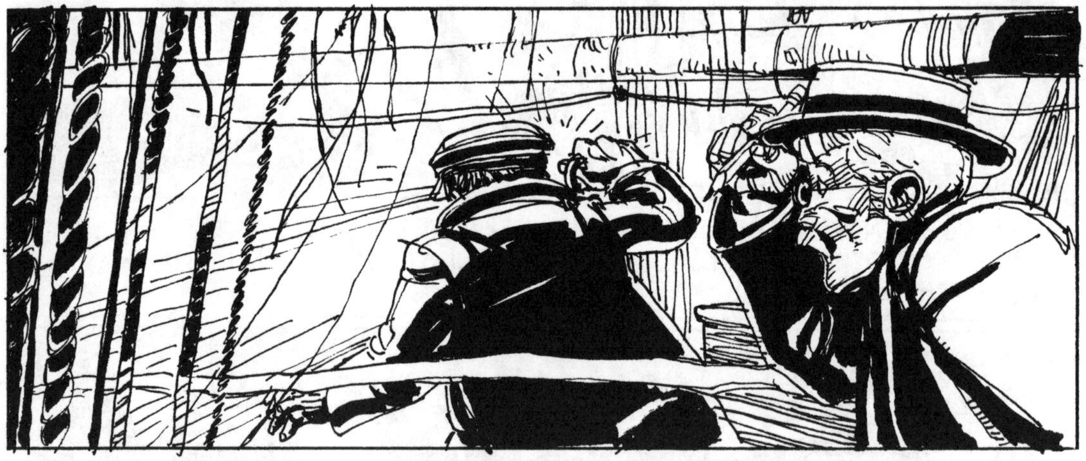

HE RAN AFT AND BENT OVER THE WHEEL TO EXAMINE IT...

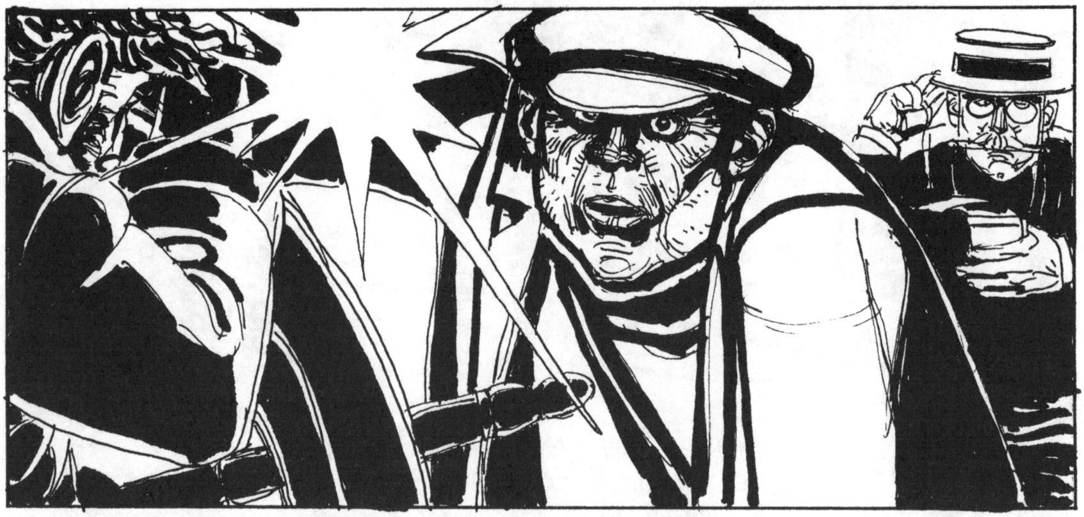

THEN RECOILED, AS IF FROM SUDDEN EMOTION.

THE SHIP, AS IF BY SOME MIRACLE, HAD FOUND ITS HARBOR UNSTEERED, SAVE BY THE HAND OF A DEAD MAN.

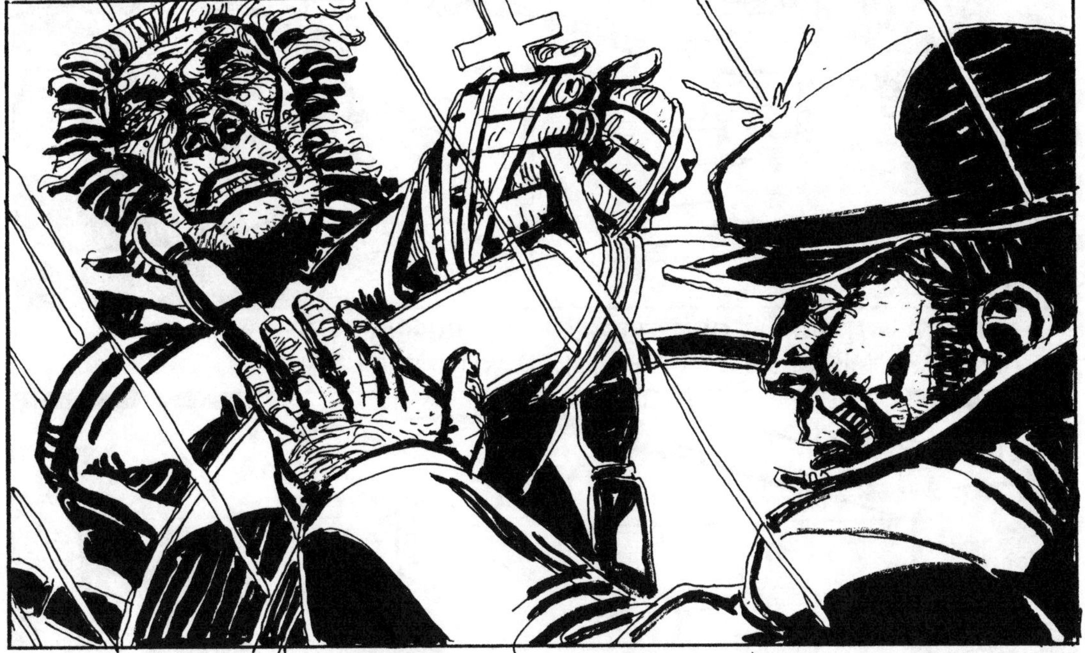

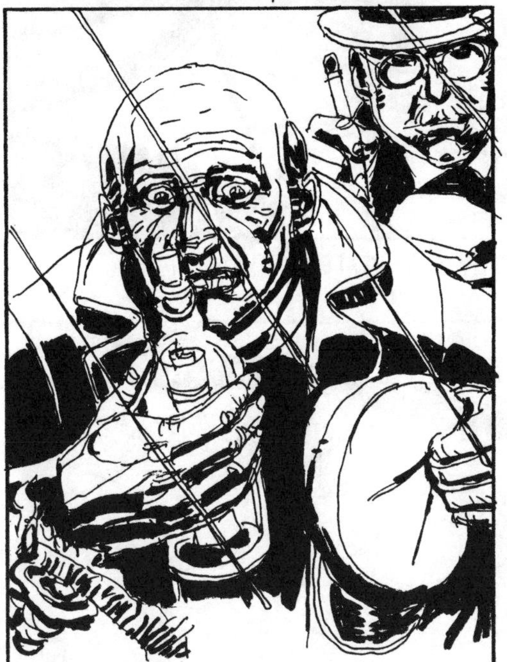
THE COAST GUARD SAID THAT THE MAN MUST HAVE TIED HIS OWN HANDS TO THE WHEEL, FASTENING THE KNOTS WITH HIS TEETH.

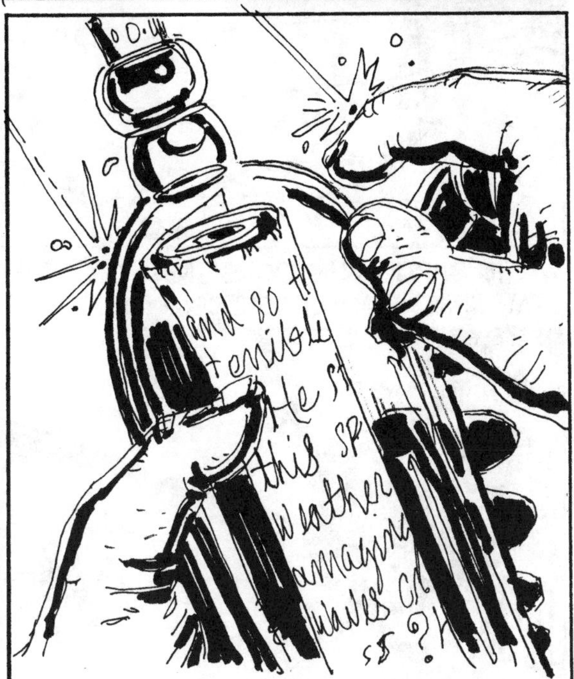
IN HIS POCKET WAS A CAREFULLY CORKED BOTTLE, EMPTY, SAVE FOR A LITTLE ROLL OF PAPER WHICH PROVED TO BE AN ADDENDUM TO THE SHIP'S LOG...

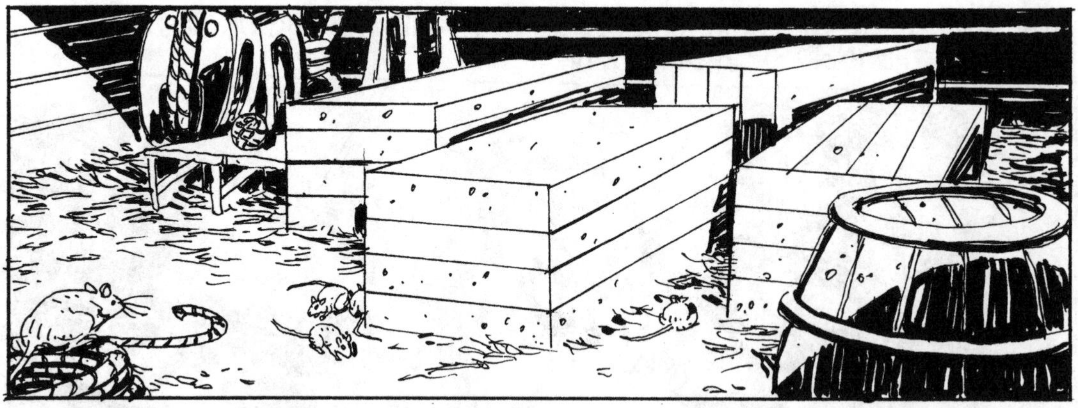

9 AUGUST – IT TURNS OUT THE SHIP IS A RUSSIAN FROM VARNA, ITS CARGO A NUMBER OF CRATES FILLED WITH MOULD.

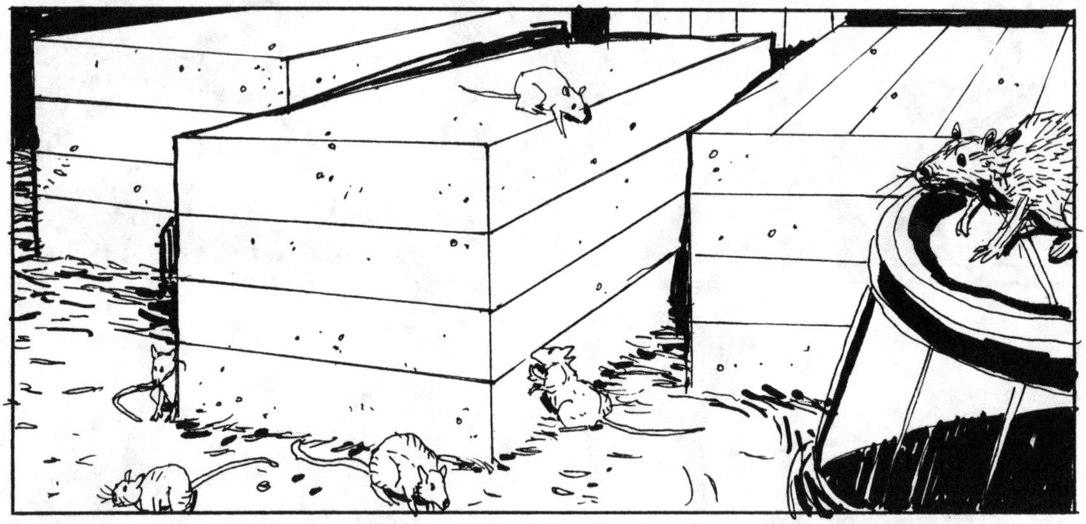

THE CARGO WAS CONSIGNED TO A WHITBY SOLICITOR WHO THIS MORNING TOOK POSSESSION...

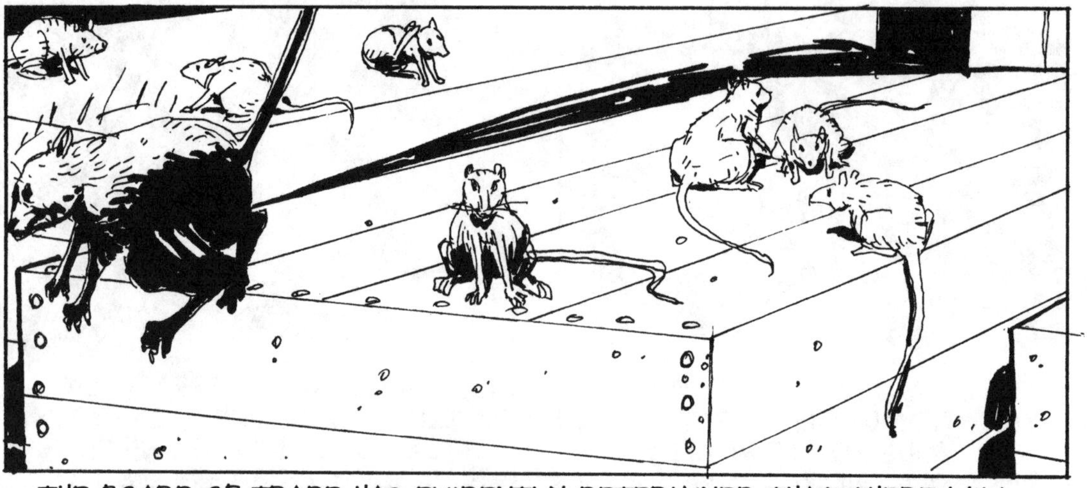

THE BOARD OF TRADE HAS EVIDENTLY DETERMINED THAT THERE WILL BE NO CAUSE FOR COMPLAINT.

MEMBERS OF THE LOCAL S.P.C.A. HAVE EXPRESSED A GOOD DEAL OF INTEREST CONCERNING THE DOG WHICH ESCAPED FROM THE SHIP...

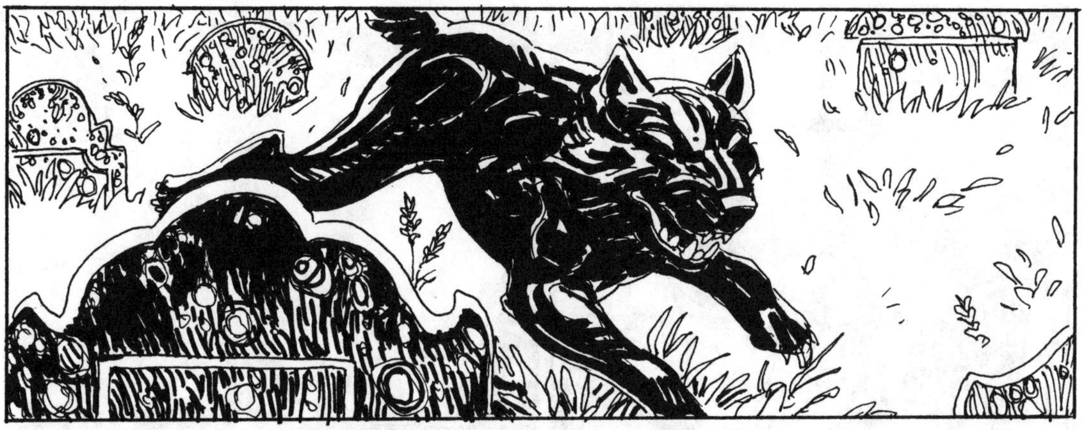

THEIR DESIRE TO BEFRIEND THE DOG HAS BEEN THWARTED BY THE FACT THAT IT IS NOWHERE TO BE FOUND.

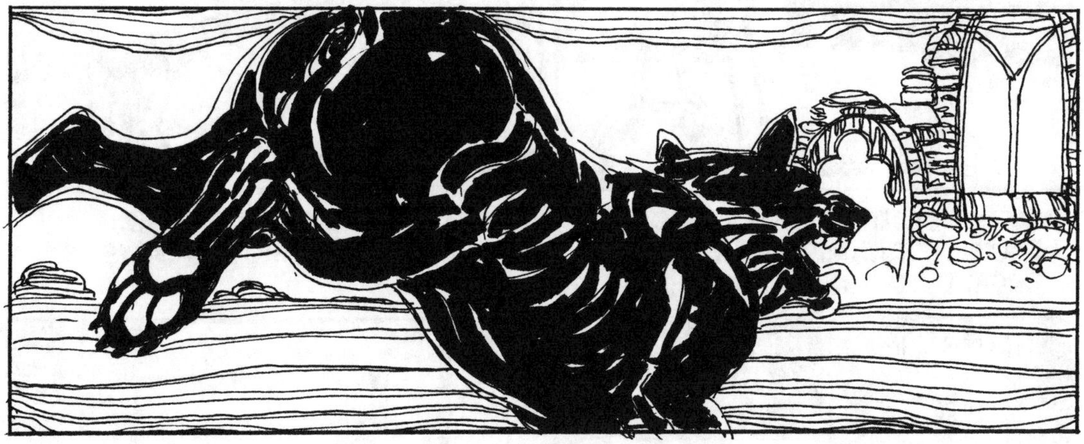

IT IS FEARED THAT THE BEAST MAY BE FRIGHTENED AND HIDING IN THE MOORS.

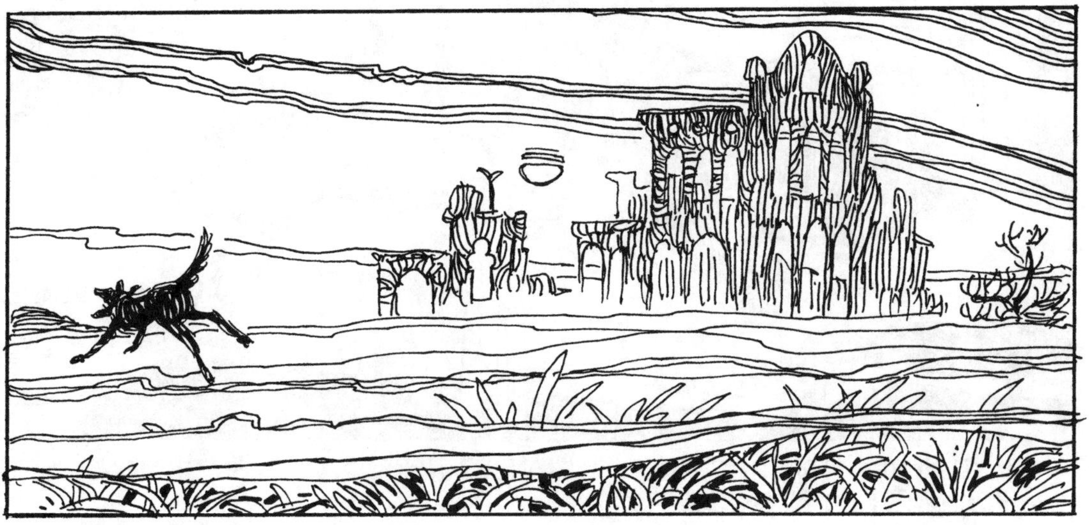

BY THE KINDNESS OF THE BOARD OF TRADE INSPECTOR, I HAVE BEEN PERMITTED TO LOOK OVER THE LOG OF THE DEMETER...

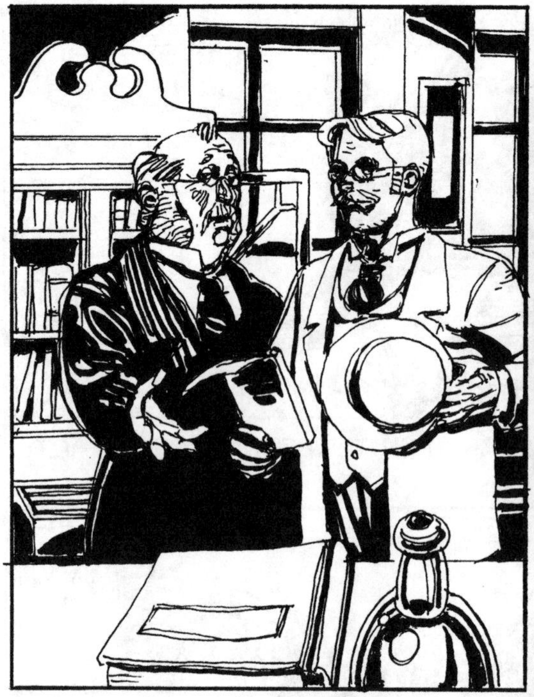

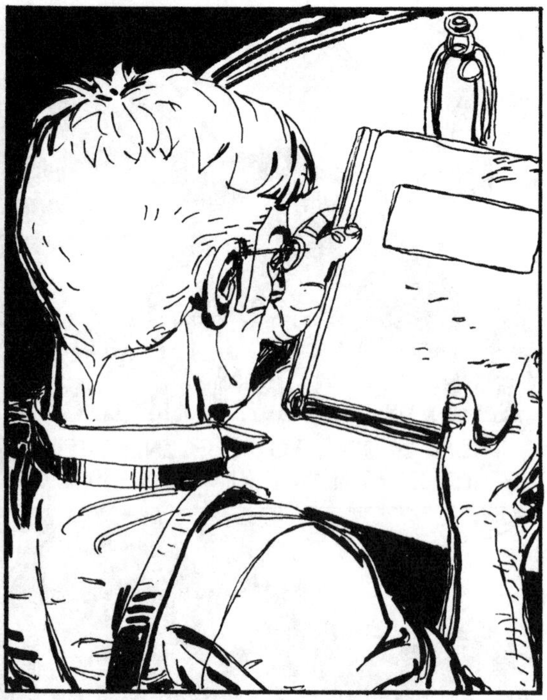

BUT IT CONTAINS NOTHING OF SPECIAL INTEREST, EXCEPT TO THE FACT OF THE MISSING MEN. THE GREATEST INTEREST, HOWEVER, IS IN REGARD TO THE M.S. IN THE BOTTLE...

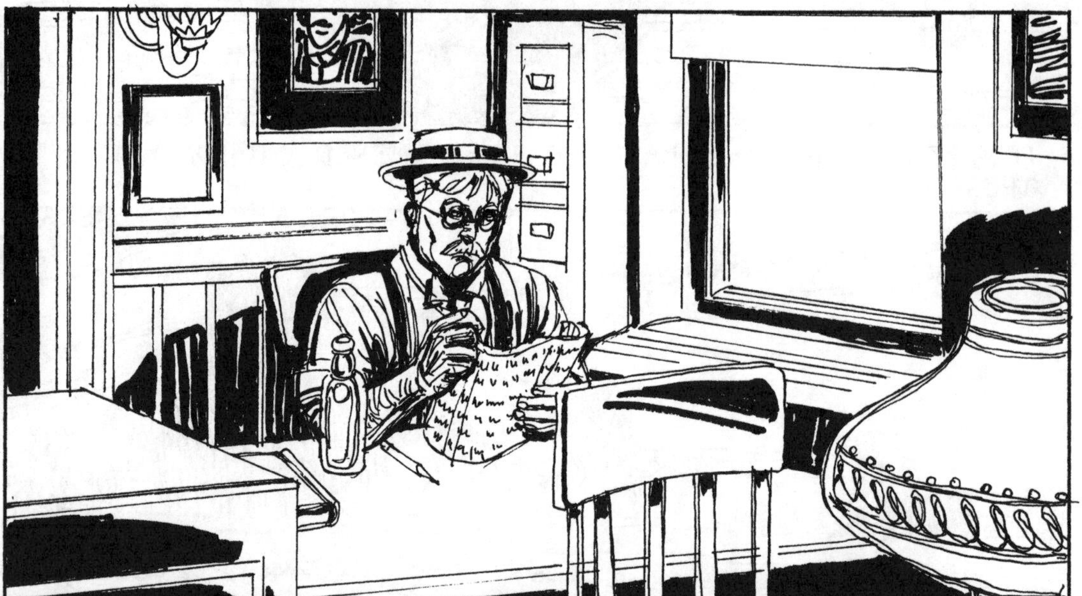

I HAVE NEVER COME ACROSS A STRANGER NARRATIVE THAN THE ONE WHICH UNFOLDS BETWEEN THE TWO DOCUMENTS!

LOG OF THE 'DEMETER,' VARNA TO WHITBY:

6 JULY – WE FINISHED TAKING IN CARGO. AT NOON SET SAIL…

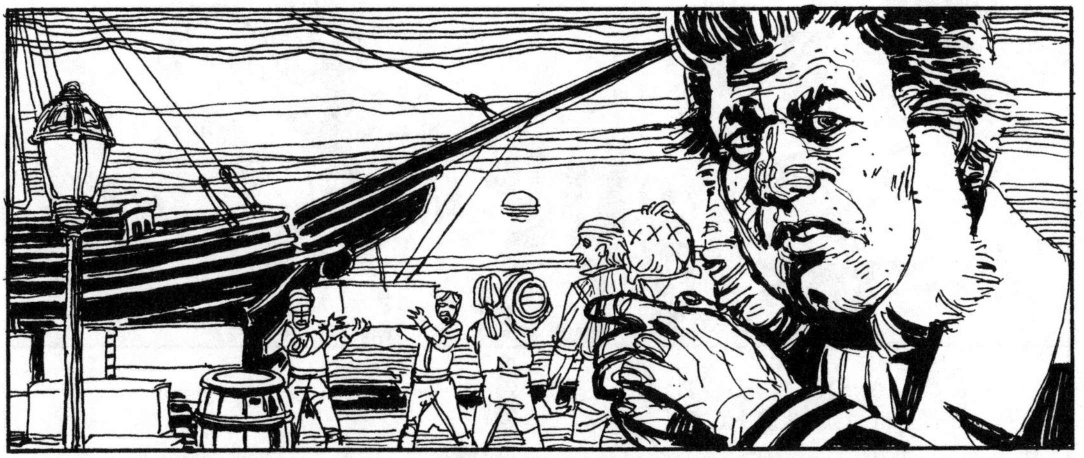

11 JULY – AT DAWN WE ENTERED BOSPHORUS… BOARDED BY TURKISH CUSTOMS OFFICERS, ALL CORRECT. UNDER WAY, 4 P.M.…

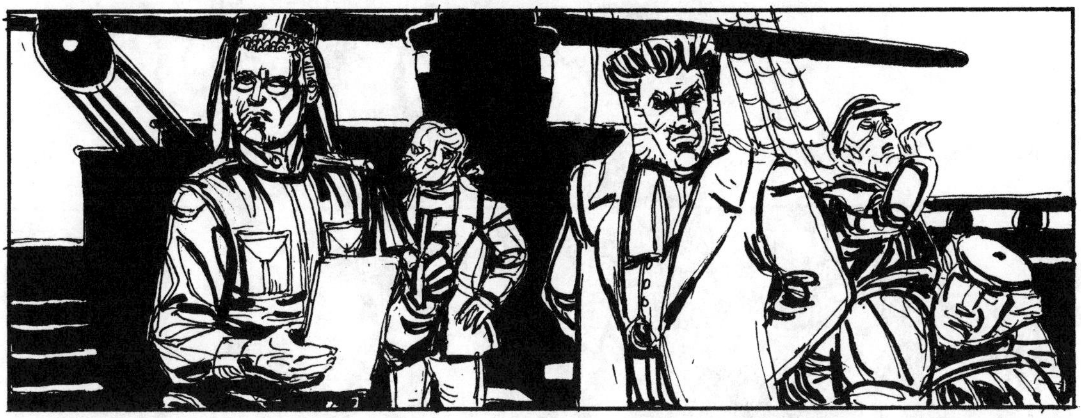

12 JULY – THROUGH DARDANELLES. CUSTOMS OFFICERS AGAIN. WANT US OFF SOON…

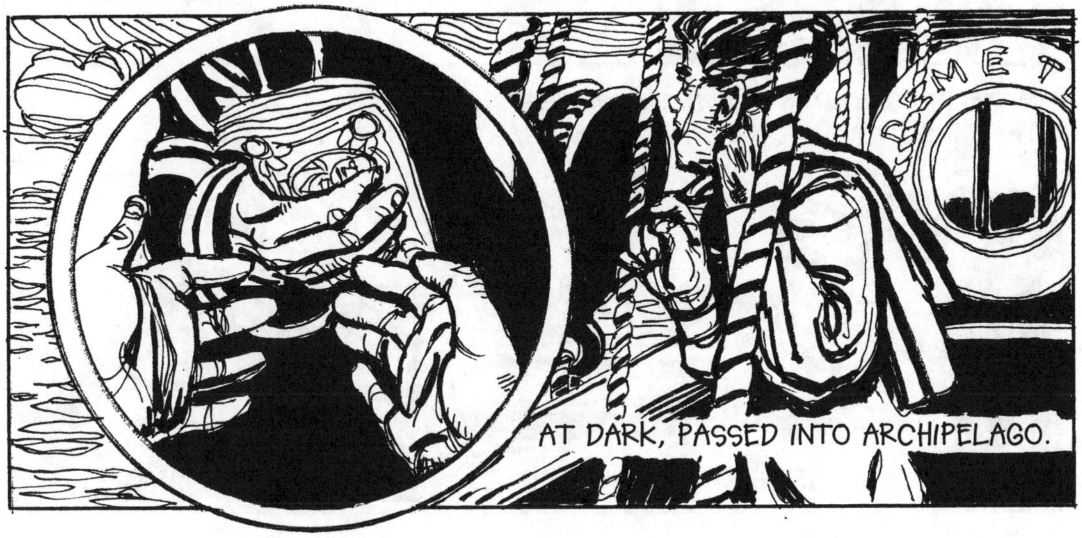
AT DARK, PASSED INTO ARCHIPELAGO.

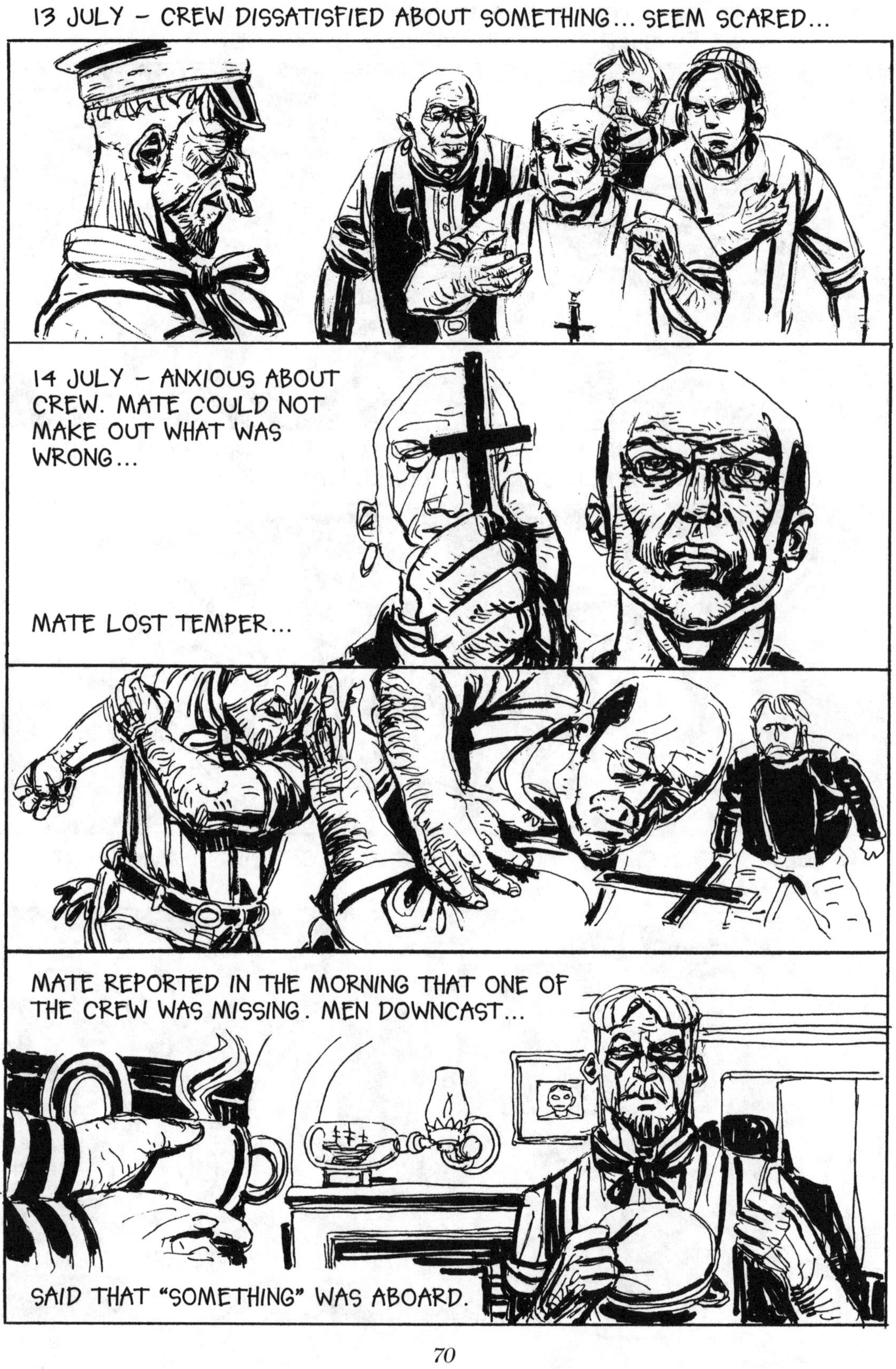
13 JULY – CREW DISSATISFIED ABOUT SOMETHING… SEEM SCARED…
14 JULY – ANXIOUS ABOUT CREW. MATE COULD NOT MAKE OUT WHAT WAS WRONG…
MATE LOST TEMPER…
MATE REPORTED IN THE MORNING THAT ONE OF THE CREW WAS MISSING. MEN DOWNCAST…
SAID THAT "SOMETHING" WAS ABOARD.

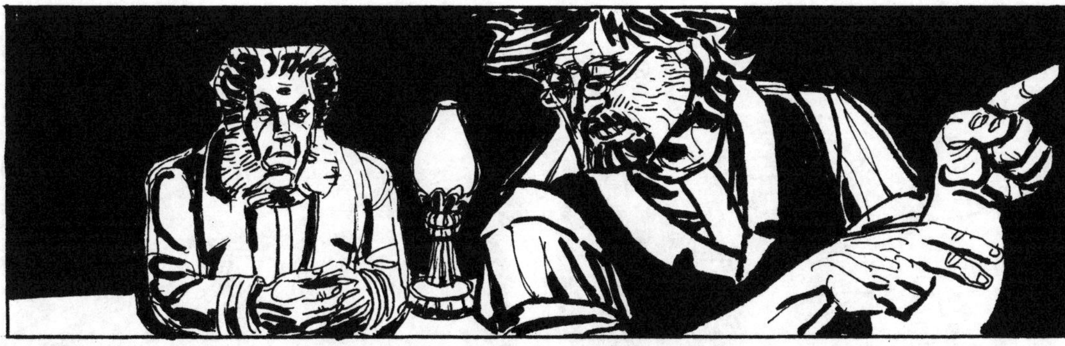

17 JULY – ONE OF THE MEN CAME TO MY CABIN AND IN AN AWESTRUCK WAY CONFIDED TO ME THAT A STRANGE MAN WAS ABOARD...

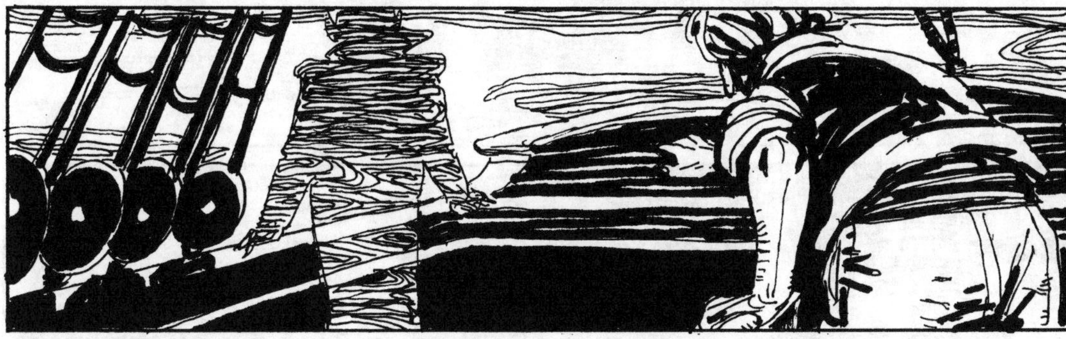

A TALL MAN, UNLIKE ANY OF THE CREW. HE WENT ALONG THE DECK FORWARD, THEN DISAPPEARED.

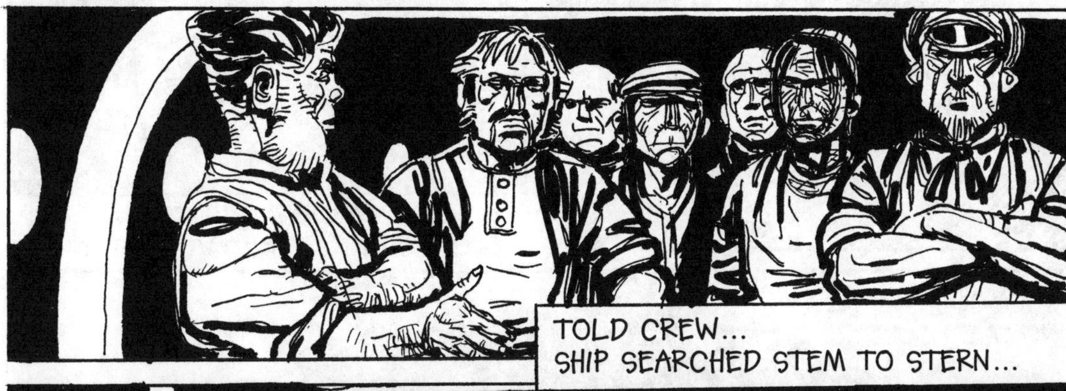
TOLD CREW...
SHIP SEARCHED STEM TO STERN...

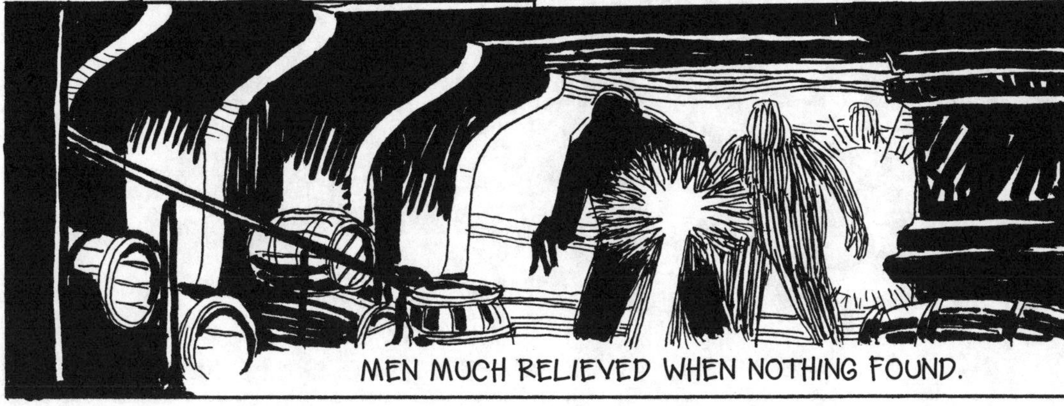
MEN MUCH RELIEVED WHEN NOTHING FOUND.

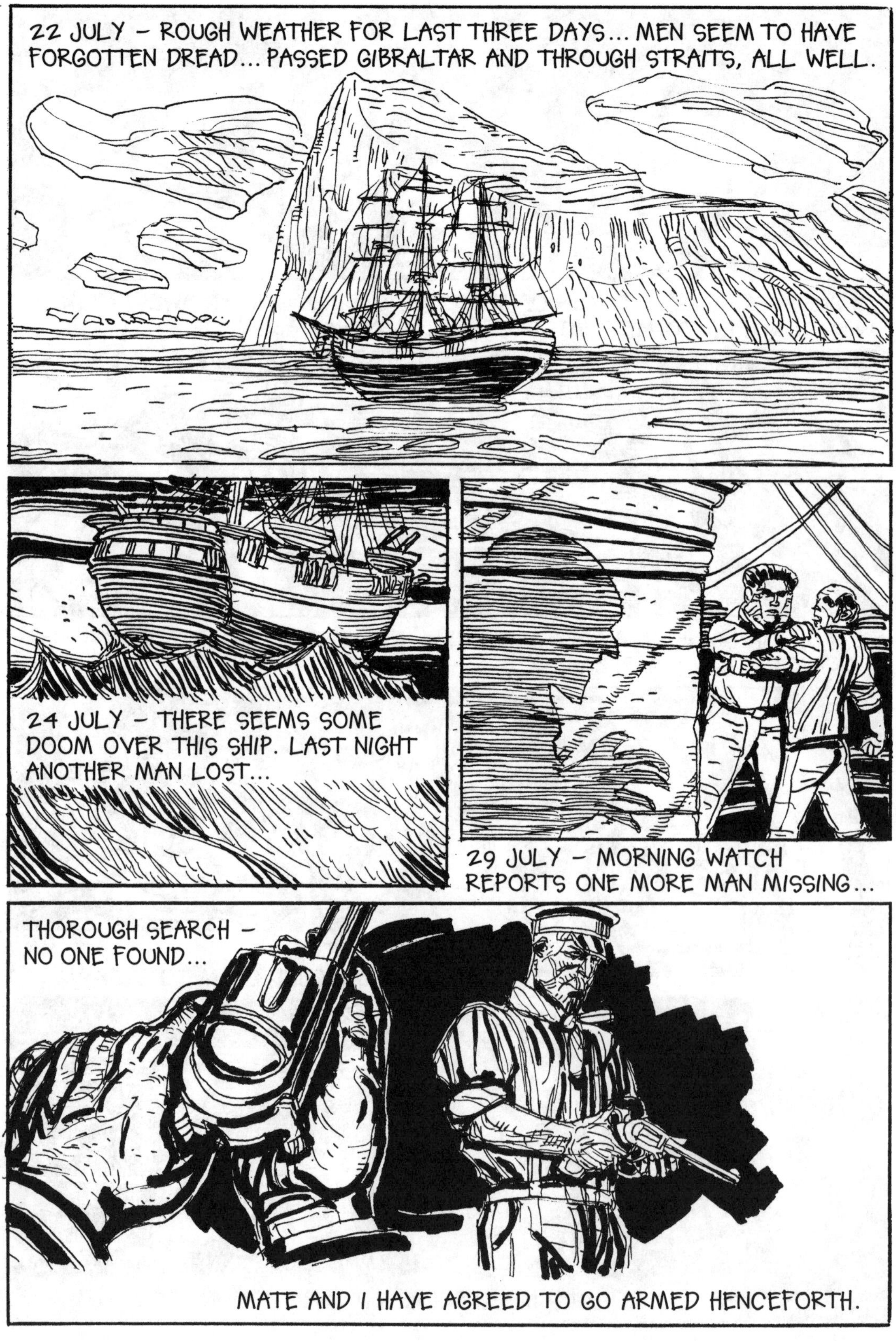
22 JULY – ROUGH WEATHER FOR LAST THREE DAYS... MEN SEEM TO HAVE FORGOTTEN DREAD... PASSED GIBRALTAR AND THROUGH STRAITS, ALL WELL.
24 JULY – THERE SEEMS SOME DOOM OVER THIS SHIP. LAST NIGHT ANOTHER MAN LOST...
29 JULY – MORNING WATCH REPORTS ONE MORE MAN MISSING...
THOROUGH SEARCH – NO ONE FOUND...
MATE AND I HAVE AGREED TO GO ARMED HENCEFORTH.

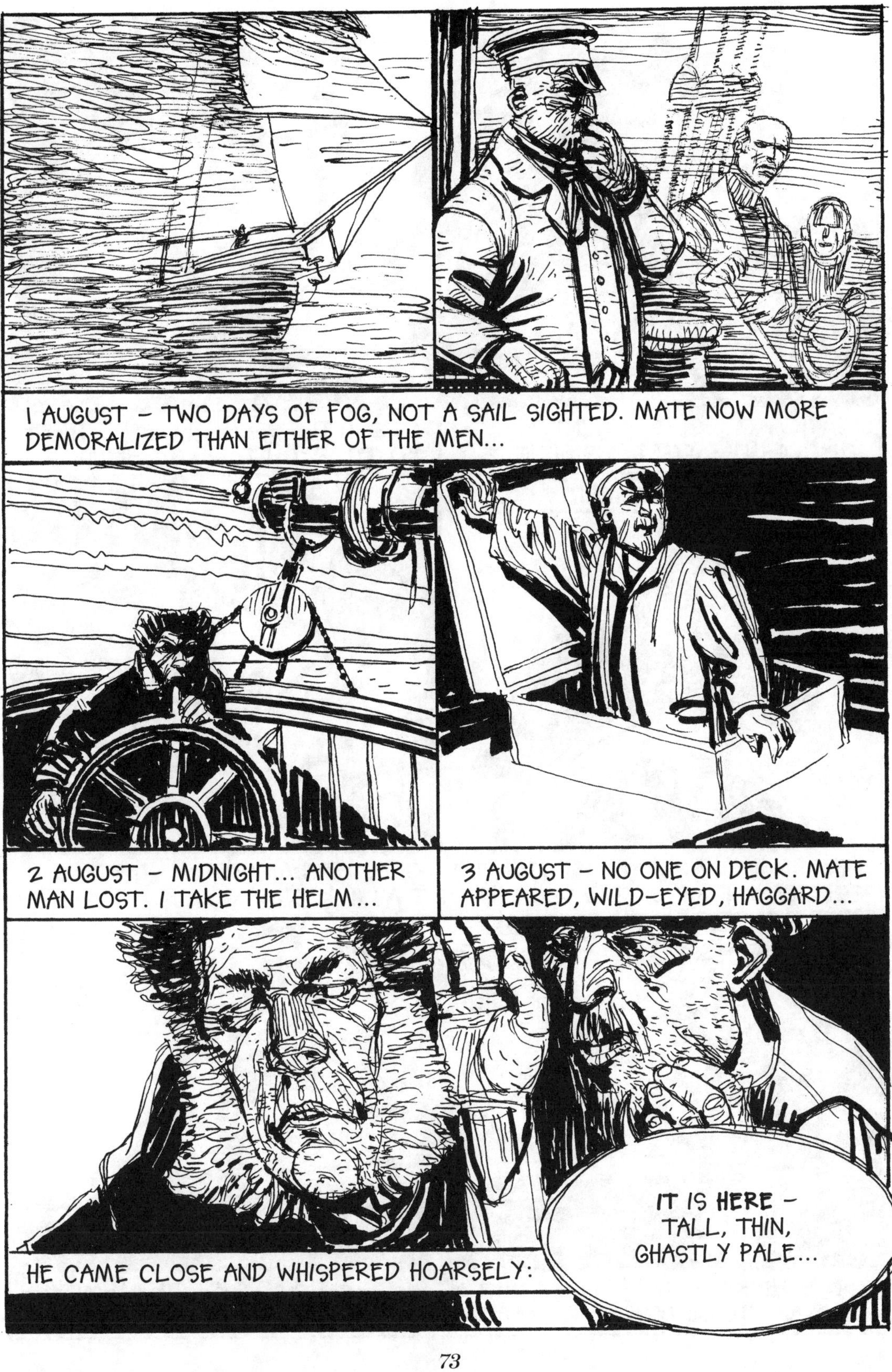
I AUGUST – TWO DAYS OF FOG, NOT A SAIL SIGHTED. MATE NOW MORE DEMORALIZED THAN EITHER OF THE MEN...
2 AUGUST – MIDNIGHT... ANOTHER MAN LOST. I TAKE THE HELM...
3 AUGUST – NO ONE ON DECK. MATE APPEARED, WILD-EYED, HAGGARD...
HE CAME CLOSE AND WHISPERED HOARSELY:
IT IS HERE – TALL, THIN, GHASTLY PALE...

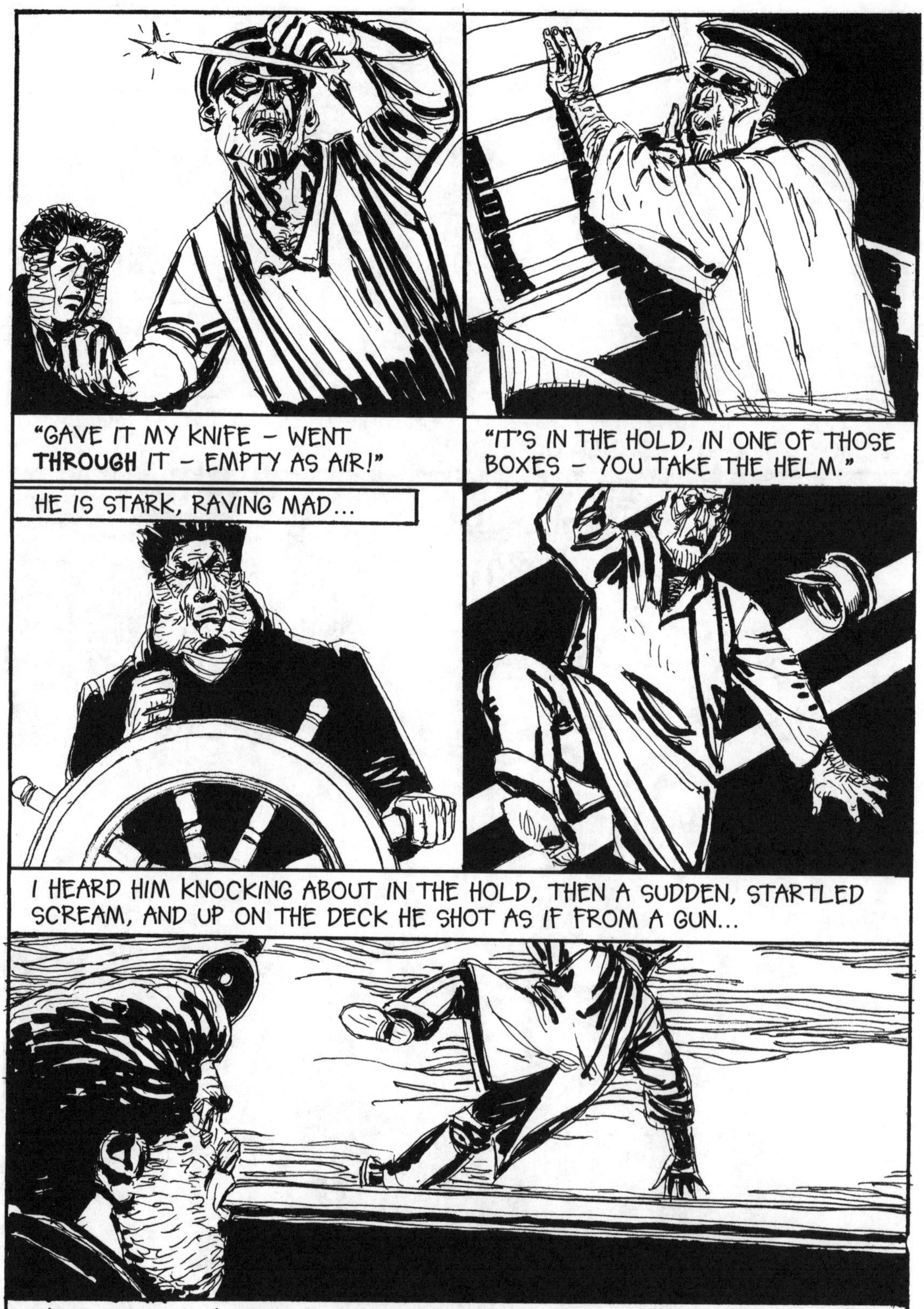
"GAVE IT MY KNIFE – WENT THROUGH IT – EMPTY AS AIR!"
"IT'S IN THE HOLD, IN ONE OF THOSE BOXES – YOU TAKE THE HELM."
HE IS STARK, RAVING MAD...
I HEARD HIM KNOCKING ABOUT IN THE HOLD, THEN A SUDDEN, STARTLED SCREAM, AND UP ON THE DECK HE SHOT AS IF FROM A GUN...
"HE IS THERE! I KNOW THE SECRET NOW!!" – AND BEFORE I COULD MOVE FORWARD TO SEIZE HIM, HE SPRANG OVERBOARD!

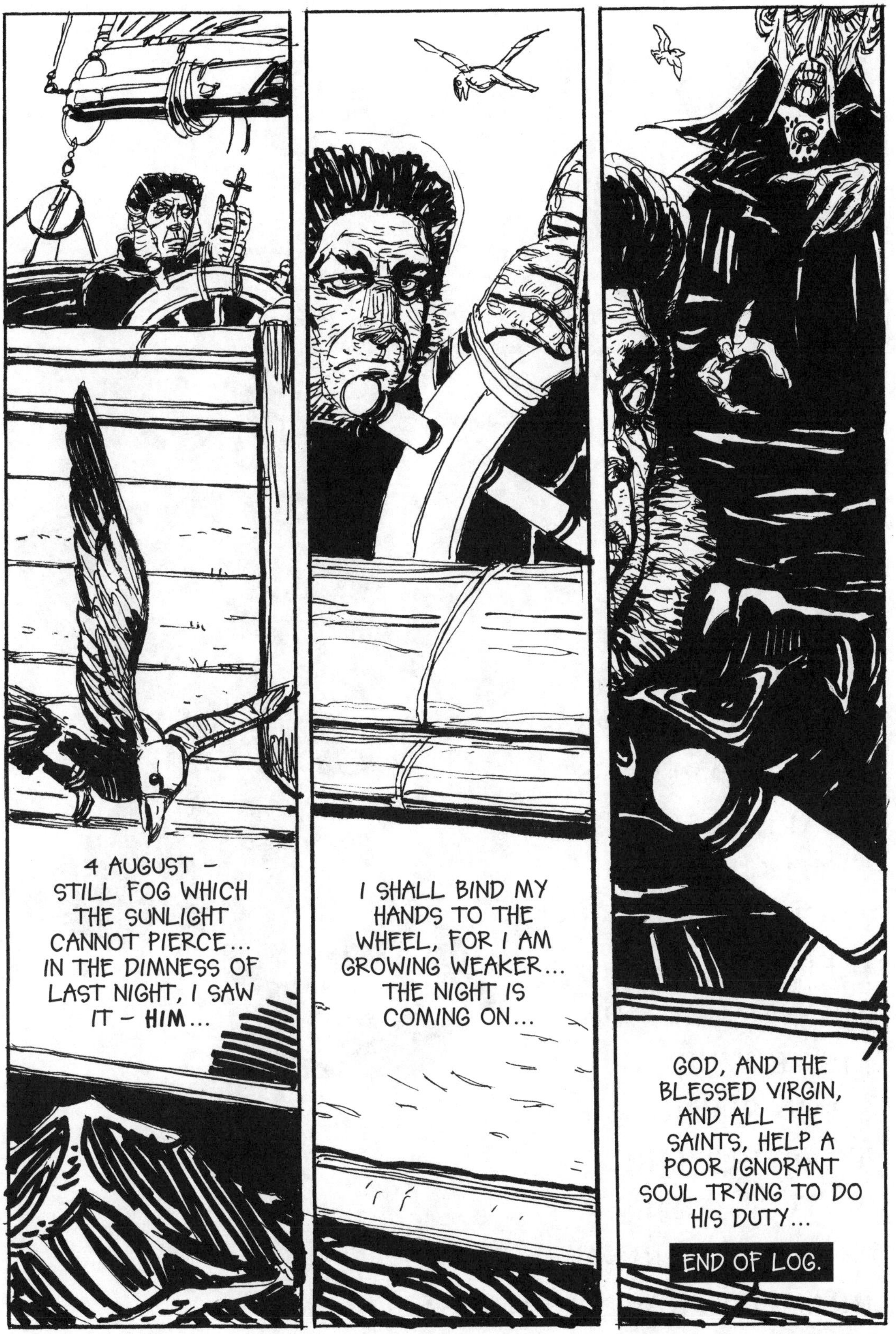
4 AUGUST – STILL FOG WHICH THE SUNLIGHT CANNOT PIERCE... IN THE DIMNESS OF LAST NIGHT, I SAW IT – **HIM**...
I SHALL BIND MY HANDS TO THE WHEEL, FOR I AM GROWING WEAKER... THE NIGHT IS COMING ON...
GOD, AND THE BLESSED VIRGIN, AND ALL THE SAINTS, HELP A POOR IGNORANT SOUL TRYING TO DO HIS DUTY...
END OF LOG.

The Dracula Gallery

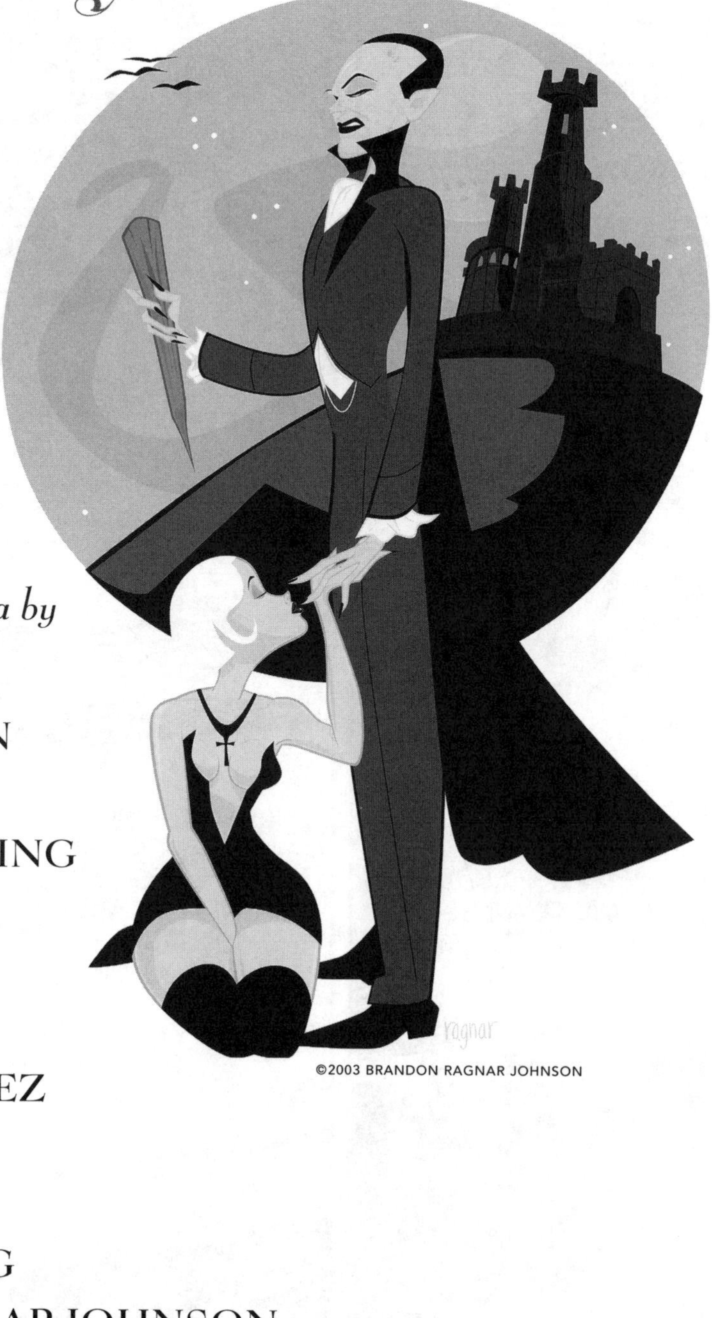
ragnar

illustrations based on Bram Stoker's Dracula by

KOSTAS ARONIS
NEALE BLANDEN
SKOT OLSEN
MICHAEL MANNING
JEFF GAITHER
MAXON CRUMB
LISA K. WEBER
SPAIN RODRIGUEZ
TODD SCHORR
ANTON EMDIN
TODD LOVERING
BRANDON RAGNAR JOHNSON

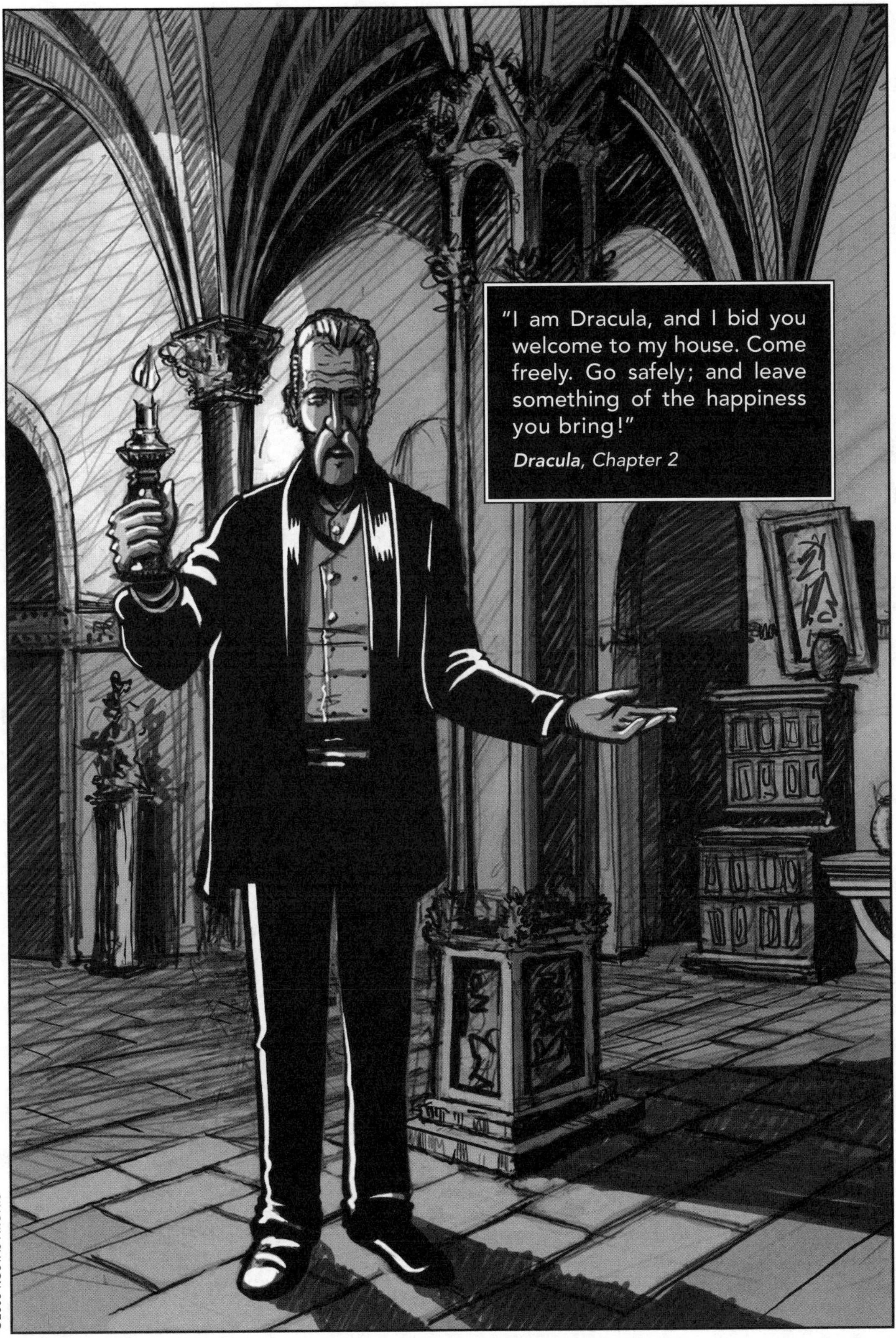
"I am Dracula, and I bid you welcome to my house. Come freely. Go safely; and leave something of the happiness you bring!"
Dracula, Chapter 2

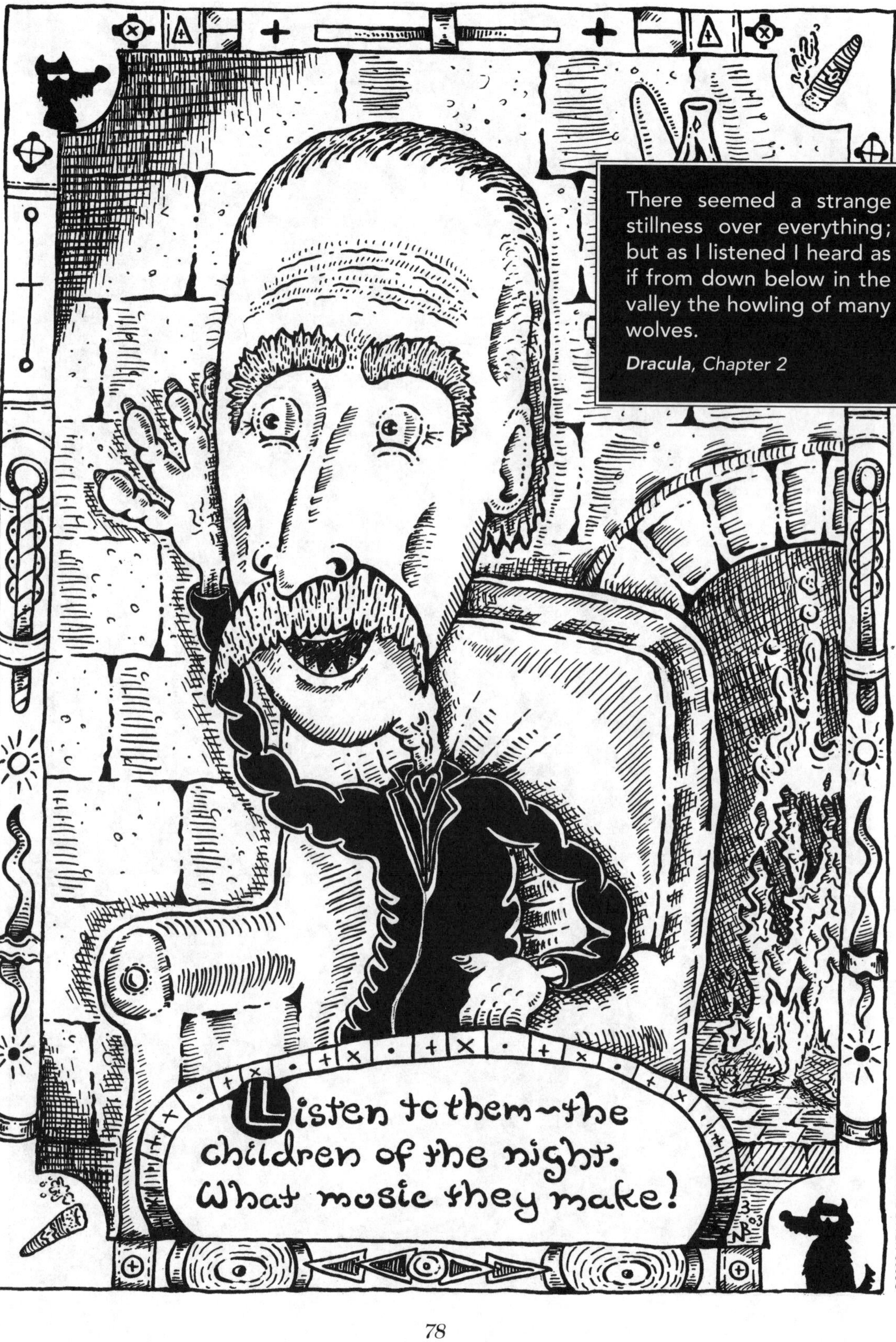
There seemed a strange stillness over everything; but as I listened I heard as if from down below in the valley the howling of many wolves.
Dracula, Chapter 2
Listen to them—the children of the night. What music they make!

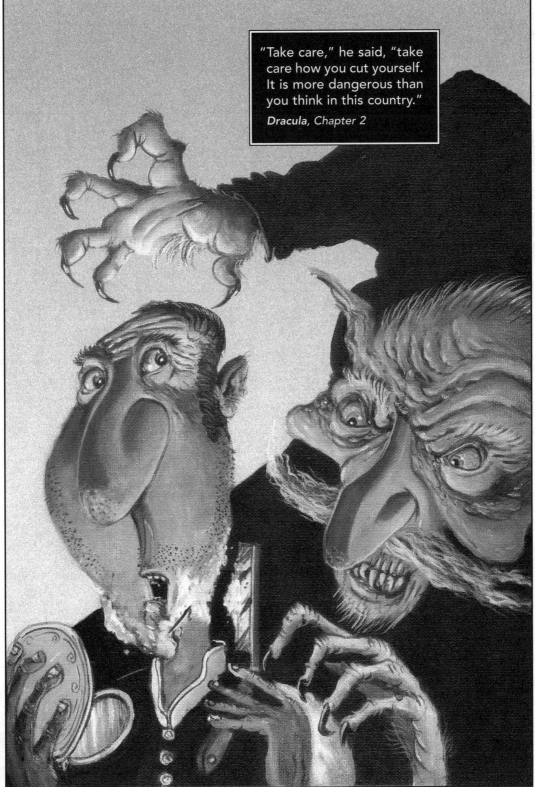

"Take care," he said, "take care how you cut yourself. It is more dangerous than you think in this country."
Dracula, Chapter 2

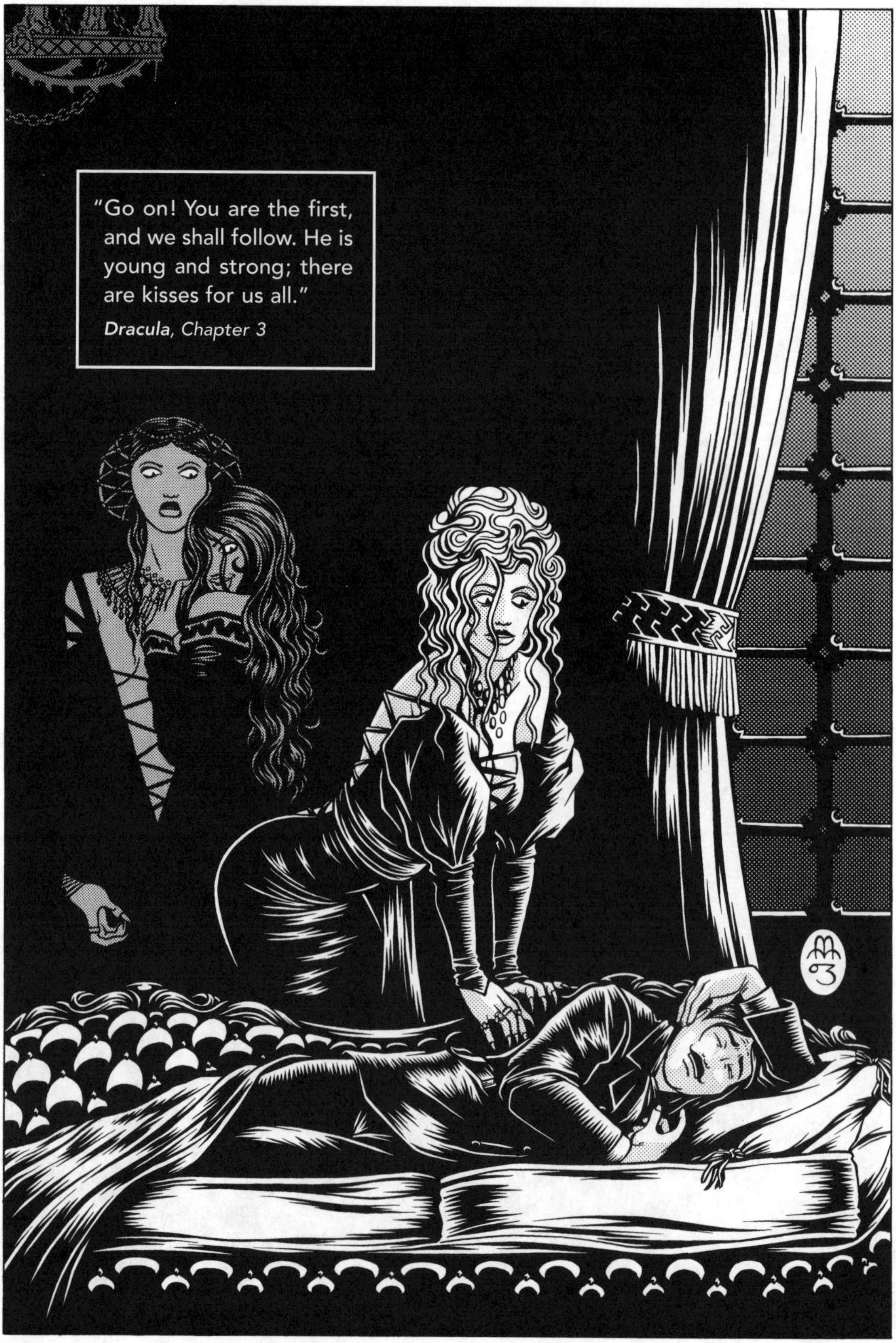
"Go on! You are the first, and we shall follow. He is young and strong; there are kisses for us all."
Dracula, Chapter 3

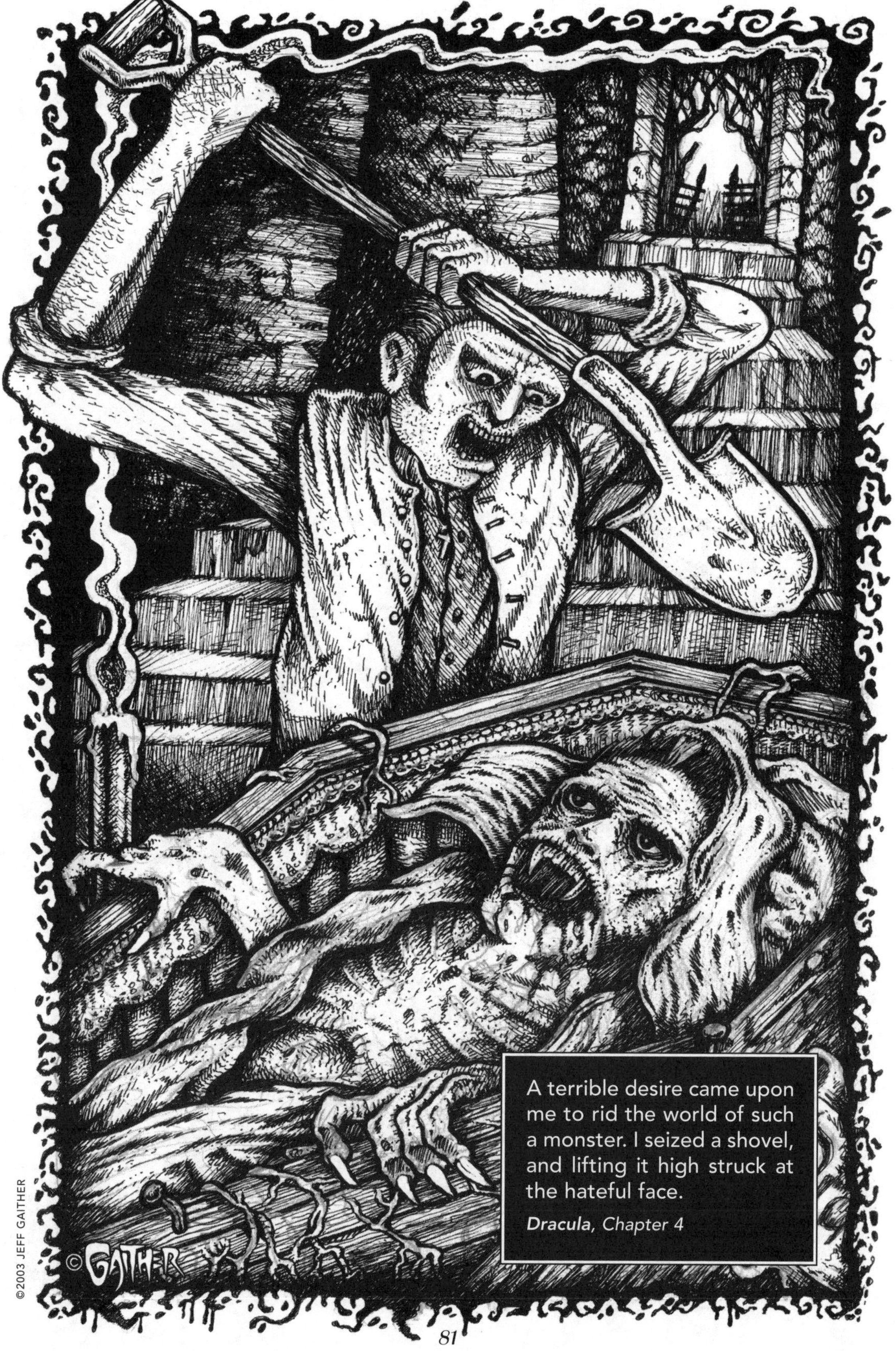
©GAITHER

A terrible desire came upon me to rid the world of such a monster. I seized a shovel, and lifting it high struck at the hateful face.

Dracula, Chapter 4

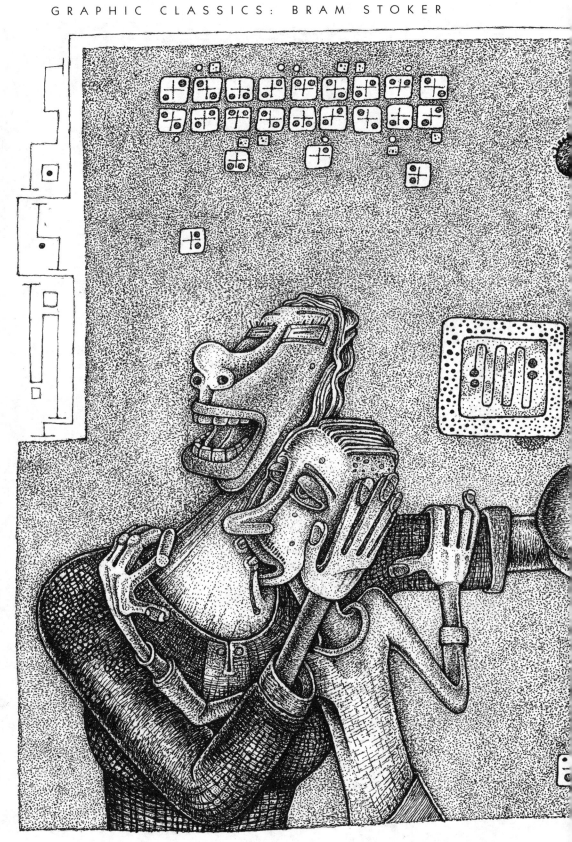

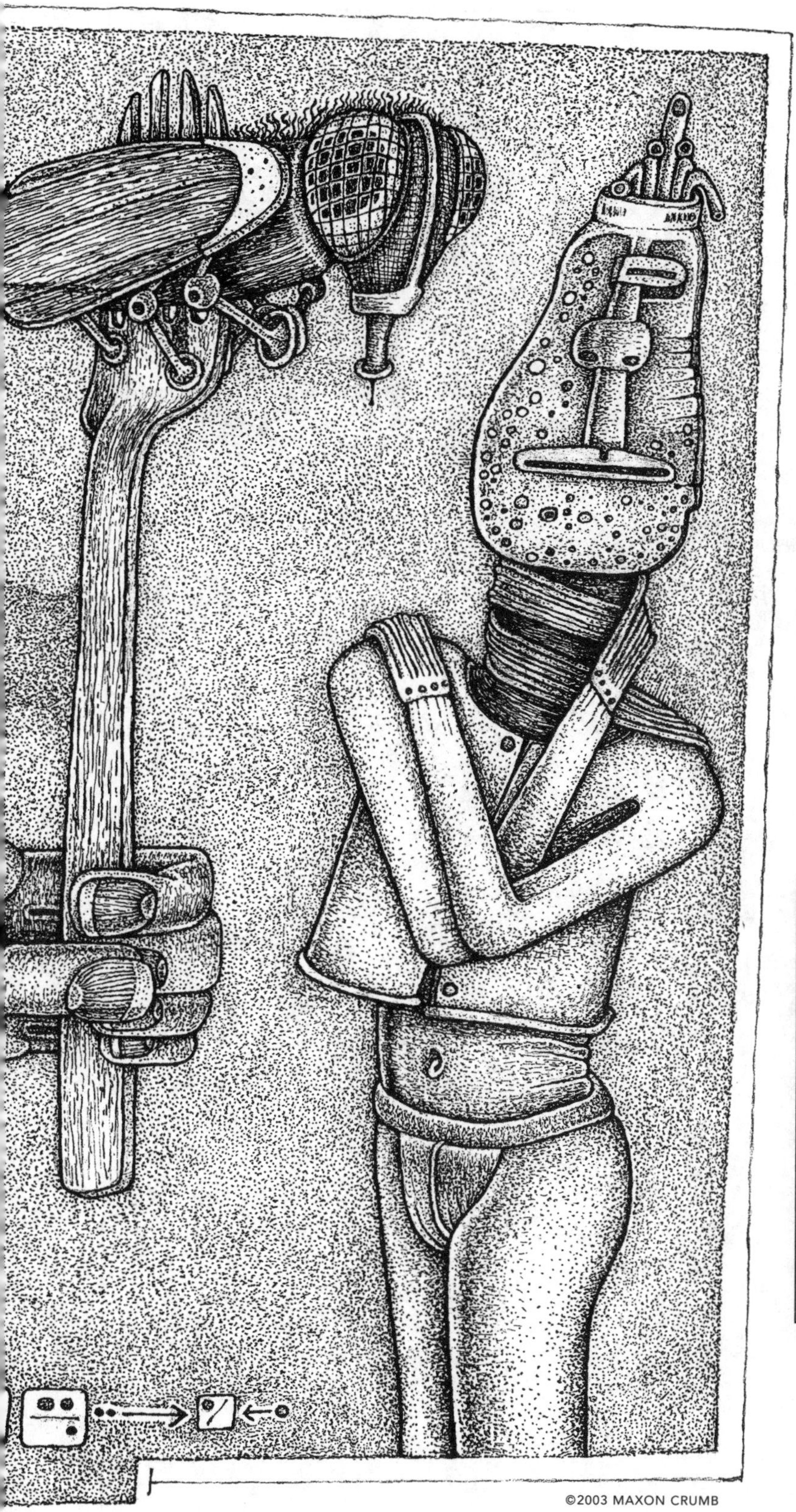

My homicidal maniac is of a peculiar kind. I shall have to call him a zoophagous (life-eating) maniac: what he desires is to absorb as many lives as he can, and he has laid himself out to achieve it in a cumulative way.

***Dracula**, Chapter 6*

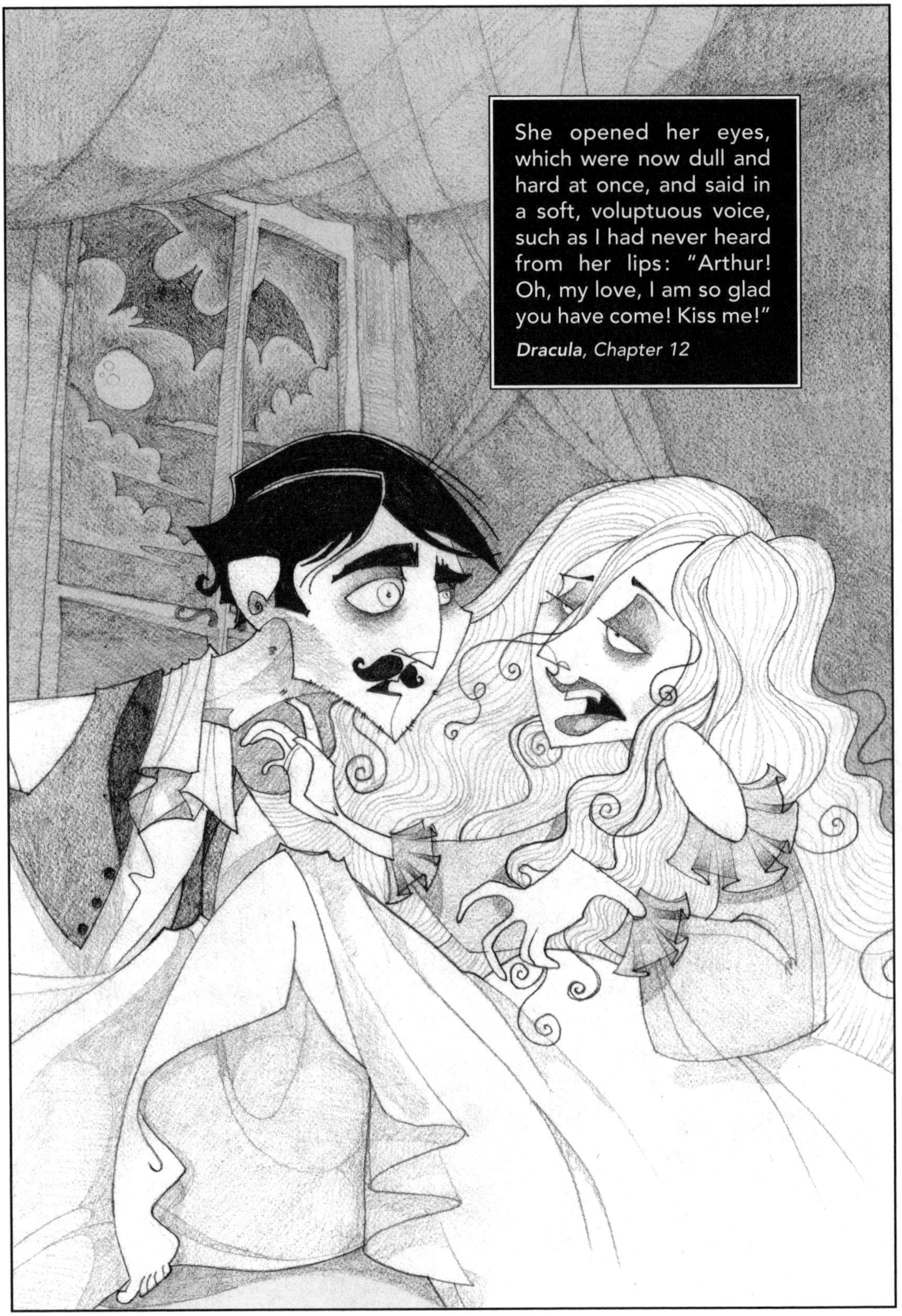
She opened her eyes, which were now dull and hard at once, and said in a soft, voluptuous voice, such as I had never heard from her lips: "Arthur! Oh, my love, I am so glad you have come! Kiss me!"
Dracula, Chapter 12

"Take this stake in your left hand, ready to place the point over her heart, and the hammer in your right. Then strike in God's name, that so all may be well with the dead that we love, and that the Un-Dead pass away."

***Dracula**, Chapter 16*

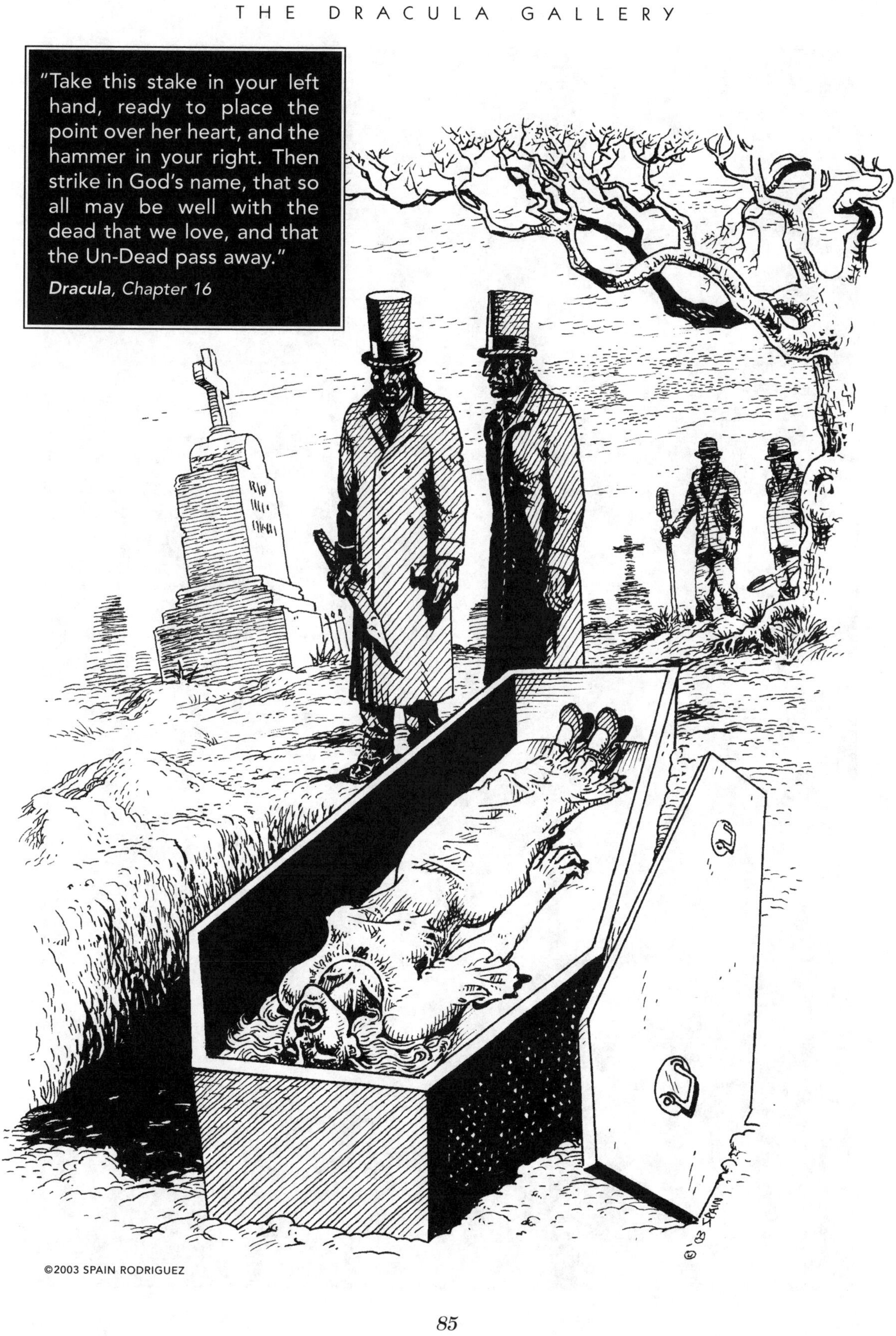
© '03 SPAIN

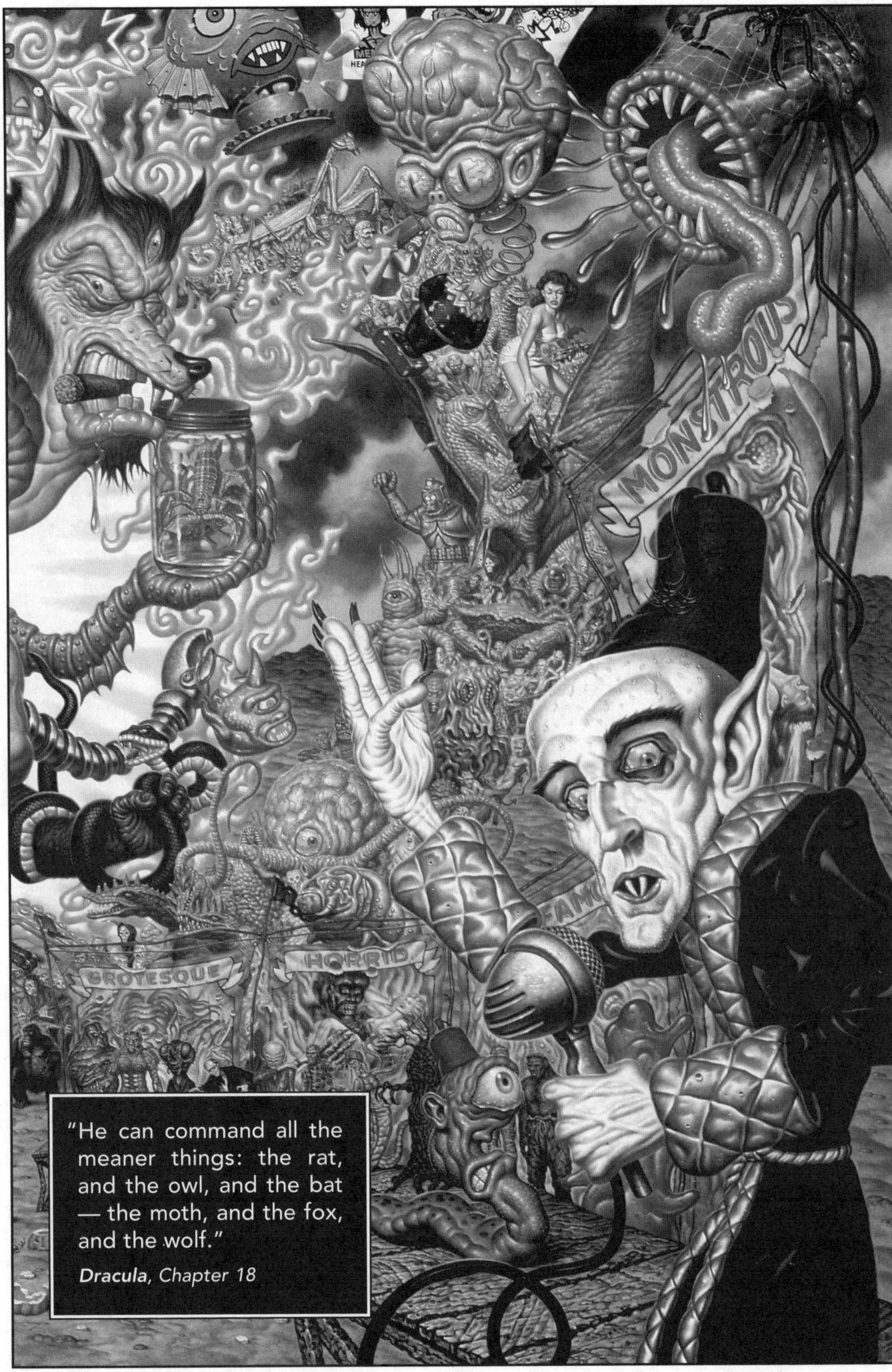
MONSTROUS
GROTESQUE
HORRID

"He can command all the meaner things: the rat, and the owl, and the bat — the moth, and the fox, and the wolf."

***Dracula**, Chapter 18*

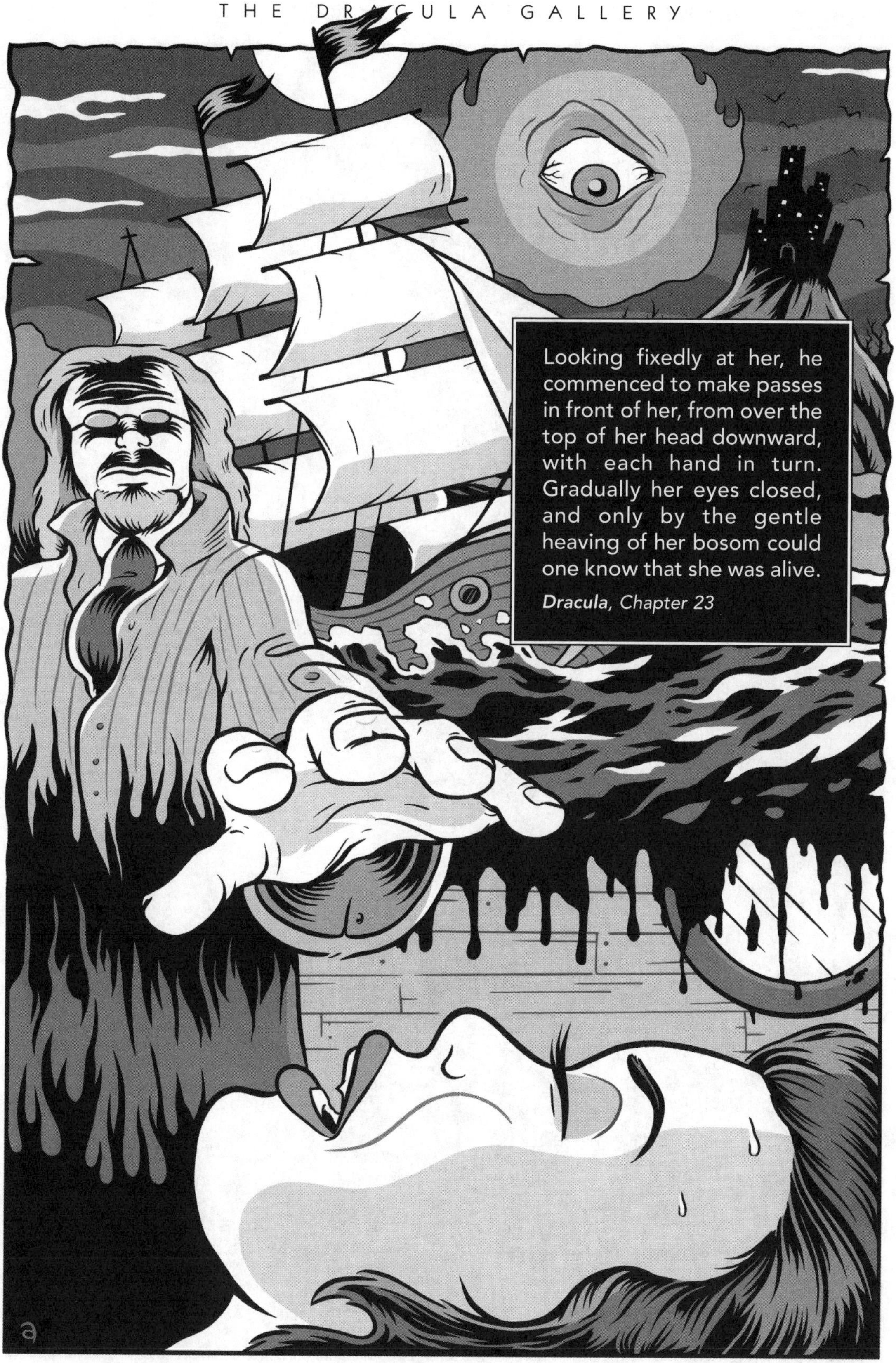
Looking fixedly at her, he commenced to make passes in front of her, from over the top of her head downward, with each hand in turn. Gradually her eyes closed, and only by the gentle heaving of her bosom could one know that she was alive.
Dracula, Chapter 23

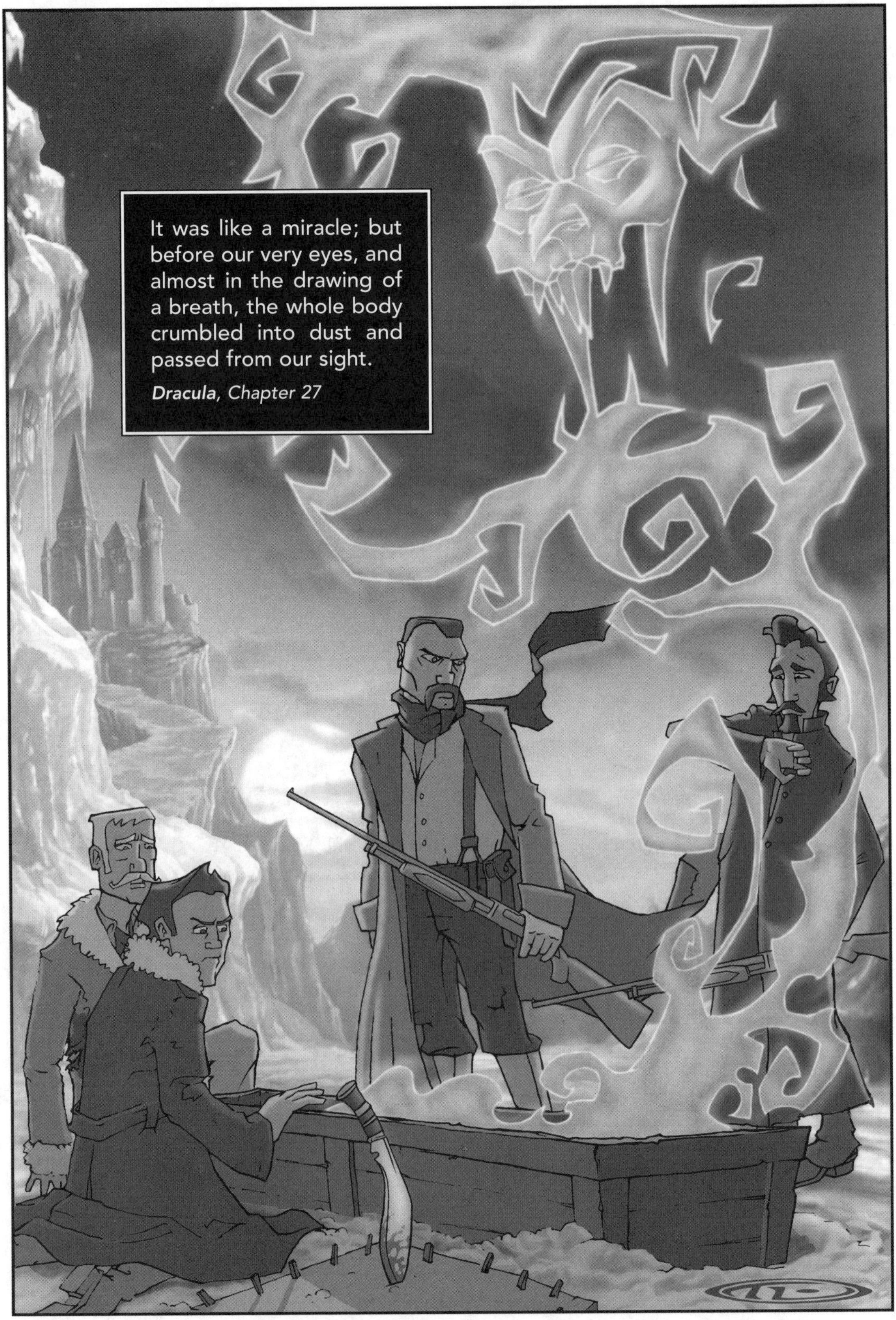
It was like a miracle; but before our very eyes, and almost in the drawing of a breath, the whole body crumbled into dust and passed from our sight.
Dracula, Chapter 27

Professor Abraham Van Helsing's

Vampire Hunter's Guide

illustrated by

HUNT EMERSON

an excerpt from Dracula by

BRAM STOKER

freely adapted by Tom Pomplun

I think it good that I tell you something of the enemy with which we have to deal. I shall then make known to you something of its power, which has been ascertained for me. So we then can decide how we shall act, and can take our measure according.

There *are* such beings as vampires, some of us have evidence that they exist. Even had we not the proof of our own unhappy experience, the teachings and the records of the past give proof enough for sane peoples. I admit that at the first I was sceptic. Alas! Had I known at first what now I know, precious life would have been spared. But that is gone, and we must so work, that other poor souls perish not, whilst we can save.

STRENGTHS OF THE VAMPIRE:

1. The nosferatu do not die like the bee when he sting once. He become only stronger, with yet more power to work his evil.

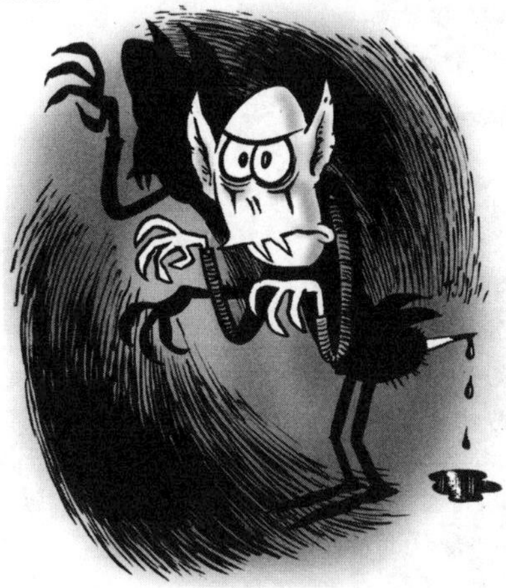

2. The vampire is of himself so strong in person as twenty men, and he is of cunning more than mortal, for his cunning be the growth of ages.

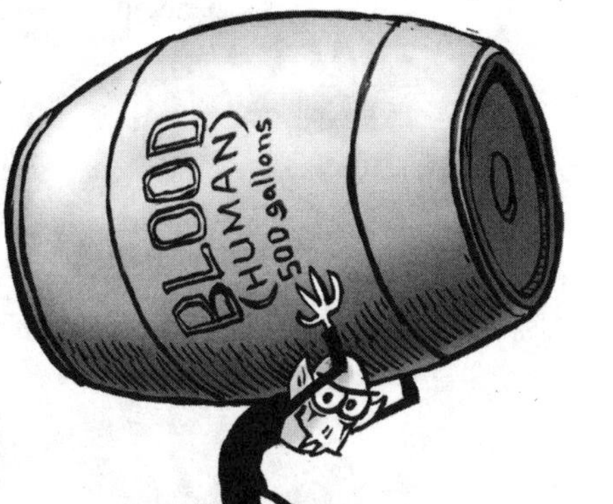
BLOOD
(HUMAN)
500 gallons

3. He have the aids of necromancy, and all the dead that he can come nigh to are for him at command.

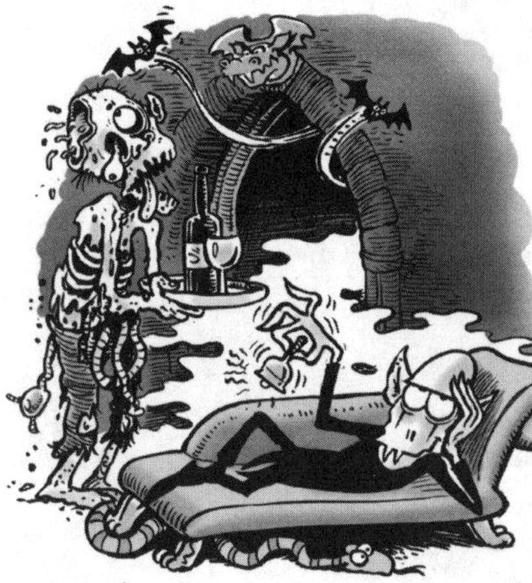

4. He can, within his range, direct the elements: the storm, the fog and the thunder.

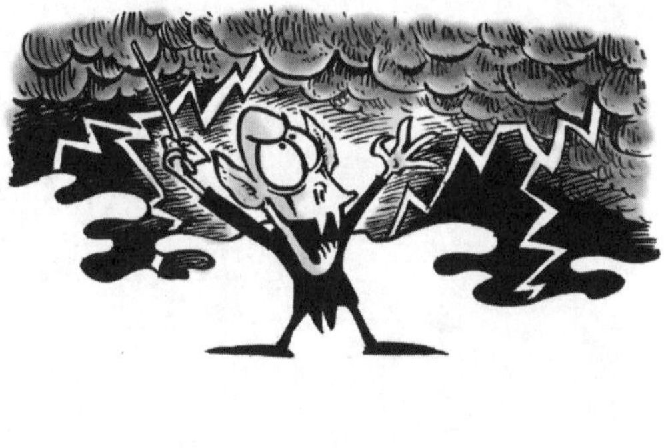

5. He can command all the meaner things: the rat, the owl, the bat, the moth, the fox and the wolf.

6. He can transform himself to wolf, or he can be as bat. He can grow and become small, and he can at times vanish and come unknown.

7. The vampire live on, and cannot die by mere passing of the time. He can flourish when that he can fatten on the blood of the living.

8. Even more, he can grow younger, and his vital faculties can refresh themselves when his special pabulum is plenty.

9. He can come in mist which he create around himself, and he come on moonlight rays as elemental dust.

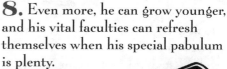

10. He can see in the dark, no small power this, in a world which is one half shut from the light.

So, you know what we have to contend against, but we too, are not without strength. We have on our side power of combination, a power denied to the vampire kind, we have sources of science, we are free to act and think, and the hours of the day and the night are ours equally. We have self devotion in a cause and an end to achieve which is not a selfish one. These things are much.

WEAKNESSES OF THE VAMPIRE:

1. The vampire cannot flourish without his special diet, he eat not as others.

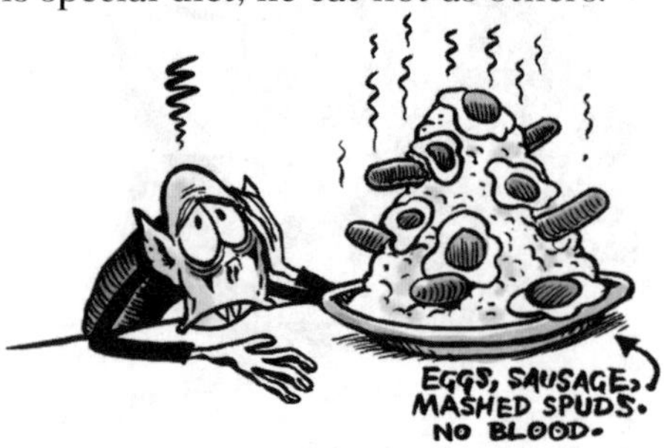
EGGS, SAUSAGE, MASHED SPUDS. NO BLOOD.

2. He throws no shadow, and he make in the mirror no reflect.

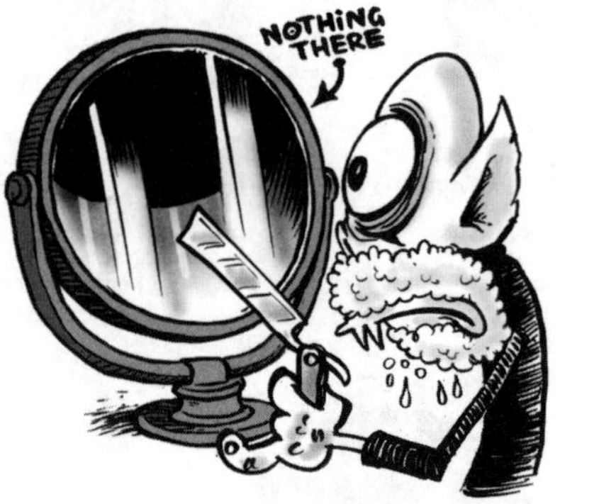
NOTHING THERE

3. He may not enter anywhere at the first, unless there be some one of the household who bid him to come, though afterwards he can come as he please.

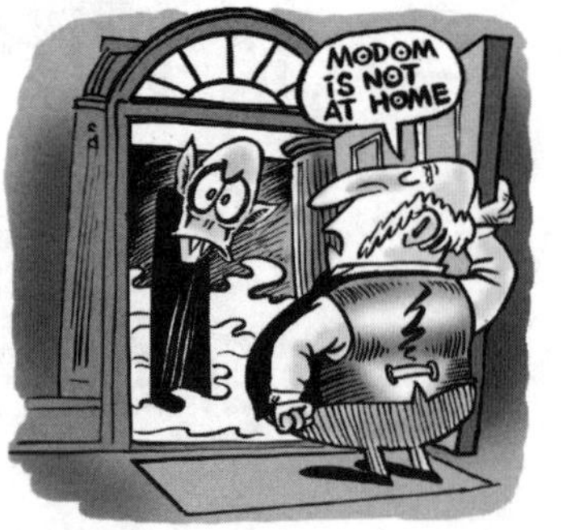
MODOM IS NOT AT HOME

4. His power ceases, as does that of all evil things, at the coming of the day.

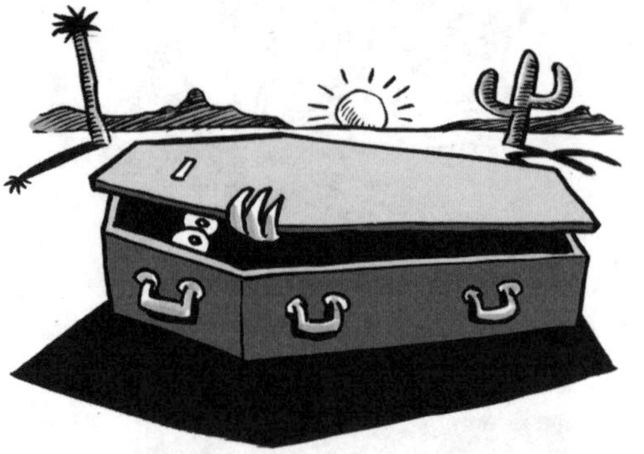

5. It is said, too, that he can only pass running water at the slack or the flood of the tide.

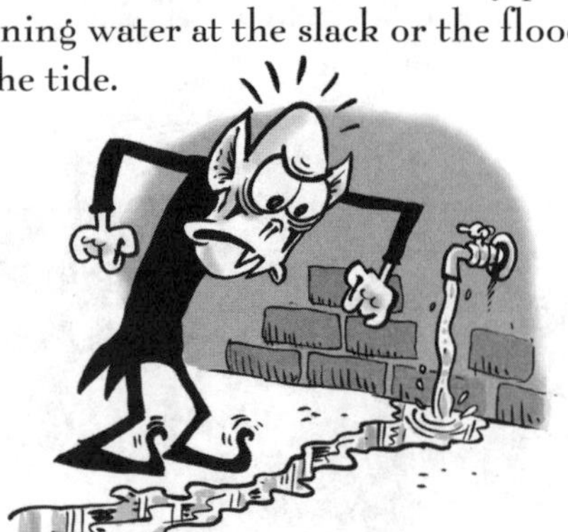

6. Then there are things which so afflict him that he has no power, as the garlic that we know of.

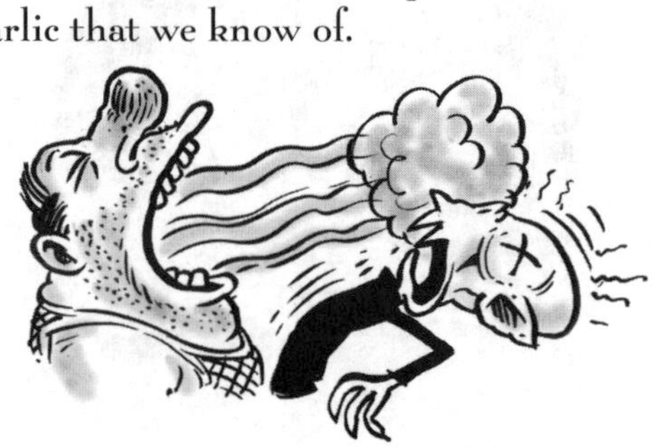

7. And as for things sacred, as my crucifix, when we have faith, to them he is nothing, but in their presence he take his place far off and silent with respect.

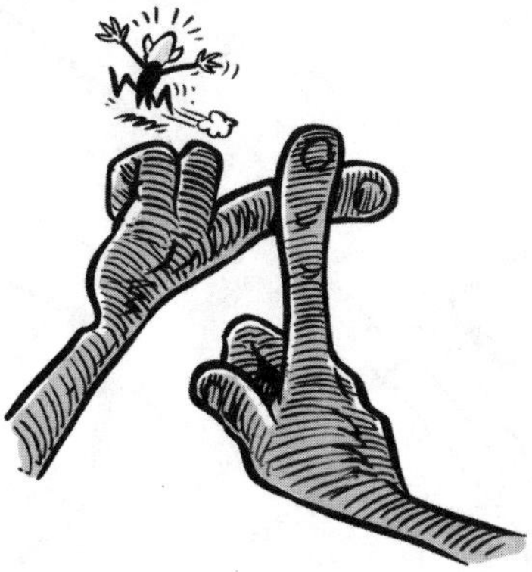

8. A branch of wild rose on his coffin keep him that he move not from it.

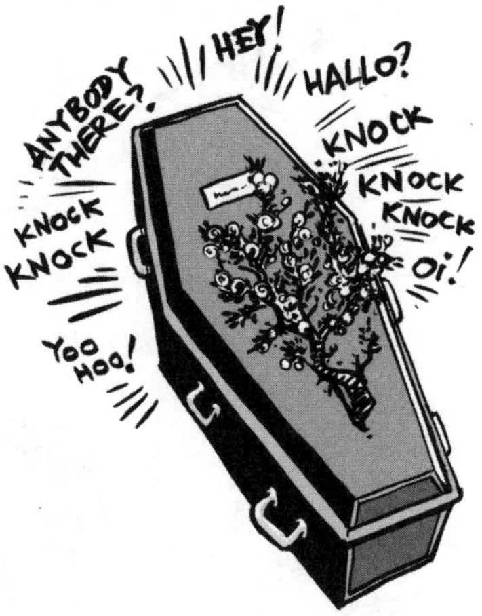
ANYBODY THERE?
HEY!
HALLO?
KNOCK
KNOCK
KNOCK
KNOCK KNOCK
OI!
YOO HOO!

9. A sacred bullet or a wooden stake through the heart kill him so that he be true dead.

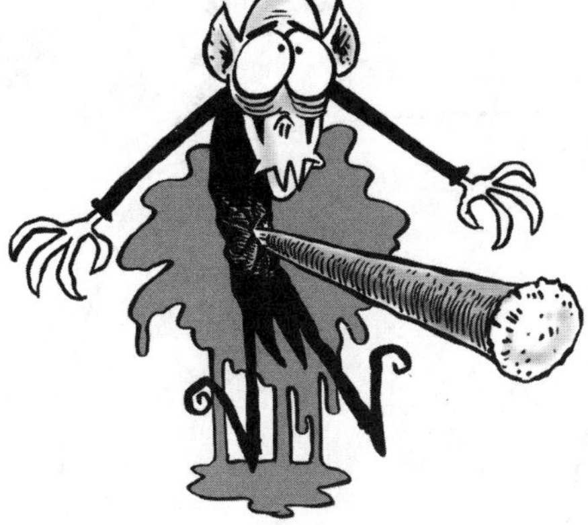

10. Or to cut off the head will giveth final rest. We have seen it with our eyes.

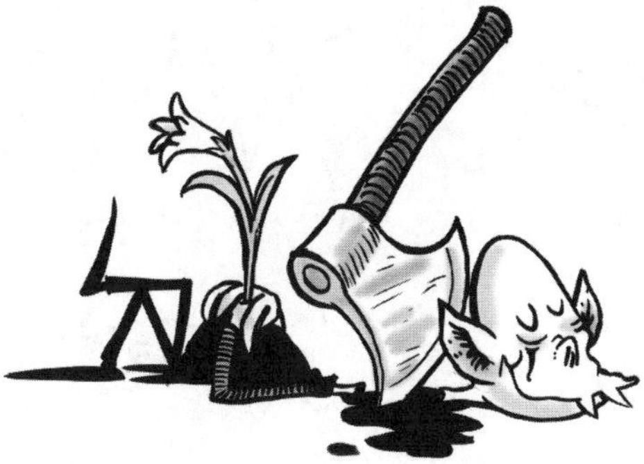

My friends, it is a terrible task that we undertake, and there may be consequence to make the brave shudder. Life is nothings, I heed him not. But to fail here, is not mere life or death. It is that we become as him, that we henceforward become foul things of the night like him, without heart or conscience, preying on the bodies and the souls of those we love best. To us forever are the gates of heaven shut, and we go on for all time abhorred by all, a blot on the face of God's sunshine, an arrow in the side of Him who died for man. But we are face to face with duty, and in such case must we shrink? For me, I say no. What say you?

Van Helsing

Professor Abraham Van Helsing, M.D., D.Ph., D.Lit., etc., etc.,
30 September, 1897, Amsterdam.

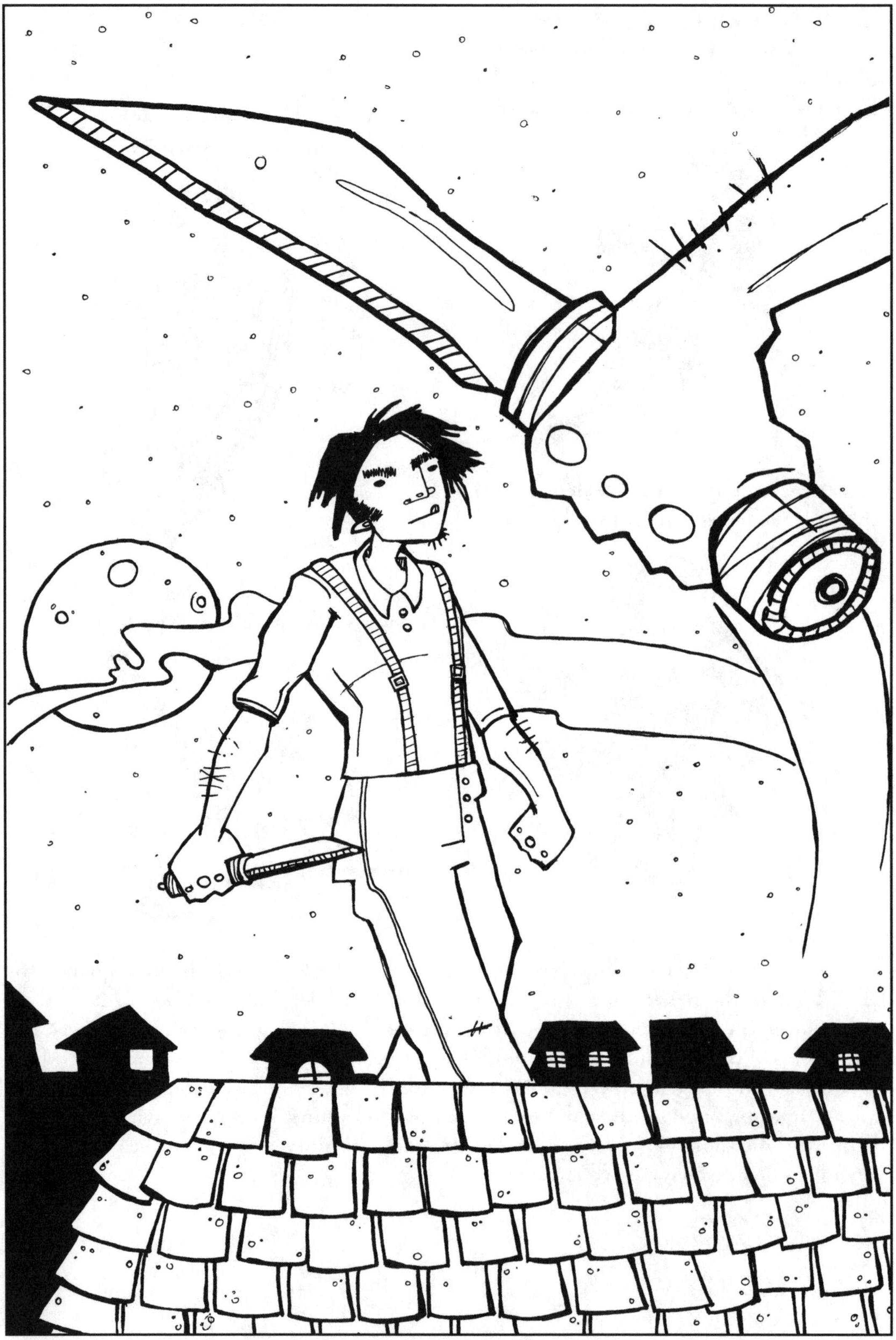

THE DUALITISTS
— or —
THE DEATH-DOOM
OF THE DOUBLE-BORN

story by **Bram Stoker**
edited by Tom Pomplun
illustrated by **Lesley Reppeteaux**

THERE WAS JOY in the house of Bubb. For ten long years had Ephraim and Sophonisba Bubb mourned the loneliness of their life. Unavailingly had they gazed into the emporia of baby-linen, and fixed their glances on the basket-makers' warehouses where the cradles hung in rows. In vain had they prayed, and wished, and waited, but never had even a ray of hope been held out by the family physician.

But now at last the moment had arrived. Ephraim Bubb sat on the stairs, and tried to catch the strain of blissful music from the lips of his first-born. Finally, from the chamber within came a sharp cry, which shortly after was repeated, and soon the doctor came forth.

"My dear sir, allow me to offer twofold felicitations. Mr. Bubb, you are the father of Twins!"

They were the finest children that ever were seen — so at least said the cognoscenti, and the parents were not slow to believe. The twins grew apace, were weaned, teethed, and at length arrived at the stage of three years.

HARRY MERFORD and Tommy Santon lived in the same range of villas as Ephraim Bubb. Harry's parents had taken up their abode in Number 25, and Tommy's were in Number 27. Between these two residences Ephraim Bubb reared his blossoms in Number 26. Harry and Tommy had been accustomed from the earliest times to meet each other daily. Their primal method of communication had been by the housetops, until their respective sires had been obliged to pay Bubb for damages to his roof and dormer windows, and from that time they had been forbidden to meet, while their mutual neighbour had taken the precaution of having his garden walls topped with broken glass to prevent their incursions. Harry and Tommy, however, being gifted with daring souls and strong seats to their trousers, defied the rugged walls of Bubb and continued to meet in secret.

Day by day, and often night by night, would these two brave the perils of nurse, and father, and mother, of whip and imprisonment to meet together. What they discussed in secret none other knew. What deeds of darkness were perpetrated in their symposia none could tell.

There was in the garden of Bubb a summer house surrounded by young poplars which the fond father had planted on his children's natal day. These trees quite obscured the house, and here Harry and Tommy held their conclaves.

The boys had each been given at Christmas a new knife, and for a long time these knives, similar in size and pattern, were their chief delights. With them they cut and hacked in their respective homes all things which would not be likely to be noticed, for the young gentlemen had no wish that their moments of pleasure should be atoned for by moments of pain. The insides of drawers, and desks, the underparts of tables and chairs, even the floors, where corners of the carpets could surreptitiously be turned up, all bore marks of their craftsmanship, and to compare notes on these artistic triumphs was a source of joy.

At length, however, a critical time came, for the old joys had begun to pall, and it was absolutely necessary that the existing schemes of destruction should be enlarged.

They met in the arbor to discuss this grave situation. Tommy unfolded with much pride a scheme which he had in contemplation of cutting a series of holes in the sounding board of the piano, so as to destroy its musical properties. Harry had conceived the project of cutting the canvas at the back of his great grandfather's portrait, so that in time when the picture should be moved, the head would fall bodily out from the frame.

At this point of the council a brilliant thought occurred to Tommy. "Why should not the enjoyment be doubled, and the musical instruments and family pictures of both establishments be sacrificed on the altar of pleasure?" This was agreed to, and the meeting adjourned for dinner.

When they next met it came out that all the schemes of domestic reform had been foiled by maternal vigilance. Sadly the two forlorn youths took out their knives and regarded them. So like were the knives that but for the initials scratched in the handles neither boy could have been sure which was his own. After a while they began mutually to brag of the superior excellence of their respective weapons. Tommy insisted that his was the sharper, and Harry asserted that his was the stronger. Hotter and hotter grew the war of words. With one impulse the boys suggested that they should test the quality of their knives by the ordeal of the Hack.

No sooner said than done. Harry held out his knife edge uppermost, and Tommy, grasping his firmly by the handle, brought down the edge of the blade crosswise on Harry's. The process was then reversed, and Harry became in turn the aggressor. Then they paused and eagerly looked for the result. It was not hard to see; in each knife were two great dents of equal depth; and so it was necessary to renew the contest, and seek a further proof.

It was well into the evening when, wearied and jaded, Harry and Tommy sought their respective homes. Alas! the splendor of the knives was gone. Naught remained but two useless wrecks, with their keen edges destroyed forever.

But though they mourned for their fondly cherished weapons, the hearts of the boys were glad; for the bygone day had opened a prospect of pleasure as boundless as the limits of the world.

FROM THAT DAY a new era dawned in the lives of Harry and Tommy. So long as the resources of the parental establishments could hold out, so long would their new amusement continue. They obtained

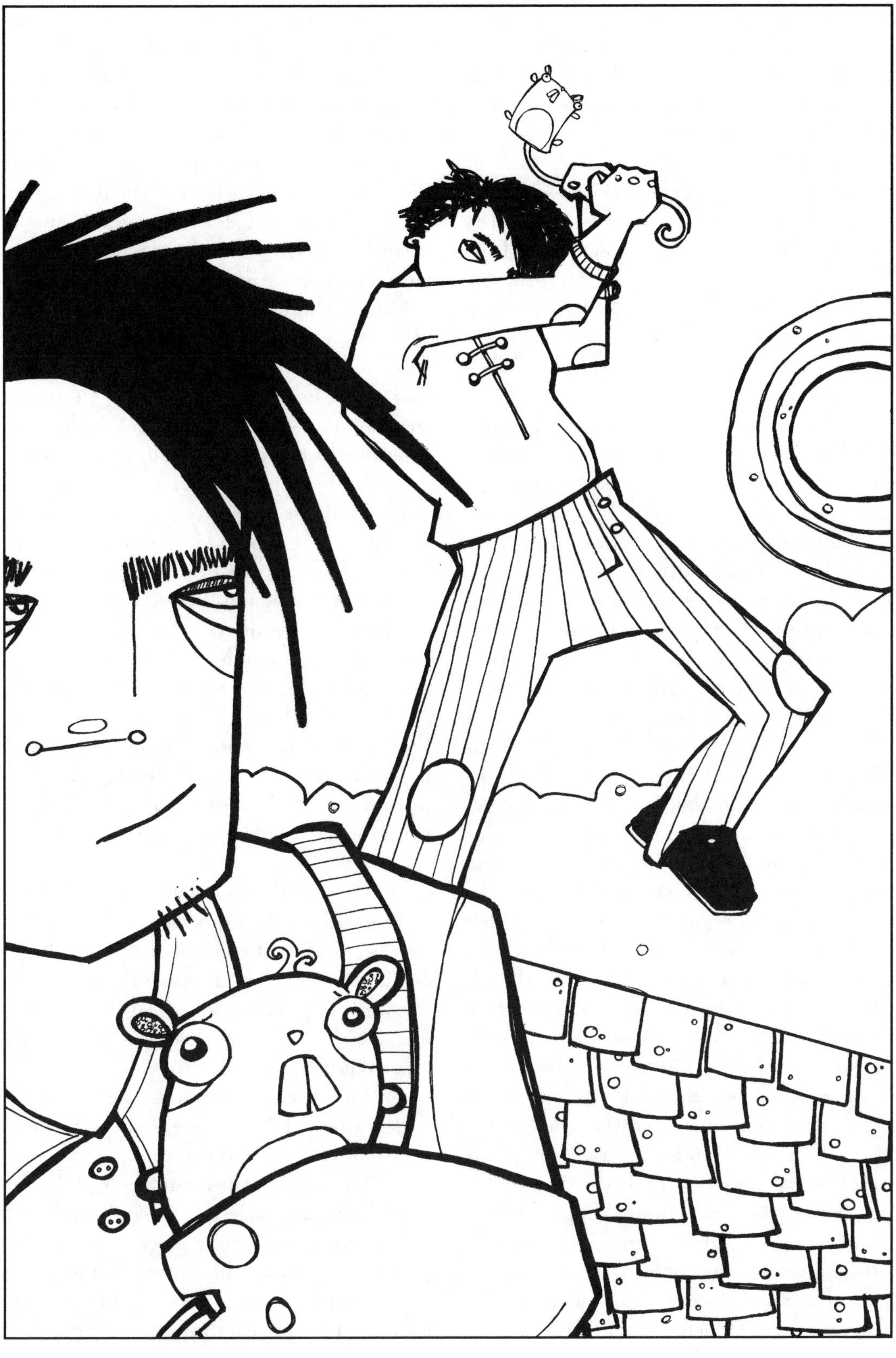

surreptitious possession of articles of family cutlery not in general use, and brought them to their rendezvous. These came fair and spotless from the butlers' pantries. Alas! they returned not as they came.

But in course of time the stock of available cutlery became exhausted, and again the inventive faculties of the youths were called upon. They reasoned thus: "The knife game is played out, but the excitement of the Hack is not. Let us carry this Great Idea into new worlds; let us continue to hack, but with objects other than knives."

It was done. Spoons and forks were daily flattened and beaten out of shape; pepper castor met pepper castor in combat, and both were borne dying from the field; candlesticks met in fray to part no more on this side of the grave.

At last all the resources of the butler's pantry became exhausted, and then began a system of miscellaneous destruction that proved in little time ruinous to the furniture of the respective homes of Harry and Tommy. Mrs. Santon and Mrs. Merford began to notice that the wear and tear in their households became excessive. Day after day some new domestic calamity seemed to have occurred. Today a valuable edition of some book would appear to have suffered some dire misfortune, for the edges were frayed and broken and the back loose if not altogether displaced; tomorrow the legs of some chair or table would show signs of extraordinary hardship. Even in the nursery the sounds of lamentation were heard. It was a thing of daily occurrence for the little girls to state that when going to bed at night they had laid their dollies in their beds with tender care, but they had found them with legs and arms amputated and faces beaten from all semblance of human form.

Then articles of crockery began to be missed. Mrs. Merford and Mrs. Santon mourned their losses, but Harry and Tommy gloated daily over their spoils.

At length one awful day arrived. The butlers of the houses of Merford and Santon, finding their breakage accounts in excess of their wages, determined to discover the true authors of the damages.

It was then that Harry and Tommy, according to their concerted scheme of action, stepped forward and relieved their minds of the deadly weight that had for long in secret borne them down. The story of each ran that time after time he had seen their butler, when he thought that nobody was looking, knocking knives together in the pantry, chairs and books and pictures in the drawing-room and study, dolls in the nursery, and plates in the kitchen. Then, indeed, was the master of each household stern and uncompromising in his demands for justice. Each butler was committed to an officer of the law under the double charge of drunkenness and wilful destruction of property.

Sweetly slept Harry and Tommy in their beds that night. The rewards given by proud and grateful parents lay in their pockets, and in their hearts the happy consciousness of having done their duty.

ON THE DAY FOLLOWING the revelation of the butlers' dire misdeeds, Harry and Tommy met in the arbour to plan a new campaign. In the hour when the narrowing walls of possibility hedged them in on every side, thus ran the conclusion of these dauntless youths:

"We have played out the meaner things that are inanimate and inert; why not then trench on the domains of life?"

That night they met when both households had retired to sleep. Each bore a domestic rabbit and a piece of sticking-plaster. Then, in the quiet moonlight, commenced a work of mystery, blood, and gloom. The proceedings began by the fixing of a piece of sticking-plaster over the mouth of each rabbit to prevent it making a noise, if so inclined. Then Tommy held up his rabbit by its hind legs, and it hung wriggling, a white mass in the moonlight. Slowly Harry raised his rabbit, and when level with his head brought it down on Tommy's client.

Deep into the night the game was kept up, and the Eastern sky began to show signs of approaching day as each boy bore triumphantly the corpse of his bunny and placed it within its hutch.

Next night the same game was renewed with a new rabbit on each side, and for more than a week — so long as the hutches supplied the wherewithal — the battle was sustained. True that there were red eyes in the juveniles of Santon and Merford as one by one the beloved pets were found dead, but Harry and Tommy, with the hearts of heroes steeled to the pitiful cries of childhood, still fought the good fight on to the bitter end.

When the supply of rabbits was exhausted, other munition was not wanting, and for some days the war was continued with guinea pigs, pigeons, canaries, poodles, tortoises, and cats. At last, however, all the animals available were sacrificed; but the passion for hacking still remained. How was it all to end?

THE NEXT DAY Tommy and Harry sat in the arbour dejected and disconsolate. At last the conviction had been forced upon them that the resources available for hacking were exhausted. That very morning they had had a desperate battle, and their attire showed the ravages of direful war. Their hats were battered into shapeless masses, their shoes were soleless and heelless and their trousers were frayed.

Maddened by the equal success of arms, and with the lust for victory still unsated, they longed more fiercely than ever for some new pleasure: like tigers that have tasted blood they thirsted for a larger and more potent libation.

As they sat, with their souls in a tumult of desire and despair, some evil genius guided into the garden the twin blossoms of the tree of Bubb. Hand in hand Zacariah and Zerubbabel advanced from the back door; they had escaped from their nurses, and with the exploring instinct of humanity, advanced boldly into the great world. In the course of time they approached the hedge of poplars, from behind which the anxious eyes of Harry and Tommy viewed their approach.

It was a touching sight, these lovely babes, alike in form, feature, size, and dress. When the startling similarity was recognized by Harry and Tommy, each suddenly turned, and, grasping the other by the shoulder, spoke in a keen whisper, "They are exactly equal! This is the very apotheosis of our art!"

With excited faces and trembling hands they lured the unsuspecting babes within the precincts of their charnelhouse. Tommy held Zacariah across his arm with his baby moon-face smiling up at the cobwebs on the arbour roof, and Harry, with a mighty effort, raised the cherubic Zerubbabel aloft.

Each nerved himself for a great endeavour, Harry to give, Tommy to endure a shock, and then the form of Zerubbabel was seen whirling through the air around Harry's glowing and determined face. There was a sickening crash and the arm of Tommy yielded visibly.

The pasty face of Zerubbabel had fallen fair on that of Zacariah, for Tommy and Harry were by this time artists of too great experience to miss so simple a mark. The putty-like noses collapsed, the cheeks became for a moment flattened, and when in an instant more they parted, the faces of both were dabbled in gore. Immediately

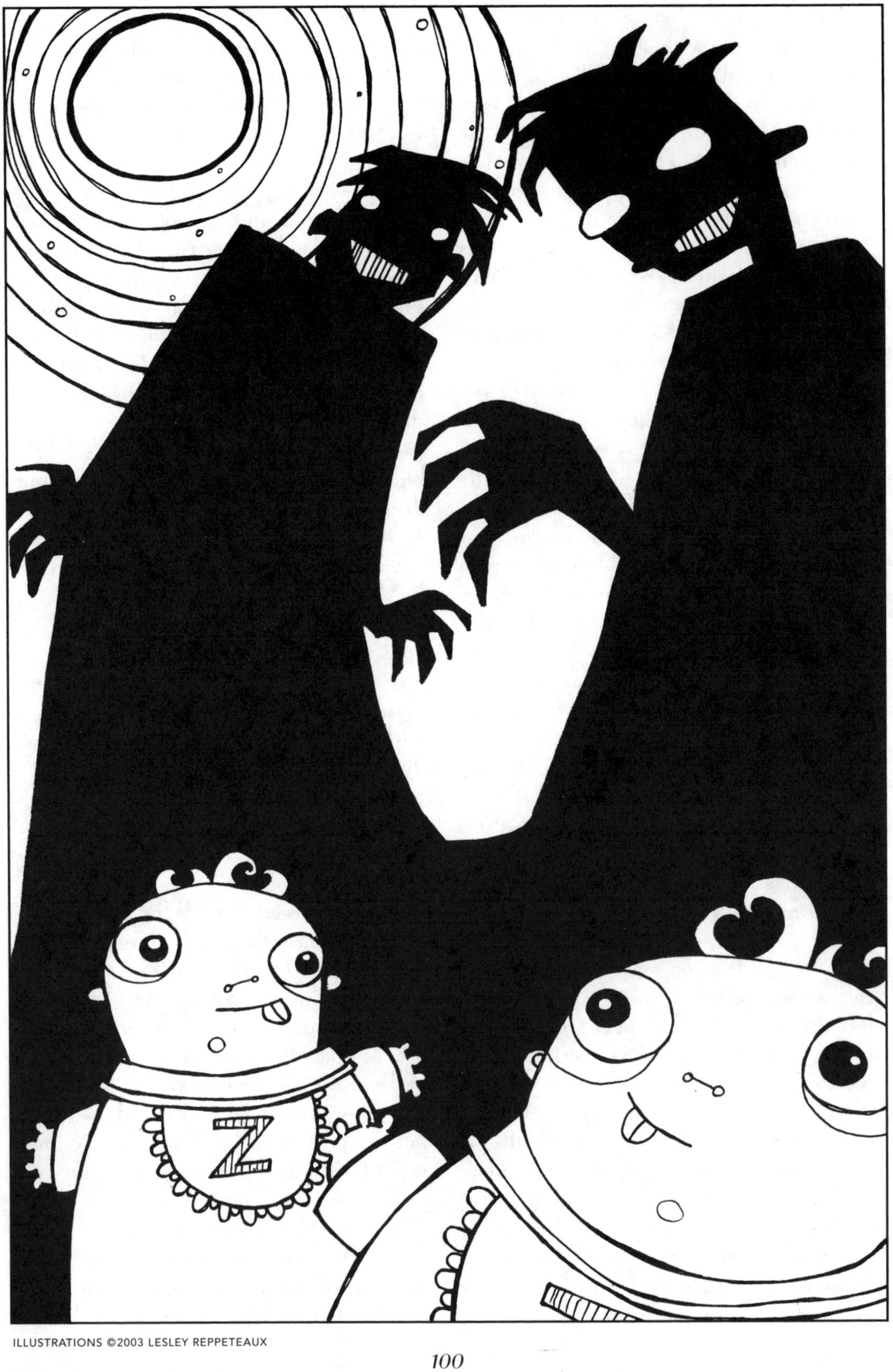
Z

the firmament was rent with a series of such yells as might have awakened the dead. Forthwith from the house of Bubb came parental cries and footsteps. As the sounds of scurrying feet rang through the mansion, Harry cried to Tommy, "They will be on us soon. Let us cut to the roof of the stable."

Tommy answered by a nod, and the two boys, regardless of consequences, and bearing each a twin, ascended to the roof by means of a ladder which they pulled up after them.

As Ephraim Bubb issued from his house in pursuit of his lost darlings, the sight which met his gaze froze his very soul. There, on the stable roof, stood Harry and Tommy renewing their game. The twins were each in turn lifted high in air and let fall with stunning force on the supine form of its fellow.

Loudly did Ephraim and also Sophonisba, who had now appeared upon the scene, shriek in vain for aid, but no eyes save their own saw the work of butchery or heard the shrieks of anguish and despair. Wildly did Ephraim strive, but in vain, to scale the stable wall.

Baffled in every effort, he rushed into the house and appeared in a moment bearing in his hands a double-barrelled gun, into which he poured the contents of a shot pouch as he ran. He came anigh the stable and hailed the murderous youths, "Drop them twins and come down here or I'll shoot you like a brace of dogs."

"Never!" exclaimed the heroic two with one impulse, and continued their awful pastime with a zest tenfold as they knew that the agonized eyes of parents wept at the cause of their joy.

"Then die!" shrieked Ephraim, as he fired both barrels at the hackers.

But, alas! love for his darlings shook the hand that never shook before. As the smoke cleared off and Ephraim recovered from the kick of his gun, he heard a twofold laugh of triumph and saw Harry and Tommy, all unhurt, waving in the air the trunks of the twins—the fond father had blown the heads completely off his own offspring.

Tommy and Harry shrieked in glee, and after playing catch with the bodies for some time, flung them high in the air. Ephraim leaped forward to catch what had once been Zacariah, and Sophonisba grabbed wildly for the loved remains of her Zerubbabel.

But the weight of the bodies and the height from which they fell were not reckoned by either parent. Ephraim and Sophonisba were stricken dead by the falling twins, who were thus posthumously guilty of the crime of parricide.

A CORONER'S JURY found the parents guilty of the crimes of infanticide and suicide, on the evidence of Harry and Tommy, who swore, reluctantly, that the inhuman monsters, maddened by drink, had killed their offspring by shooting them into the air out of a cannon — since stolen — whence like curses they had fallen on their own heads; and that therefore they had slain themselves with their own hands.

Harry and Tommy were each rewarded with honors and were knighted, even at their tender years.

Fortune seemed to smile upon them all the long after years, and they lived to a ripe old age, hale of body, and respected and beloved of all.

Often in the golden summer eves, when all nature seemed at rest, when the oldest cask was opened and the largest lamp was lit, when the chestnuts glowed in the embers and the kid turned on the spit, with shouting and with laughter they were accustomed to tell the tale of "The Dualitists, or, The Death-Doom of the Double-Born."

BRAM STOKER'S

THE JUDGE'S HOUSE

ADAPTED BY:
GERRY ALANGUILAN
2003

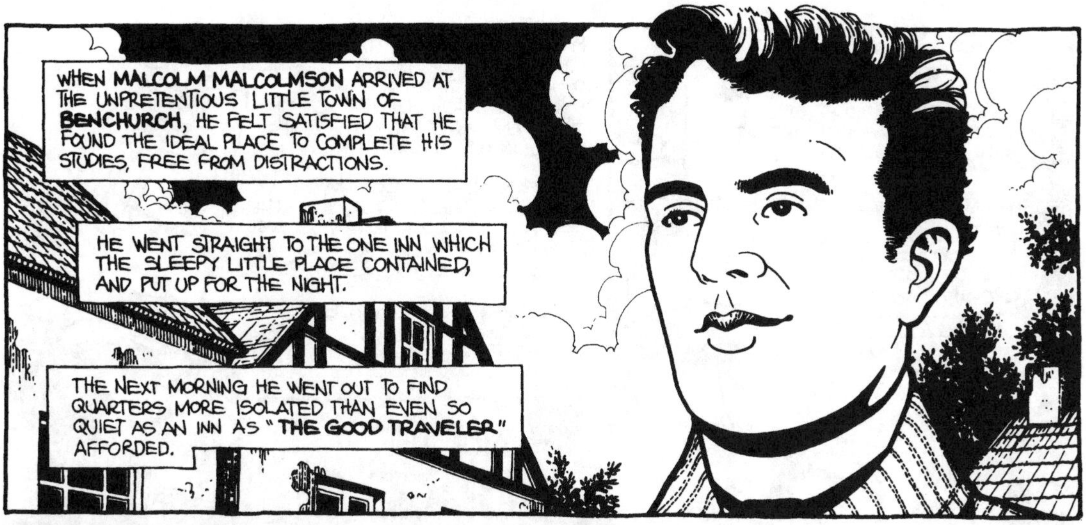
WHEN MALCOLM MALCOLMSON ARRIVED AT THE UNPRETENTIOUS LITTLE TOWN OF BENCHURCH, HE FELT SATISFIED THAT HE FOUND THE IDEAL PLACE TO COMPLETE HIS STUDIES, FREE FROM DISTRACTIONS.
HE WENT STRAIGHT TO THE ONE INN WHICH THE SLEEPY LITTLE PLACE CONTAINED, AND PUT UP FOR THE NIGHT.
THE NEXT MORNING HE WENT OUT TO FIND QUARTERS MORE ISOLATED THAN EVEN SO QUIET AS AN INN AS "THE GOOD TRAVELER" AFFORDED.

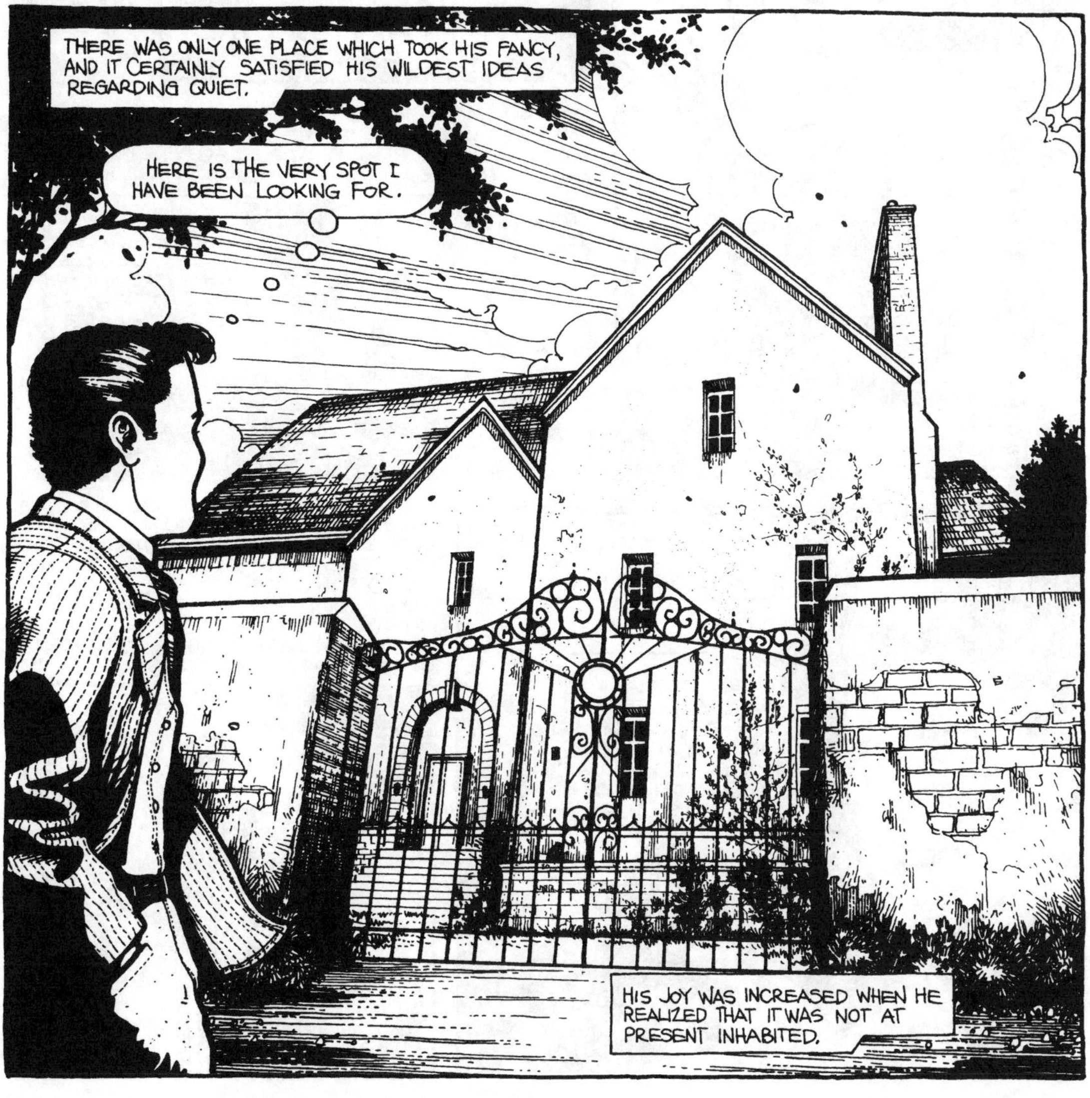
THERE WAS ONLY ONE PLACE WHICH TOOK HIS FANCY, AND IT CERTAINLY SATISFIED HIS WILDEST IDEAS REGARDING QUIET.
HERE IS THE VERY SPOT I HAVE BEEN LOOKING FOR.
HIS JOY WAS INCREASED WHEN HE REALIZED THAT IT WAS NOT AT PRESENT INHABITED.

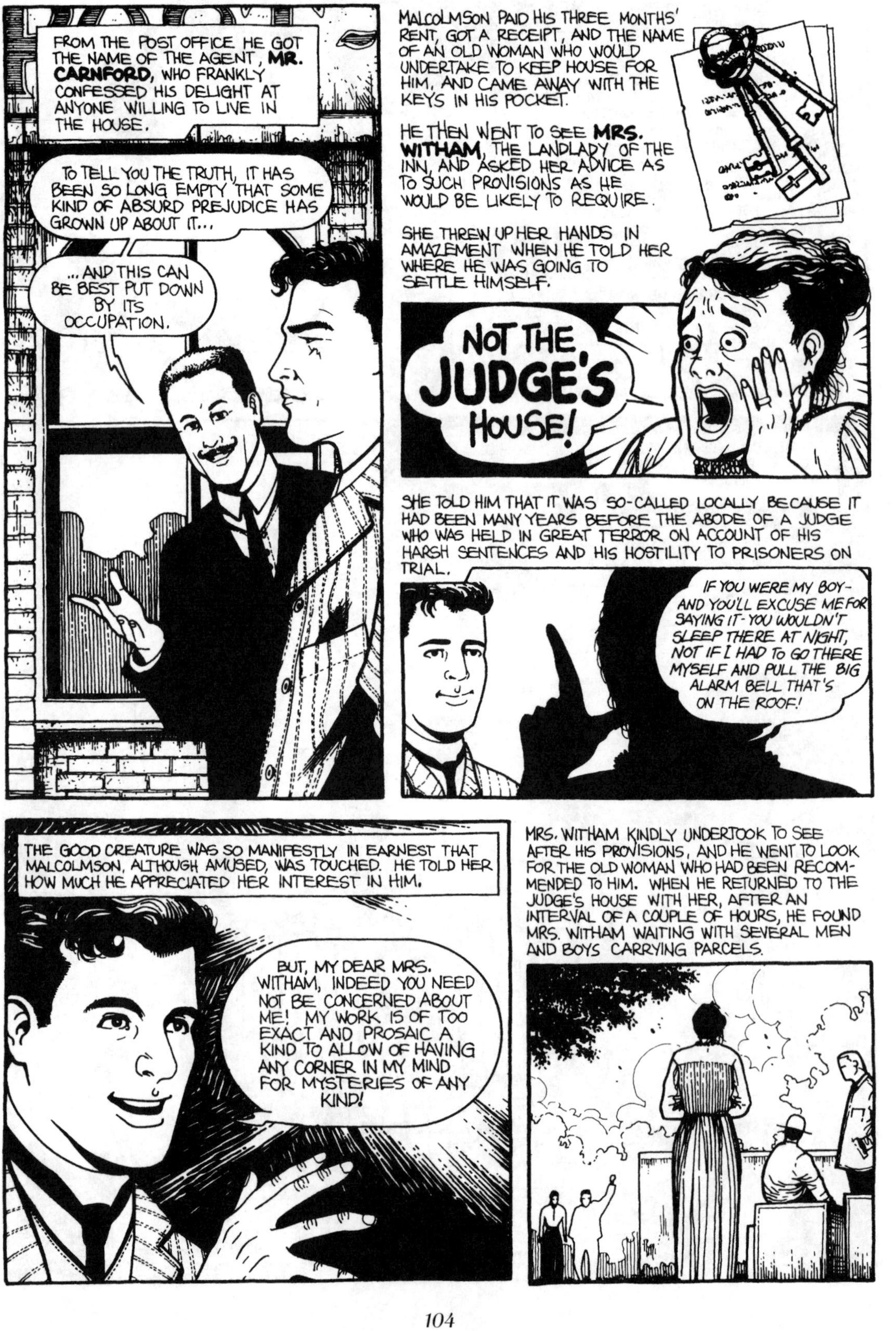
FROM THE POST OFFICE HE GOT THE NAME OF THE AGENT, MR. CARNFORD, WHO FRANKLY CONFESSED HIS DELIGHT AT ANYONE WILLING TO LIVE IN THE HOUSE.
TO TELL YOU THE TRUTH, IT HAS BEEN SO LONG EMPTY THAT SOME KIND OF ABSURD PREJUDICE HAS GROWN UP ABOUT IT...
...AND THIS CAN BE BEST PUT DOWN BY ITS OCCUPATION.
MALCOLMSON PAID HIS THREE MONTHS' RENT, GOT A RECEIPT, AND THE NAME OF AN OLD WOMAN WHO WOULD UNDERTAKE TO KEEP HOUSE FOR HIM, AND CAME AWAY WITH THE KEYS IN HIS POCKET.
HE THEN WENT TO SEE MRS. WITHAM, THE LANDLADY OF THE INN, AND ASKED HER ADVICE AS TO SUCH PROVISIONS AS HE WOULD BE LIKELY TO REQUIRE.
SHE THREW UP HER HANDS IN AMAZEMENT WHEN HE TOLD HER WHERE HE WAS GOING TO SETTLE HIMSELF.
NOT THE JUDGE'S HOUSE!
SHE TOLD HIM THAT IT WAS SO-CALLED LOCALLY BECAUSE IT HAD BEEN MANY YEARS BEFORE THE ABODE OF A JUDGE WHO WAS HELD IN GREAT TERROR ON ACCOUNT OF HIS HARSH SENTENCES AND HIS HOSTILITY TO PRISONERS ON TRIAL.
IF YOU WERE MY BOY- AND YOU'LL EXCUSE ME FOR SAYING IT- YOU WOULDN'T SLEEP THERE AT NIGHT, NOT IF I HAD TO GO THERE MYSELF AND PULL THE BIG ALARM BELL THAT'S ON THE ROOF!
THE GOOD CREATURE WAS SO MANIFESTLY IN EARNEST THAT MALCOLMSON, ALTHOUGH AMUSED, WAS TOUCHED. HE TOLD HER HOW MUCH HE APPRECIATED HER INTEREST IN HIM.
BUT, MY DEAR MRS. WITHAM, INDEED YOU NEED NOT BE CONCERNED ABOUT ME! MY WORK IS OF TOO EXACT AND PROSAIC A KIND TO ALLOW OF HAVING ANY CORNER IN MY MIND FOR MYSTERIES OF ANY KIND!
MRS. WITHAM KINDLY UNDERTOOK TO SEE AFTER HIS PROVISIONS, AND HE WENT TO LOOK FOR THE OLD WOMAN WHO HAD BEEN RECOMMENDED TO HIM. WHEN HE RETURNED TO THE JUDGE'S HOUSE WITH HER, AFTER AN INTERVAL OF A COUPLE OF HOURS, HE FOUND MRS. WITHAM WAITING WITH SEVERAL MEN AND BOYS CARRYING PARCELS.

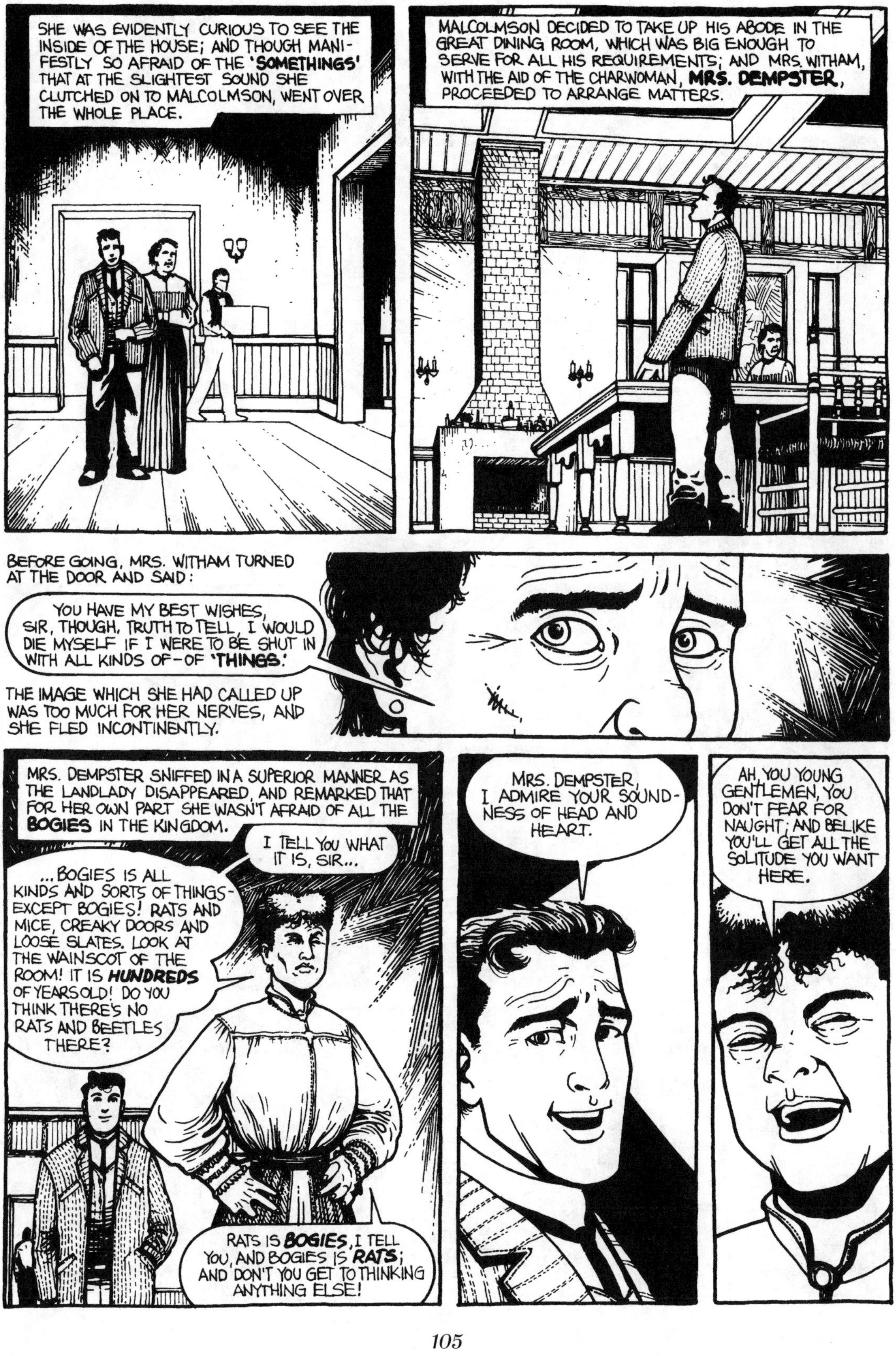
SHE WAS EVIDENTLY CURIOUS TO SEE THE INSIDE OF THE HOUSE; AND THOUGH MANIFESTLY SO AFRAID OF THE 'SOMETHINGS' THAT AT THE SLIGHTEST SOUND SHE CLUTCHED ON TO MALCOLMSON, WENT OVER THE WHOLE PLACE.
MALCOLMSON DECIDED TO TAKE UP HIS ABODE IN THE GREAT DINING ROOM, WHICH WAS BIG ENOUGH TO SERVE FOR ALL HIS REQUIREMENTS; AND MRS. WITHAM, WITH THE AID OF THE CHARWOMAN, MRS. DEMPSTER, PROCEEDED TO ARRANGE MATTERS.
BEFORE GOING, MRS. WITHAM TURNED AT THE DOOR AND SAID:
YOU HAVE MY BEST WISHES, SIR, THOUGH, TRUTH TO TELL, I WOULD DIE MYSELF IF I WERE TO BE SHUT IN WITH ALL KINDS OF—OF 'THINGS.'
THE IMAGE WHICH SHE HAD CALLED UP WAS TOO MUCH FOR HER NERVES, AND SHE FLED INCONTINENTLY.
MRS. DEMPSTER SNIFFED IN A SUPERIOR MANNER AS THE LANDLADY DISAPPEARED, AND REMARKED THAT FOR HER OWN PART SHE WASN'T AFRAID OF ALL THE BOGIES IN THE KINGDOM.
I TELL YOU WHAT IT IS, SIR...
...BOGIES IS ALL KINDS AND SORTS OF THINGS-EXCEPT BOGIES! RATS AND MICE, CREAKY DOORS AND LOOSE SLATES. LOOK AT THE WAINSCOT OF THE ROOM! IT IS HUNDREDS OF YEARS OLD! DO YOU THINK THERE'S NO RATS AND BEETLES THERE?
RATS IS BOGIES, I TELL YOU, AND BOGIES IS RATS; AND DON'T YOU GET TO THINKING ANYTHING ELSE!
MRS. DEMPSTER, I ADMIRE YOUR SOUNDNESS OF HEAD AND HEART.
AH, YOU YOUNG GENTLEMEN, YOU DON'T FEAR FOR NAUGHT; AND BELIKE YOU'LL GET ALL THE SOLITUDE YOU WANT HERE.

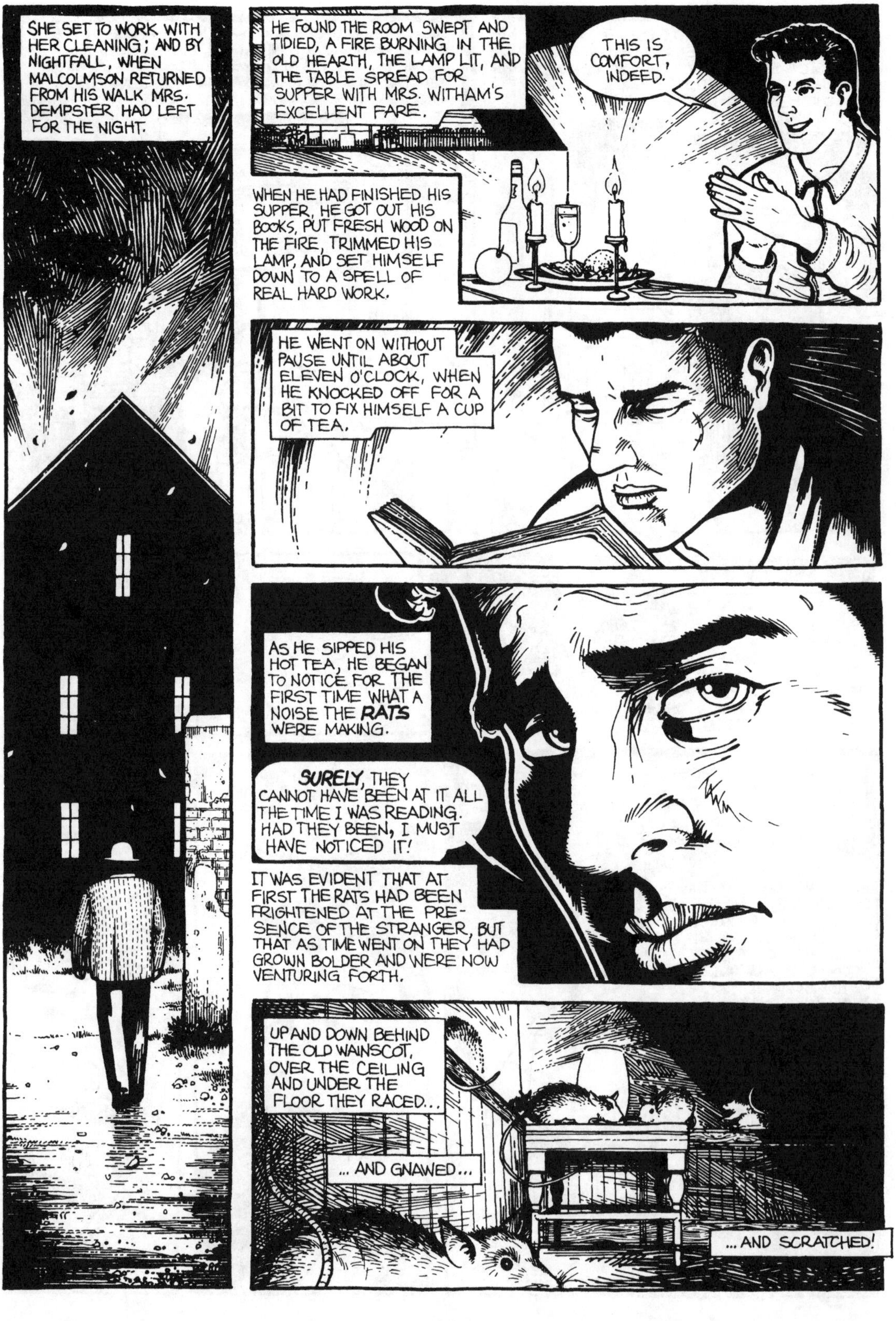
SHE SET TO WORK WITH HER CLEANING; AND BY NIGHTFALL, WHEN MALCOLMSON RETURNED FROM HIS WALK MRS. DEMPSTER HAD LEFT FOR THE NIGHT.
HE FOUND THE ROOM SWEPT AND TIDIED, A FIRE BURNING IN THE OLD HEARTH, THE LAMP LIT, AND THE TABLE SPREAD FOR SUPPER WITH MRS. WITHAM'S EXCELLENT FARE.
THIS IS COMFORT, INDEED.
WHEN HE HAD FINISHED HIS SUPPER, HE GOT OUT HIS BOOKS, PUT FRESH WOOD ON THE FIRE, TRIMMED HIS LAMP, AND SET HIMSELF DOWN TO A SPELL OF REAL HARD WORK.
HE WENT ON WITHOUT PAUSE UNTIL ABOUT ELEVEN O'CLOCK, WHEN HE KNOCKED OFF FOR A BIT TO FIX HIMSELF A CUP OF TEA.
AS HE SIPPED HIS HOT TEA, HE BEGAN TO NOTICE FOR THE FIRST TIME WHAT A NOISE THE ***RATS*** WERE MAKING.
SURELY, THEY CANNOT HAVE BEEN AT IT ALL THE TIME I WAS READING. HAD THEY BEEN, I MUST HAVE NOTICED IT!
IT WAS EVIDENT THAT AT FIRST THE RATS HAD BEEN FRIGHTENED AT THE PRESENCE OF THE STRANGER, BUT THAT AS TIME WENT ON THEY HAD GROWN BOLDER AND WERE NOW VENTURING FORTH.
UP AND DOWN BEHIND THE OLD WAINSCOT, OVER THE CEILING AND UNDER THE FLOOR THEY RACED...
... AND GNAWED...
... AND SCRATCHED!

BOGIES IS RATS, AND RATS IS BOGIES!

THE TEA BEGAN TO HAVE ITS EFFECT OF STIMULUS, AND HE ALLOWED HIMSELF THE LUXURY OF A GOOD LOOK AT THE ROOM, WONDERING THAT SO QUAINT AND BEAUTIFUL A HOUSE HAD BEEN SO LONG NEGLECTED.

HERE AND THERE AS HE WENT AROUND HE SAW SOME CRACK OR HOLE BLOCKED FOR A MOMENT BY THE FACE OF A **RAT** WITH ITS BRIGHT EYES GLITTERING IN THE LIGHT, BUT IN AN INSTANT IT WAS GONE, AND A SQUEAK AND A SCAMPER FOLLOWED.

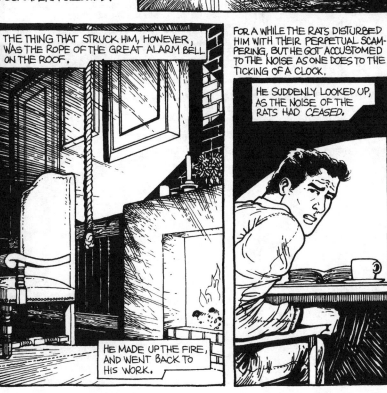

THE THING THAT STRUCK HIM, HOWEVER, WAS THE ROPE OF THE GREAT ALARM BELL ON THE ROOF.

HE MADE UP THE FIRE, AND WENT BACK TO HIS WORK.

FOR A WHILE THE RATS DISTURBED HIM WITH THEIR PERPETUAL SCAMPERING, BUT HE GOT ACCUSTOMED TO THE NOISE AS ONE DOES TO THE TICKING OF A CLOCK.

HE SUDDENLY LOOKED UP, AS THE NOISE OF THE RATS HAD *CEASED.*

THERE ON THE GREAT HIGH-BACKED CARVED OAK CHAIR BY THE SIDE OF THE FIREPLACE SAT AN ENORMOUS **RAT**...

...STEADILY GLARING AT *HIM* WITH BALEFUL EYES.

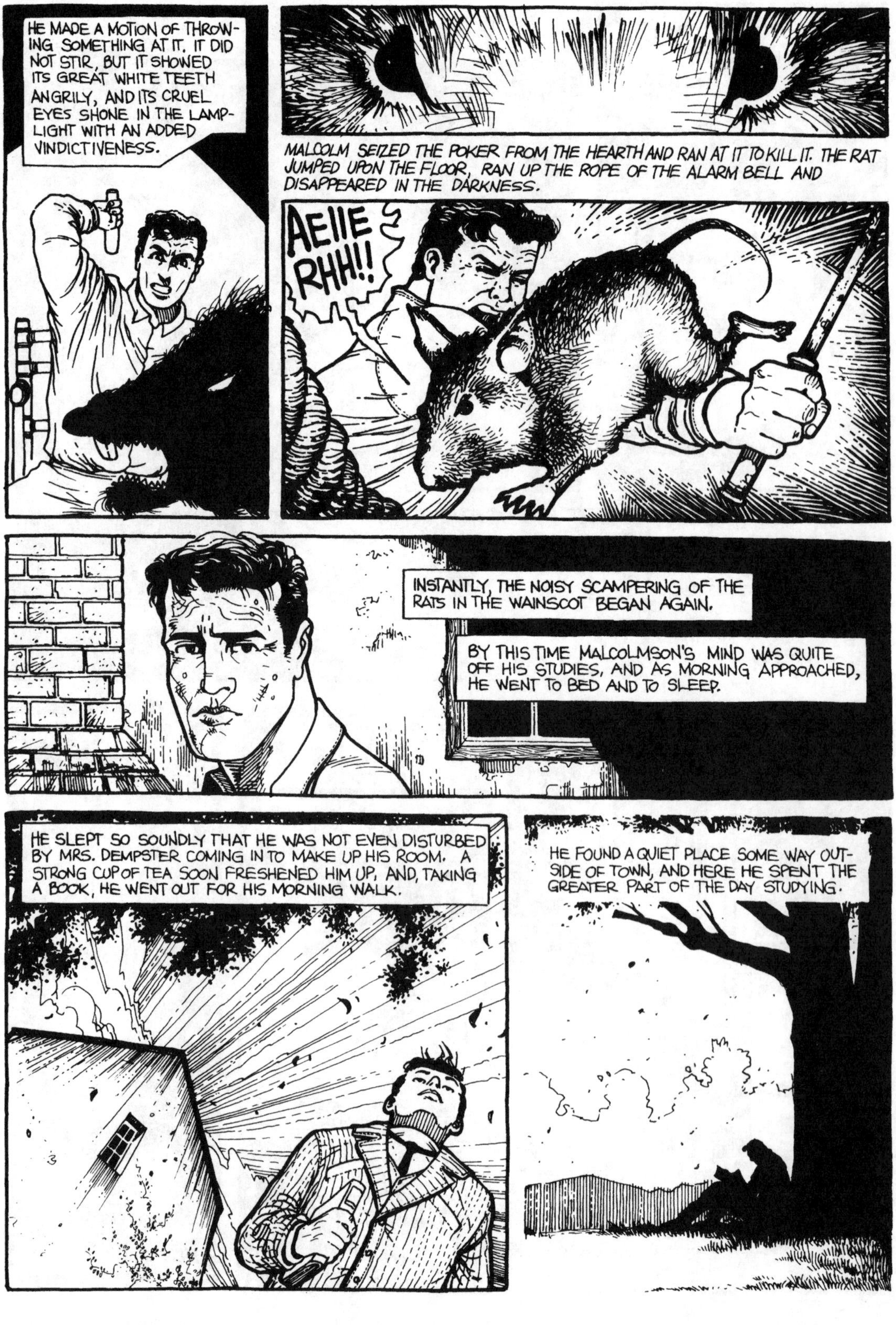
HE MADE A MOTION OF THROWING SOMETHING AT IT. IT DID NOT STIR, BUT IT SHOWED ITS GREAT WHITE TEETH ANGRILY, AND ITS CRUEL EYES SHONE IN THE LAMPLIGHT WITH AN ADDED VINDICTIVENESS.
MALCOLM SEIZED THE POKER FROM THE HEARTH AND RAN AT IT TO KILL IT. THE RAT JUMPED UPON THE FLOOR, RAN UP THE ROPE OF THE ALARM BELL AND DISAPPEARED IN THE DARKNESS.
AEIIE RHH!!
INSTANTLY, THE NOISY SCAMPERING OF THE RATS IN THE WAINSCOT BEGAN AGAIN.
BY THIS TIME MALCOLMSON'S MIND WAS QUITE OFF HIS STUDIES, AND AS MORNING APPROACHED, HE WENT TO BED AND TO SLEEP.
HE SLEPT SO SOUNDLY THAT HE WAS NOT EVEN DISTURBED BY MRS. DEMPSTER COMING IN TO MAKE UP HIS ROOM. A STRONG CUP OF TEA SOON FRESHENED HIM UP, AND, TAKING A BOOK, HE WENT OUT FOR HIS MORNING WALK.
HE FOUND A QUIET PLACE SOME WAY OUTSIDE OF TOWN, AND HERE HE SPENT THE GREATER PART OF THE DAY STUDYING.

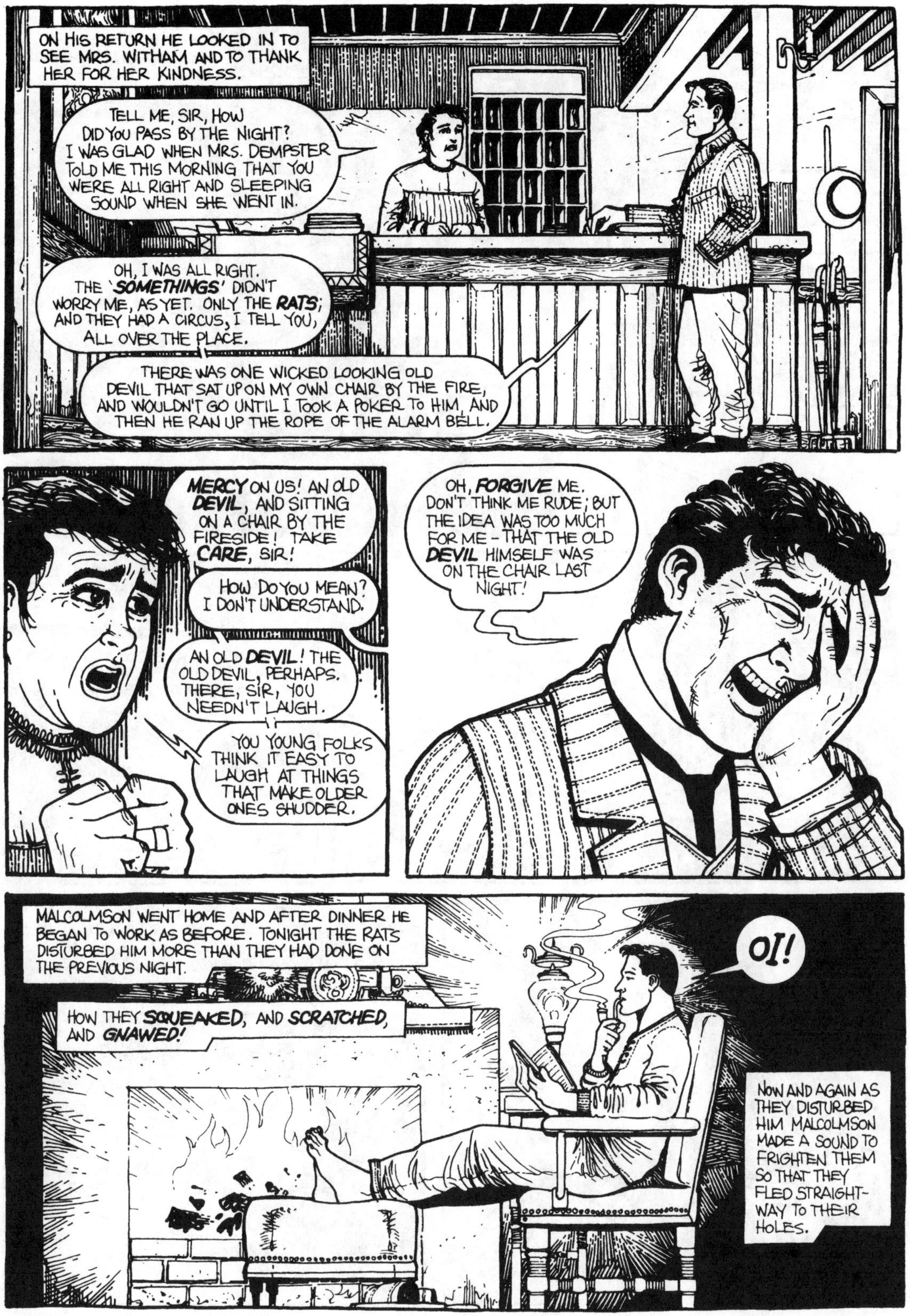
ON HIS RETURN HE LOOKED IN TO SEE MRS. WITHAM AND TO THANK HER FOR HER KINDNESS.
TELL ME, SIR, HOW DID YOU PASS BY THE NIGHT? I WAS GLAD WHEN MRS. DEMPSTER TOLD ME THIS MORNING THAT YOU WERE ALL RIGHT AND SLEEPING SOUND WHEN SHE WENT IN.
OH, I WAS ALL RIGHT. THE 'SOMETHINGS' DIDN'T WORRY ME, AS YET. ONLY THE RATS; AND THEY HAD A CIRCUS, I TELL YOU, ALL OVER THE PLACE.
THERE WAS ONE WICKED LOOKING OLD DEVIL THAT SAT UP ON MY OWN CHAIR BY THE FIRE, AND WOULDN'T GO UNTIL I TOOK A POKER TO HIM, AND THEN HE RAN UP THE ROPE OF THE ALARM BELL.
MERCY ON US! AN OLD DEVIL, AND SITTING ON A CHAIR BY THE FIRESIDE! TAKE CARE, SIR!
HOW DO YOU MEAN? I DON'T UNDERSTAND.
AN OLD DEVIL! THE OLD DEVIL, PERHAPS. THERE, SIR, YOU NEEDN'T LAUGH.
YOU YOUNG FOLKS THINK IT EASY TO LAUGH AT THINGS THAT MAKE OLDER ONES SHUDDER.
OH, FORGIVE ME. DON'T THINK ME RUDE; BUT THE IDEA WAS TOO MUCH FOR ME - THAT THE OLD DEVIL HIMSELF WAS ON THE CHAIR LAST NIGHT!
MALCOLMSON WENT HOME AND AFTER DINNER HE BEGAN TO WORK AS BEFORE. TONIGHT THE RATS DISTURBED HIM MORE THAN THEY HAD DONE ON THE PREVIOUS NIGHT.
OI!
HOW THEY SQUEAKED, AND SCRATCHED, AND GNAWED!
NOW AND AGAIN AS THEY DISTURBED HIM MALCOLMSON MADE A SOUND TO FRIGHTEN THEM SO THAT THEY FLED STRAIGHTWAY TO THEIR HOLES.

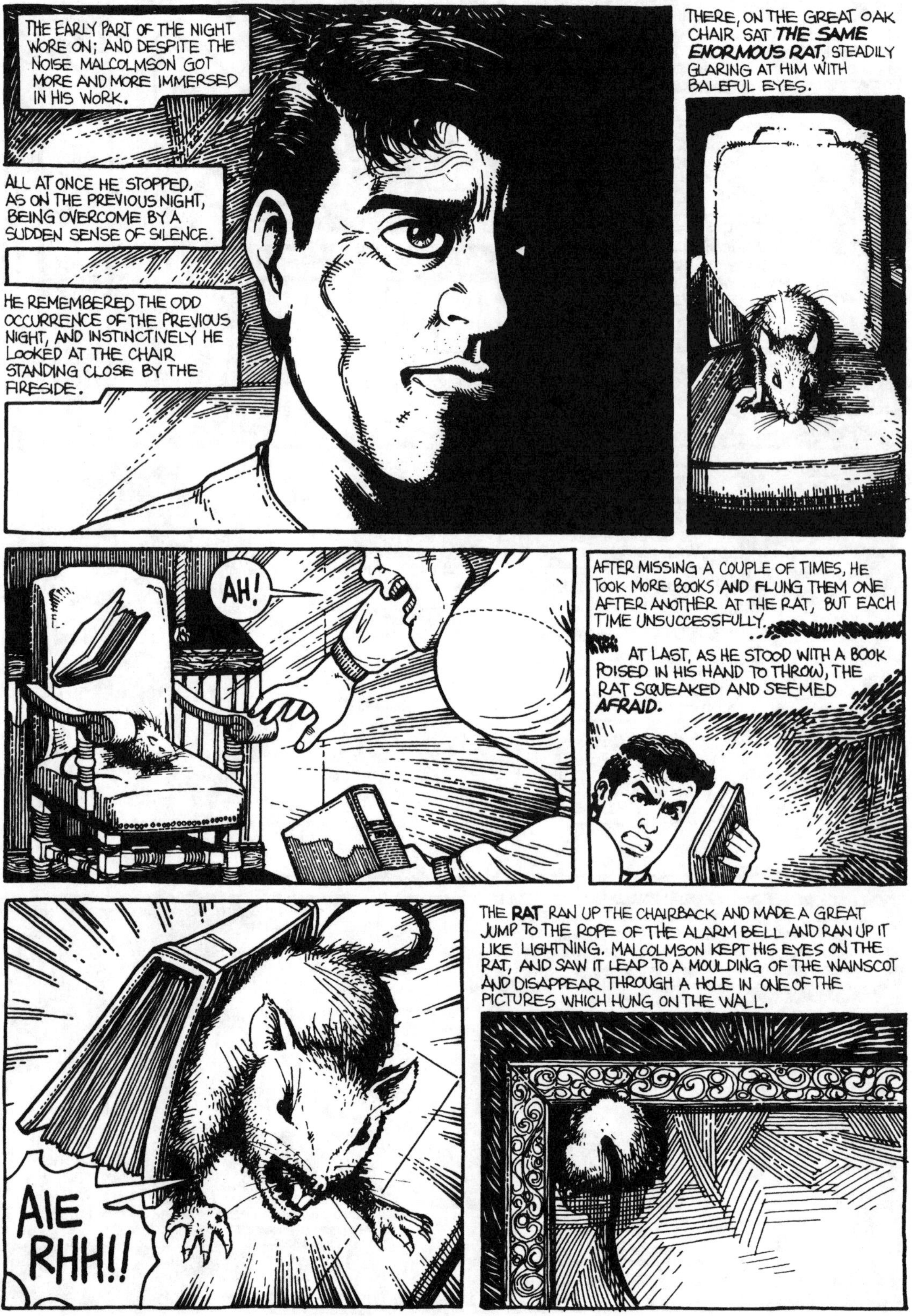
THE EARLY PART OF THE NIGHT WORE ON; AND DESPITE THE NOISE MALCOLMSON GOT MORE AND MORE IMMERSED IN HIS WORK.
ALL AT ONCE HE STOPPED, AS ON THE PREVIOUS NIGHT, BEING OVERCOME BY A SUDDEN SENSE OF SILENCE.
HE REMEMBERED THE ODD OCCURRENCE OF THE PREVIOUS NIGHT, AND INSTINCTIVELY HE LOOKED AT THE CHAIR STANDING CLOSE BY THE FIRESIDE.
THERE, ON THE GREAT OAK CHAIR SAT **THE SAME ENORMOUS RAT**, STEADILY GLARING AT HIM WITH BALEFUL EYES.
AH!
AFTER MISSING A COUPLE OF TIMES, HE TOOK MORE BOOKS AND FLUNG THEM ONE AFTER ANOTHER AT THE RAT, BUT EACH TIME UNSUCCESSFULLY.
AT LAST, AS HE STOOD WITH A BOOK POISED IN HIS HAND TO THROW, THE RAT SQUEAKED AND SEEMED **AFRAID.**
AIE RHH!!
THE **RAT** RAN UP THE CHAIRBACK AND MADE A GREAT JUMP TO THE ROPE OF THE ALARM BELL AND RAN UP IT LIKE LIGHTNING. MALCOLMSON KEPT HIS EYES ON THE RAT, AND SAW IT LEAP TO A MOULDING OF THE WAINSCOT AND DISAPPEAR THROUGH A HOLE IN ONE OF THE PICTURES WHICH HUNG ON THE WALL.

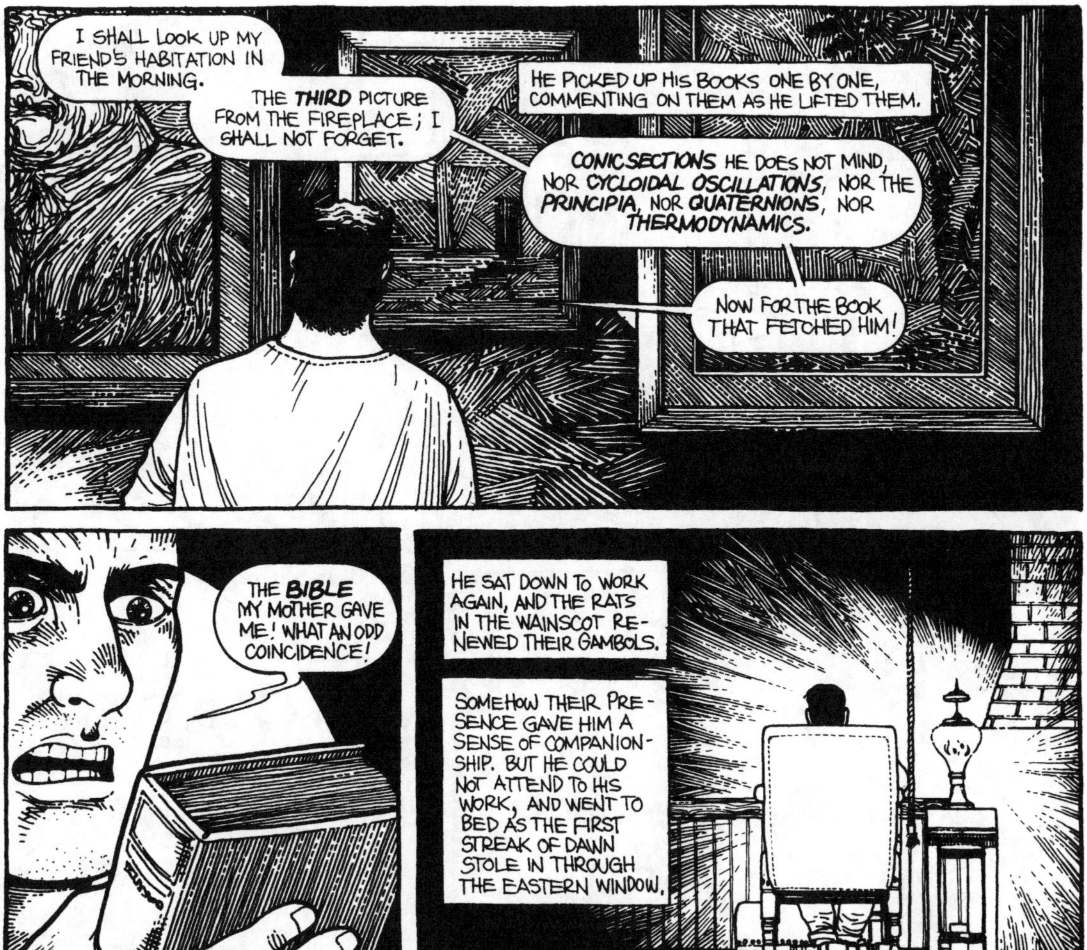
I SHALL LOOK UP MY FRIEND'S HABITATION IN THE MORNING.
THE THIRD PICTURE FROM THE FIREPLACE; I SHALL NOT FORGET.
HE PICKED UP HIS BOOKS ONE BY ONE, COMMENTING ON THEM AS HE LIFTED THEM.
CONIC SECTIONS HE DOES NOT MIND, NOR CYCLOIDAL OSCILLATIONS, NOR THE PRINCIPIA, NOR QUATERNIONS, NOR THERMODYNAMICS.
NOW FOR THE BOOK THAT FETCHED HIM!
THE BIBLE MY MOTHER GAVE ME! WHAT AN ODD COINCIDENCE!
HE SAT DOWN TO WORK AGAIN, AND THE RATS IN THE WAINSCOT RE-NEWED THEIR GAMBOLS.
SOMEHOW THEIR PRE-SENCE GAVE HIM A SENSE OF COMPANION-SHIP. BUT HE COULD NOT ATTEND TO HIS WORK, AND WENT TO BED AS THE FIRST STREAK OF DAWN STOLE IN THROUGH THE EASTERN WINDOW.

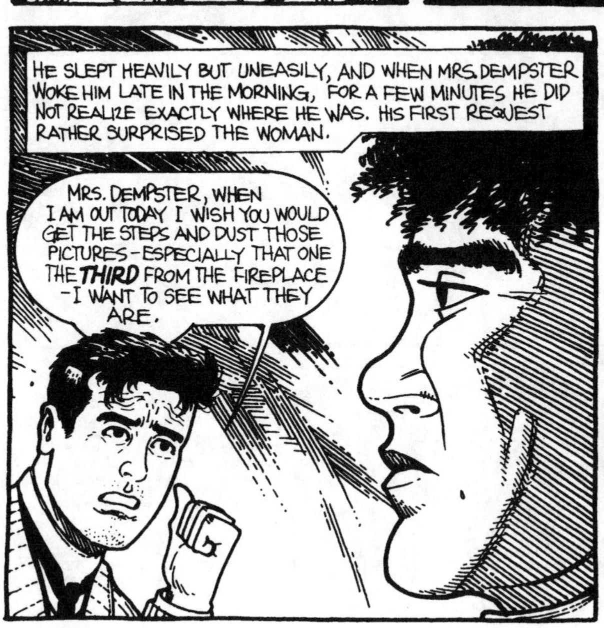
HE SLEPT HEAVILY BUT UNEASILY, AND WHEN MRS. DEMPSTER WOKE HIM LATE IN THE MORNING, FOR A FEW MINUTES HE DID NOT REALIZE EXACTLY WHERE HE WAS. HIS FIRST REQUEST RATHER SURPRISED THE WOMAN.
MRS. DEMPSTER, WHEN I AM OUT TODAY I WISH YOU WOULD GET THE STEPS AND DUST THOSE PICTURES—ESPECIALLY THAT ONE THE THIRD FROM THE FIREPLACE—I WANT TO SEE WHAT THEY ARE.

LATE IN THE AFTERNOON MALCOLMSON WORKED AT HIS BOOKS IN THE SHADED WALK, AND HE FOUND THAT HIS READING WAS PROGRESSING WELL. IT WAS IN A STATE OF JUBILATION THAT HE PAID A VISIT TO MRS. WITHAM AT "**THE GOOD TRAVELER**."

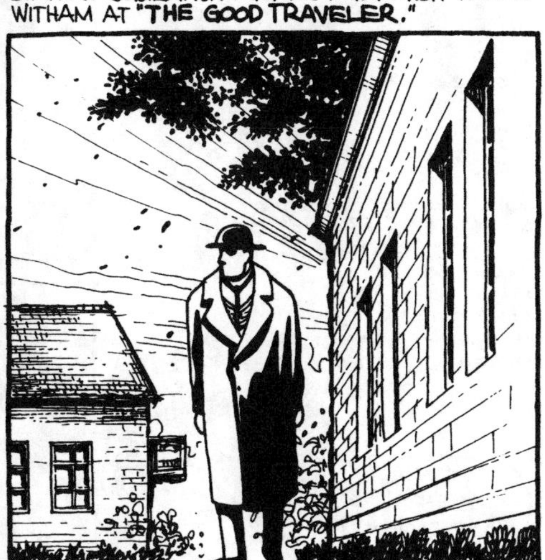

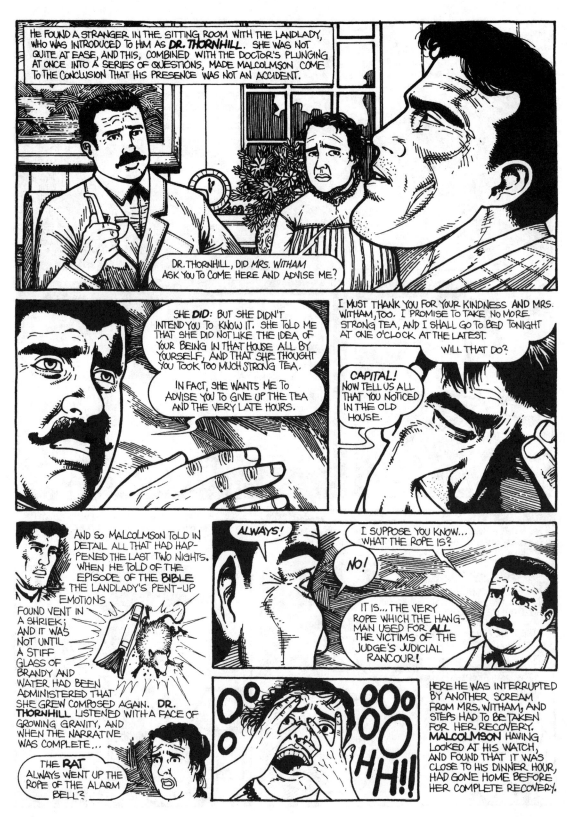

HE FOUND A STRANGER IN THE SITTING ROOM WITH THE LANDLADY, WHO WAS INTRODUCED TO HIM AS **DR. THORNHILL**. SHE WAS NOT QUITE AT EASE, AND THIS, COMBINED WITH THE DOCTOR'S PLUNGING AT ONCE INTO A SERIES OF QUESTIONS, MADE MALCOLMSON COME TO THE CONCLUSION THAT HIS PRESENCE WAS NOT AN ACCIDENT.

DR. THORNHILL, DID *MRS. WITHAM* ASK YOU TO COME HERE AND ADVISE ME?

SHE *DID*: BUT SHE DIDN'T INTEND YOU TO KNOW IT. SHE TOLD ME THAT SHE DID NOT LIKE THE IDEA OF YOUR BEING IN THAT HOUSE ALL BY YOURSELF, AND THAT SHE THOUGHT YOU TOOK TOO MUCH STRONG TEA.

IN FACT, SHE WANTS ME TO ADVISE YOU TO GIVE UP THE TEA AND THE VERY LATE HOURS.

I MUST THANK YOU FOR YOUR KINDNESS AND MRS. WITHAM, TOO. I PROMISE TO TAKE NO MORE STRONG TEA, AND I SHALL GO TO BED TONIGHT AT ONE O'CLOCK AT THE LATEST.

WILL THAT DO?

CAPITAL! NOW TELL US ALL THAT YOU NOTICED IN THE OLD HOUSE.

AND SO MALCOLMSON TOLD IN DETAIL ALL THAT HAD HAPPENED THE LAST TWO NIGHTS. WHEN HE TOLD OF THE EPISODE OF THE **BIBLE** THE LANDLADY'S PENT-UP EMOTIONS FOUND VENT IN A SHRIEK; AND IT WAS NOT UNTIL A STIFF GLASS OF BRANDY AND WATER HAD BEEN ADMINISTERED THAT SHE GREW COMPOSED AGAIN. **DR. THORNHILL** LISTENED WITH A FACE OF GROWING GRAVITY, AND WHEN THE NARRATIVE WAS COMPLETE...

THE **RAT** ALWAYS WENT UP THE ROPE OF THE ALARM BELL?

ALWAYS!

I SUPPOSE YOU KNOW... WHAT THE ROPE IS?

NO!

IT IS... THE VERY ROPE WHICH THE HANGMAN USED FOR **ALL** THE VICTIMS OF THE JUDGE'S JUDICIAL RANCOUR!

OOOOO OOHH!!

HERE HE WAS INTERRUPTED BY ANOTHER SCREAM FROM MRS. WITHAM, AND STEPS HAD TO BE TAKEN FOR HER RECOVERY. **MALCOLMSON** HAVING LOOKED AT HIS WATCH, AND FOUND THAT IT WAS CLOSE TO HIS DINNER HOUR, HAD GONE HOME BEFORE HER COMPLETE RECOVERY.

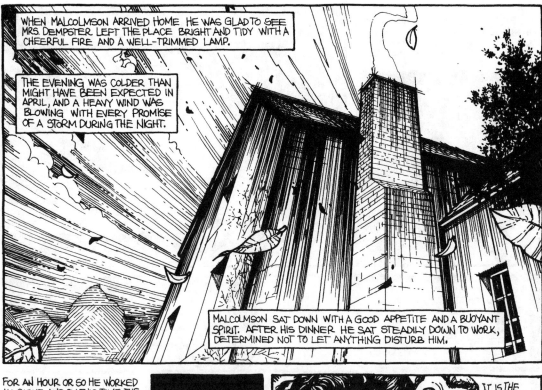

WHEN MALCOLMSON ARRIVED HOME, HE WAS GLAD TO SEE MRS. DEMPSTER LEFT THE PLACE BRIGHT AND TIDY WITH A CHEERFUL FIRE AND A WELL-TRIMMED LAMP.

THE EVENING WAS COLDER THAN MIGHT HAVE BEEN EXPECTED IN APRIL, AND A HEAVY WIND WAS BLOWING WITH EVERY PROMISE OF A STORM DURING THE NIGHT.

MALCOLMSON SAT DOWN WITH A GOOD APPETITE AND A BUOYANT SPIRIT. AFTER HIS DINNER HE SAT STEADILY DOWN TO WORK, DETERMINED NOT TO LET ANYTHING DISTURB HIM.

FOR AN HOUR OR SO HE WORKED ALL RIGHT, AND BY THIS TIME THE WIND HAD BECOME A **STORM**. THE OLD HOUSE SEEMED TO SHAKE TO ITS FOUNDATIONS, AND THE STORM RAGED THROUGH ITS MANY CHIMNEYS AND ITS QUEER OLD GABLES, PRODUCING STRANGE, UNEARTHLY SOUNDS IN THE EMPTY ROOMS AND CORRIDORS.

EVEN THE GREAT ALARM BELL ON THE ROOF MUST HAVE FELT THE FORCE OF THE WIND, FOR THE ROPE ROSE AND FELL SLIGHTLY, AS THOUGH THE BELL WERE MOVED A LITTLE FROM TIME TO TIME, AND THE LIMBER ROPE FELL ON THE OAK FLOOR WITH A HARD AND HOLLOW SOUND.

IT IS THE **ROPE** WHICH THE **HANGMAN** USED FOR THE VICTIMS OF THE JUDGE'S JUDICIAL RANCOUR!

HE WENT OVER TO THE CORNER OF THE FIREPLACE AND TOOK THE ROPE IN HIS HAND TO LOOK AT IT. HE LOST HIMSELF FOR A MOMENT IN SPECULATION AS TO WHO THESE VICTIMS WERE, AND THE GRIM WISH OF THE JUDGE TO HAVE SUCH A GHASTLY RELIC EVER UNDER HIS EYES.

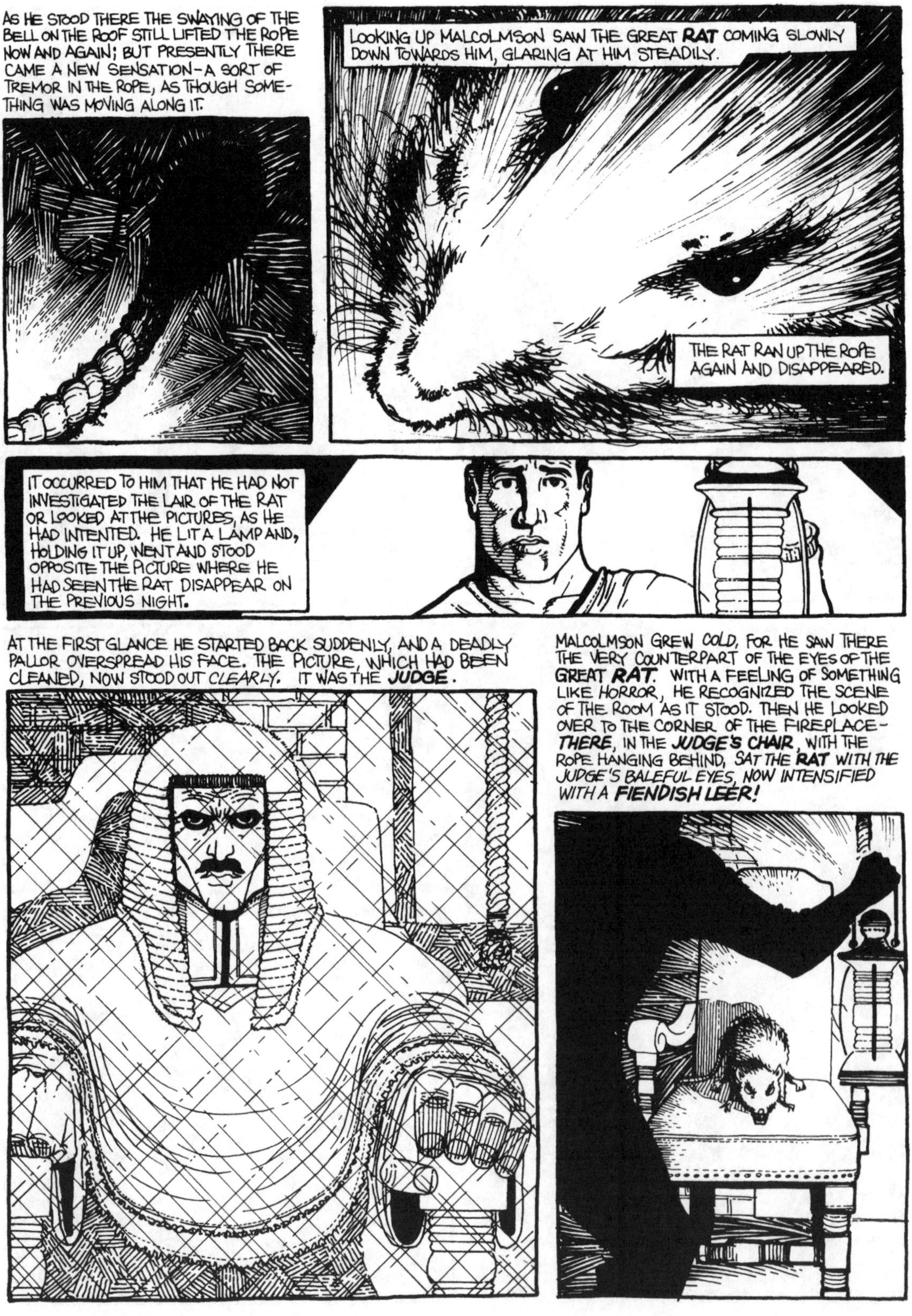
AS HE STOOD THERE THE SWAYING OF THE BELL ON THE ROOF STILL LIFTED THE ROPE NOW AND AGAIN; BUT PRESENTLY THERE CAME A NEW SENSATION–A SORT OF TREMOR IN THE ROPE, AS THOUGH SOMETHING WAS MOVING ALONG IT.
LOOKING UP MALCOLMSON SAW THE GREAT RAT COMING SLOWLY DOWN TOWARDS HIM, GLARING AT HIM STEADILY.
THE RAT RAN UP THE ROPE AGAIN AND DISAPPEARED.
IT OCCURRED TO HIM THAT HE HAD NOT INVESTIGATED THE LAIR OF THE RAT OR LOOKED AT THE PICTURES, AS HE HAD INTENTED. HE LIT A LAMP AND, HOLDING IT UP, WENT AND STOOD OPPOSITE THE PICTURE WHERE HE HAD SEEN THE RAT DISAPPEAR ON THE PREVIOUS NIGHT.
AT THE FIRST GLANCE HE STARTED BACK SUDDENLY, AND A DEADLY PALLOR OVERSPREAD HIS FACE. THE PICTURE, WHICH HAD BEEN CLEANED, NOW STOOD OUT CLEARLY. IT WAS THE JUDGE.
MALCOLMSON GREW COLD, FOR HE SAW THERE THE VERY COUNTERPART OF THE EYES OF THE GREAT RAT. WITH A FEELING OF SOMETHING LIKE HORROR, HE RECOGNIZED THE SCENE OF THE ROOM AS IT STOOD. THEN HE LOOKED OVER TO THE CORNER OF THE FIREPLACE–THERE, IN THE JUDGE'S CHAIR, WITH THE ROPE HANGING BEHIND, SAT THE RAT WITH THE JUDGE'S BALEFUL EYES, NOW INTENSIFIED WITH A FIENDISH LEER!

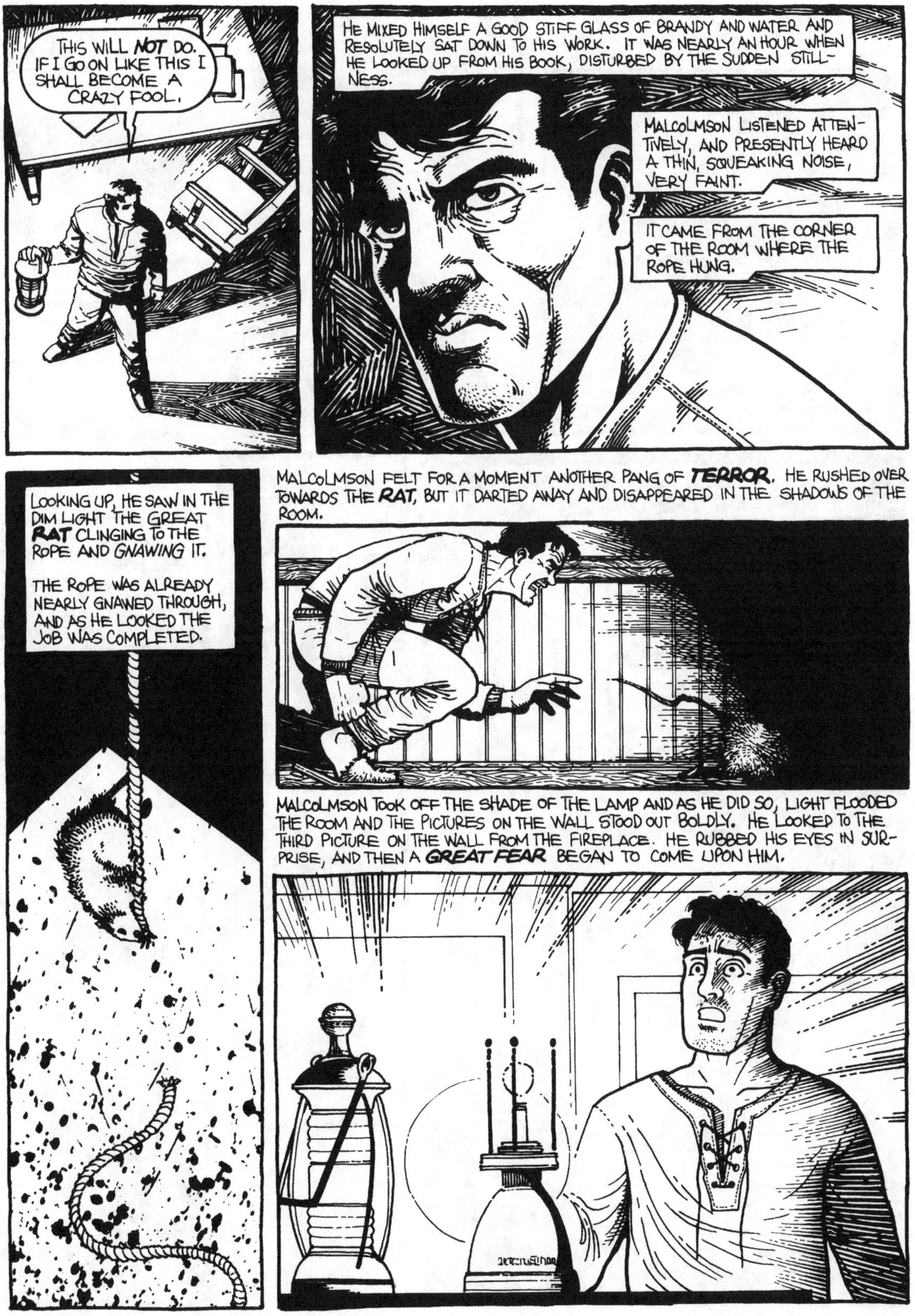
THIS WILL NOT DO. IF I GO ON LIKE THIS I SHALL BECOME A CRAZY FOOL.
HE MIXED HIMSELF A GOOD STIFF GLASS OF BRANDY AND WATER AND RESOLUTELY SAT DOWN TO HIS WORK. IT WAS NEARLY AN HOUR WHEN HE LOOKED UP FROM HIS BOOK, DISTURBED BY THE SUDDEN STILL-NESS.
MALCOLMSON LISTENED ATTEN-TIVELY, AND PRESENTLY HEARD A THIN, SQUEAKING NOISE, VERY FAINT.
IT CAME FROM THE CORNER OF THE ROOM WHERE THE ROPE HUNG.
LOOKING UP, HE SAW IN THE DIM LIGHT THE GREAT RAT CLINGING TO THE ROPE AND GNAWING IT.
THE ROPE WAS ALREADY NEARLY GNAWED THROUGH, AND AS HE LOOKED THE JOB WAS COMPLETED.
MALCOLMSON FELT FOR A MOMENT ANOTHER PANG OF TERROR. HE RUSHED OVER TOWARDS THE RAT, BUT IT DARTED AWAY AND DISAPPEARED IN THE SHADOWS OF THE ROOM.
MALCOLMSON TOOK OFF THE SHADE OF THE LAMP AND AS HE DID SO, LIGHT FLOODED THE ROOM AND THE PICTURES ON THE WALL STOOD OUT BOLDLY. HE LOOKED TO THE THIRD PICTURE ON THE WALL FROM THE FIREPLACE. HE RUBBED HIS EYES IN SUR-PRISE, AND THEN A GREAT FEAR BEGAN TO COME UPON HIM.

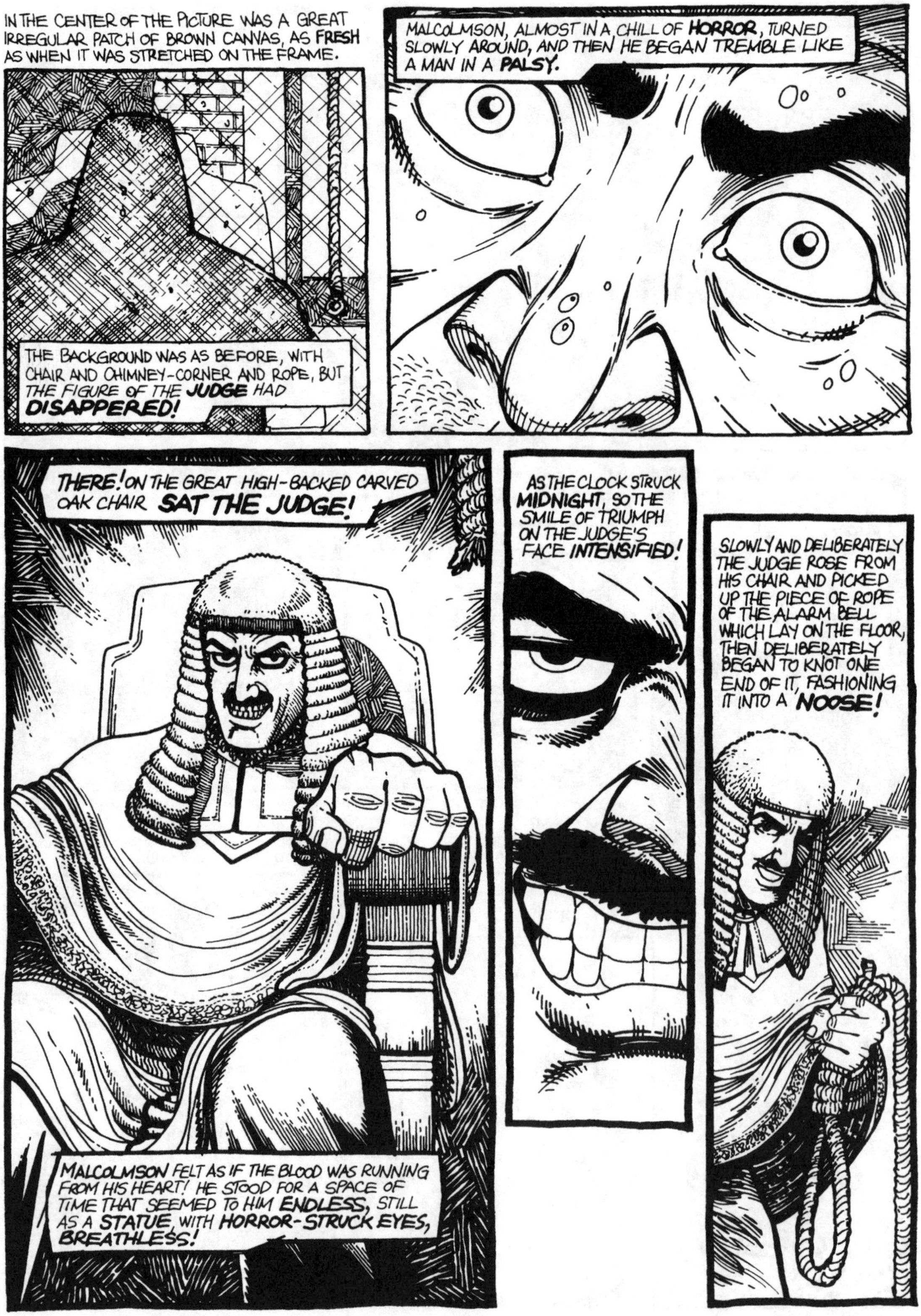
IN THE CENTER OF THE PICTURE WAS A GREAT IRREGULAR PATCH OF BROWN CANVAS, AS FRESH AS WHEN IT WAS STRETCHED ON THE FRAME.
THE BACKGROUND WAS AS BEFORE, WITH CHAIR AND CHIMNEY-CORNER AND ROPE, BUT THE FIGURE OF THE JUDGE HAD DISAPPERED!
MALCOLMSON, ALMOST IN A CHILL OF HORROR, TURNED SLOWLY AROUND, AND THEN HE BEGAN TREMBLE LIKE A MAN IN A PALSY.
THERE! ON THE GREAT HIGH-BACKED CARVED OAK CHAIR SAT THE JUDGE!
MALCOLMSON FELT AS IF THE BLOOD WAS RUNNING FROM HIS HEART! HE STOOD FOR A SPACE OF TIME THAT SEEMED TO HIM ENDLESS, STILL AS A STATUE, WITH HORROR-STRUCK EYES, BREATHLESS!
AS THE CLOCK STRUCK MIDNIGHT, SO THE SMILE OF TRIUMPH ON THE JUDGE'S FACE INTENSIFIED!
SLOWLY AND DELIBERATELY THE JUDGE ROSE FROM HIS CHAIR AND PICKED UP THE PIECE OF ROPE OF THE ALARM BELL WHICH LAY ON THE FLOOR, THEN DELIBERATELY BEGAN TO KNOT ONE END OF IT, FASHIONING IT INTO A NOOSE!

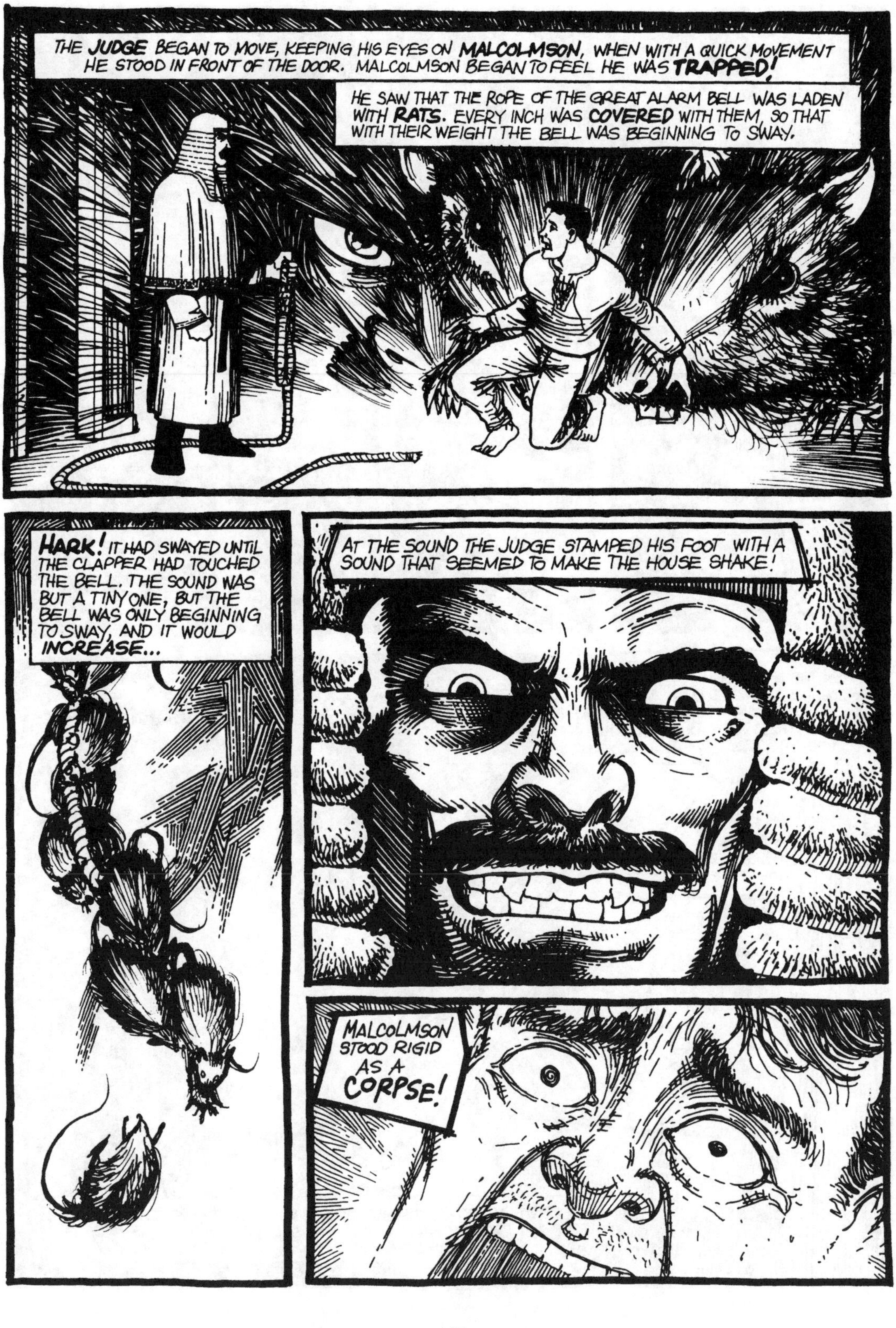
THE JUDGE BEGAN TO MOVE, KEEPING HIS EYES ON MALCOLMSON, WHEN WITH A QUICK MOVEMENT HE STOOD IN FRONT OF THE DOOR. MALCOLMSON BEGAN TO FEEL HE WAS TRAPPED!
HE SAW THAT THE ROPE OF THE GREAT ALARM BELL WAS LADEN WITH RATS. EVERY INCH WAS COVERED WITH THEM, SO THAT WITH THEIR WEIGHT THE BELL WAS BEGINNING TO SWAY.
HARK! IT HAD SWAYED UNTIL THE CLAPPER HAD TOUCHED THE BELL. THE SOUND WAS BUT A TINY ONE, BUT THE BELL WAS ONLY BEGINNING TO SWAY, AND IT WOULD INCREASE...
AT THE SOUND THE JUDGE STAMPED HIS FOOT WITH A SOUND THAT SEEMED TO MAKE THE HOUSE SHAKE!
MALCOLMSON STOOD RIGID AS A CORPSE!

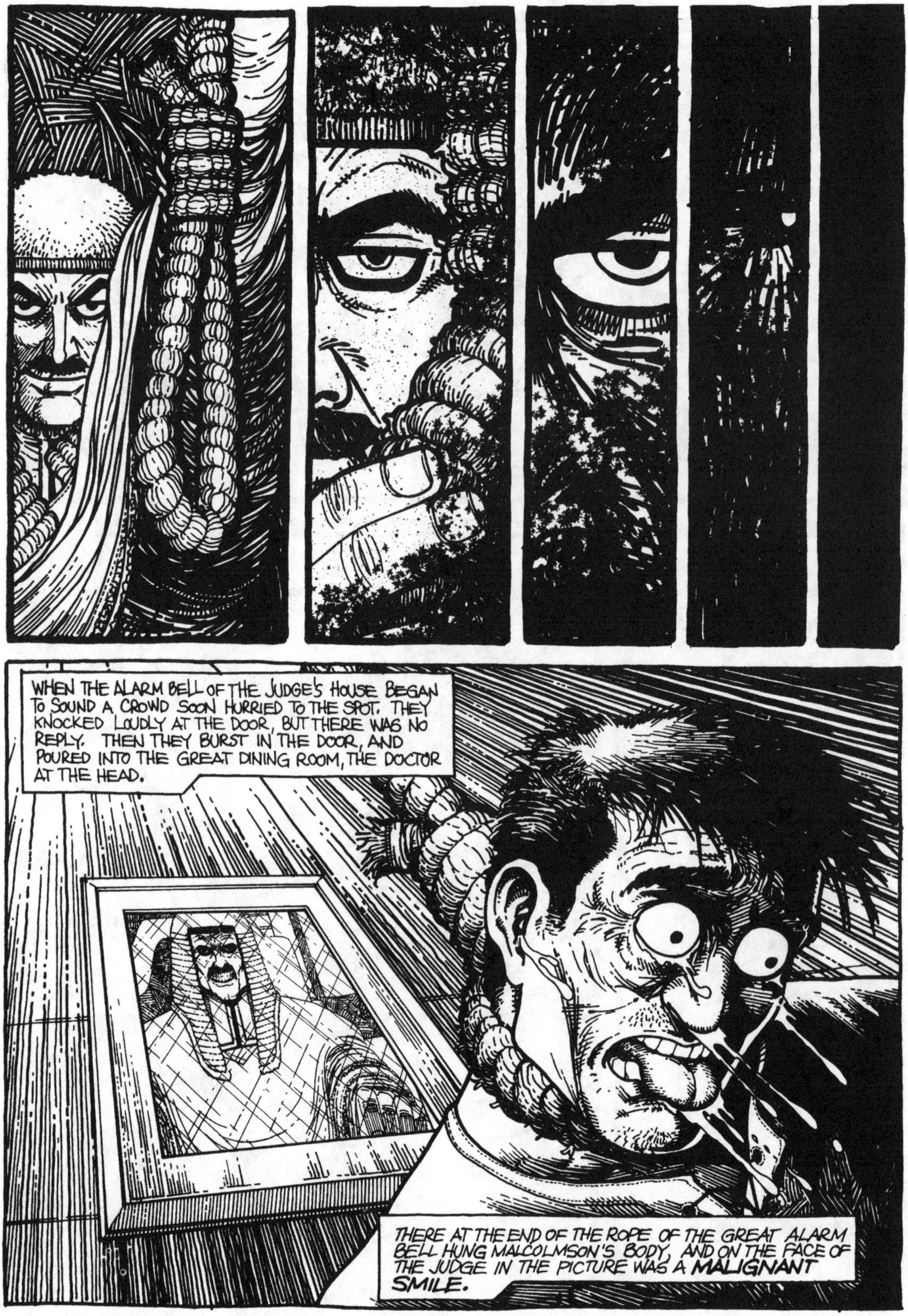
WHEN THE ALARM BELL OF THE JUDGE'S HOUSE BEGAN TO SOUND A CROWD SOON HURRIED TO THE SPOT. THEY KNOCKED LOUDLY AT THE DOOR, BUT THERE WAS NO REPLY. THEN THEY BURST IN THE DOOR, AND POURED INTO THE GREAT DINING ROOM, THE DOCTOR AT THE HEAD.
THERE AT THE END OF THE ROPE OF THE GREAT ALARM BELL HUNG MALCOLMSON'S BODY, AND ON THE FACE OF THE JUDGE IN THE PICTURE WAS A MALIGNANT SMILE.

THE BRIDAL OF DEATH

AN EXCERPT FROM THE JEWEL OF SEVEN STARS

BY BRAM STOKER

EDITED BY TOM POMPLUN

ADAPTED & ILLUSTRATED BY J. B. BONIVERT

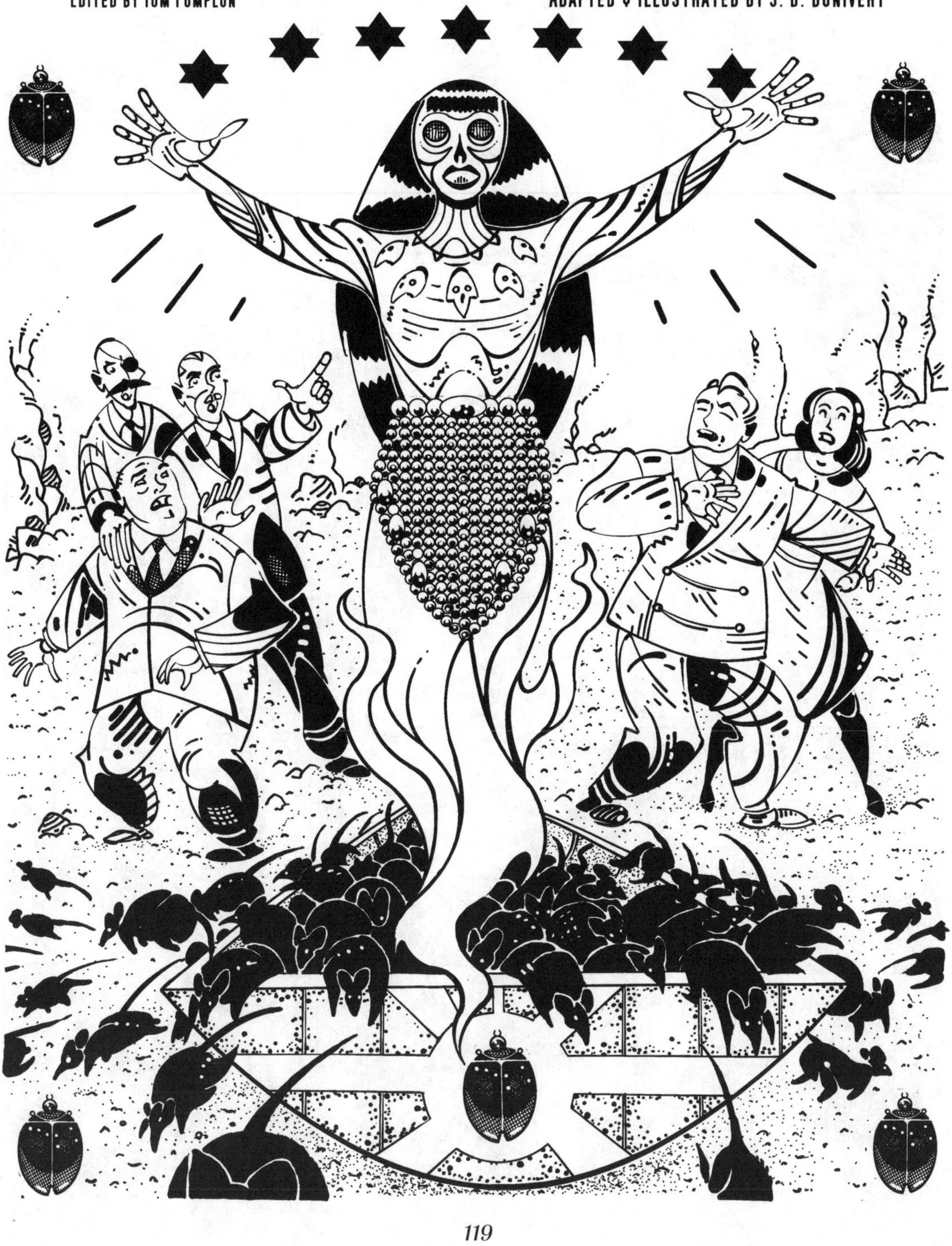

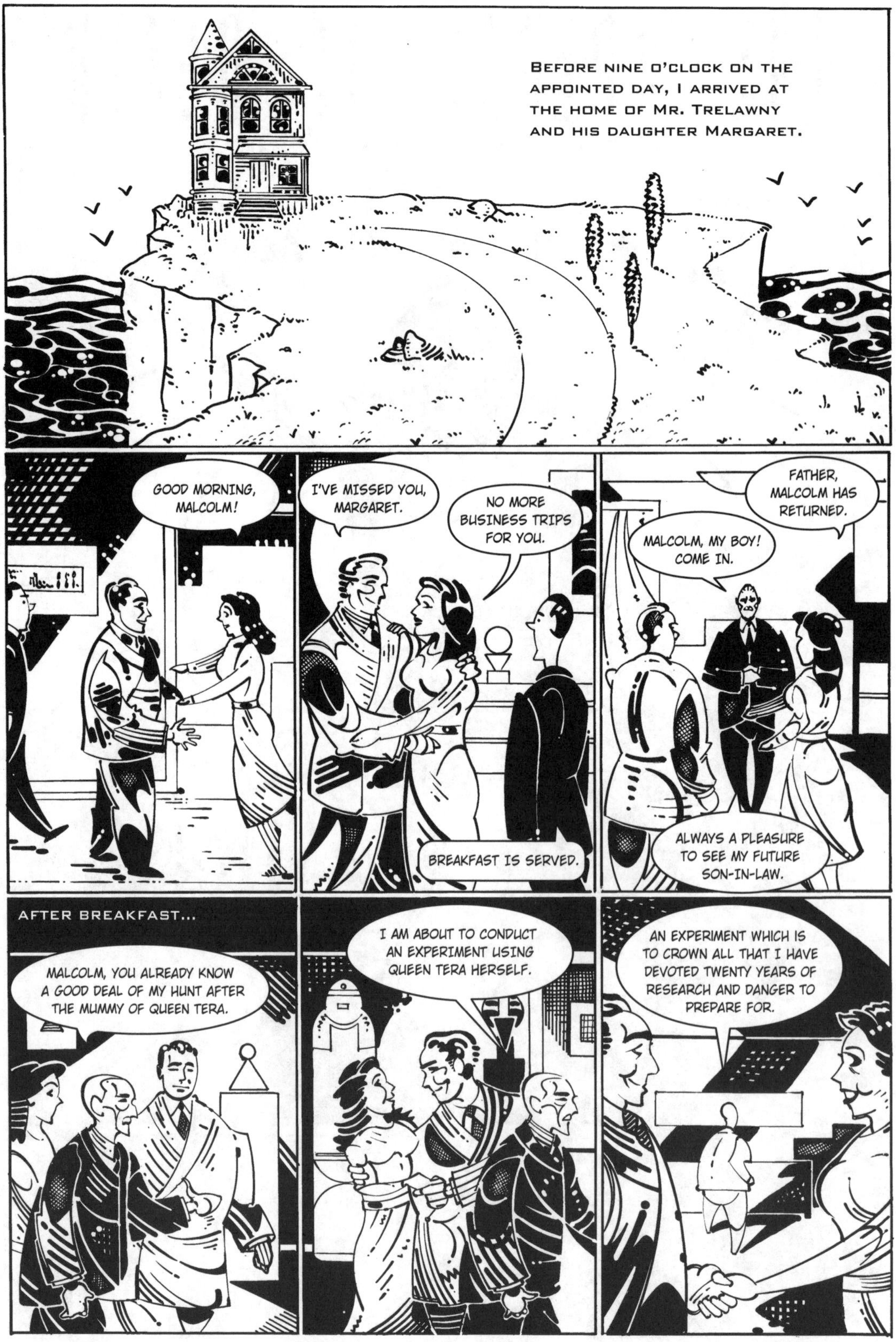
Before nine o'clock on the appointed day, I arrived at the home of Mr. Trelawny and his daughter Margaret.
GOOD MORNING, MALCOLM!
I'VE MISSED YOU, MARGARET.
NO MORE BUSINESS TRIPS FOR YOU.
BREAKFAST IS SERVED.
FATHER, MALCOLM HAS RETURNED.
MALCOLM, MY BOY! COME IN.
ALWAYS A PLEASURE TO SEE MY FUTURE SON-IN-LAW.
AFTER BREAKFAST...
MALCOLM, YOU ALREADY KNOW A GOOD DEAL OF MY HUNT AFTER THE MUMMY OF QUEEN TERA.
I AM ABOUT TO CONDUCT AN EXPERIMENT USING QUEEN TERA HERSELF.
AN EXPERIMENT WHICH IS TO CROWN ALL THAT I HAVE DEVOTED TWENTY YEARS OF RESEARCH AND DANGER TO PREPARE FOR.

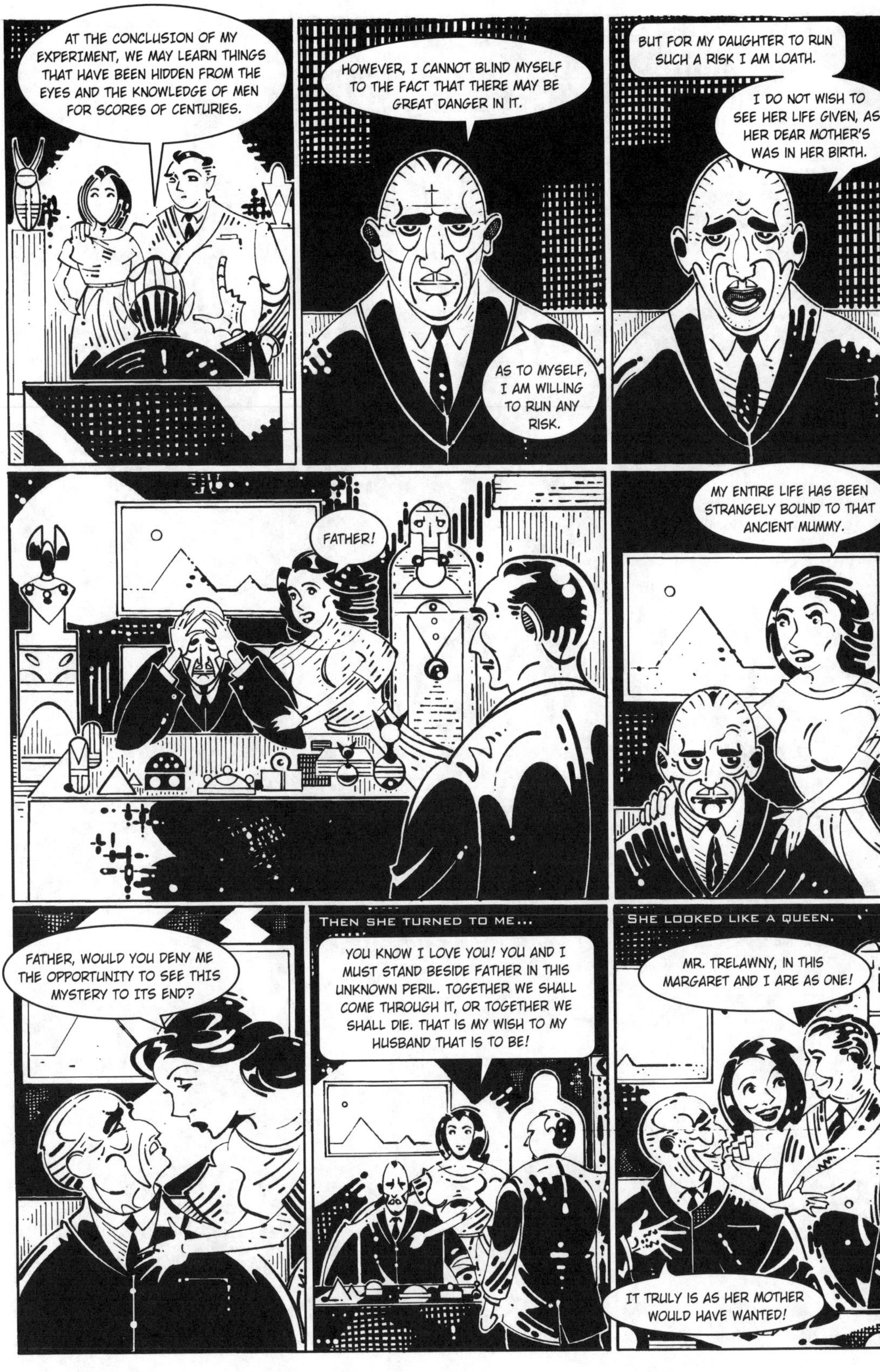
AT THE CONCLUSION OF MY EXPERIMENT, WE MAY LEARN THINGS THAT HAVE BEEN HIDDEN FROM THE EYES AND THE KNOWLEDGE OF MEN FOR SCORES OF CENTURIES.
HOWEVER, I CANNOT BLIND MYSELF TO THE FACT THAT THERE MAY BE GREAT DANGER IN IT.
AS TO MYSELF, I AM WILLING TO RUN ANY RISK.
BUT FOR MY DAUGHTER TO RUN SUCH A RISK I AM LOATH.
I DO NOT WISH TO SEE HER LIFE GIVEN, AS HER DEAR MOTHER'S WAS IN HER BIRTH.
FATHER!
MY ENTIRE LIFE HAS BEEN STRANGELY BOUND TO THAT ANCIENT MUMMY.
FATHER, WOULD YOU DENY ME THE OPPORTUNITY TO SEE THIS MYSTERY TO ITS END?
THEN SHE TURNED TO ME...
YOU KNOW I LOVE YOU! YOU AND I MUST STAND BESIDE FATHER IN THIS UNKNOWN PERIL. TOGETHER WE SHALL COME THROUGH IT, OR TOGETHER WE SHALL DIE. THAT IS MY WISH TO MY HUSBAND THAT IS TO BE!
SHE LOOKED LIKE A QUEEN.
MR. TRELAWNY, IN THIS MARGARET AND I ARE AS ONE!
IT TRULY IS AS HER MOTHER WOULD HAVE WANTED!

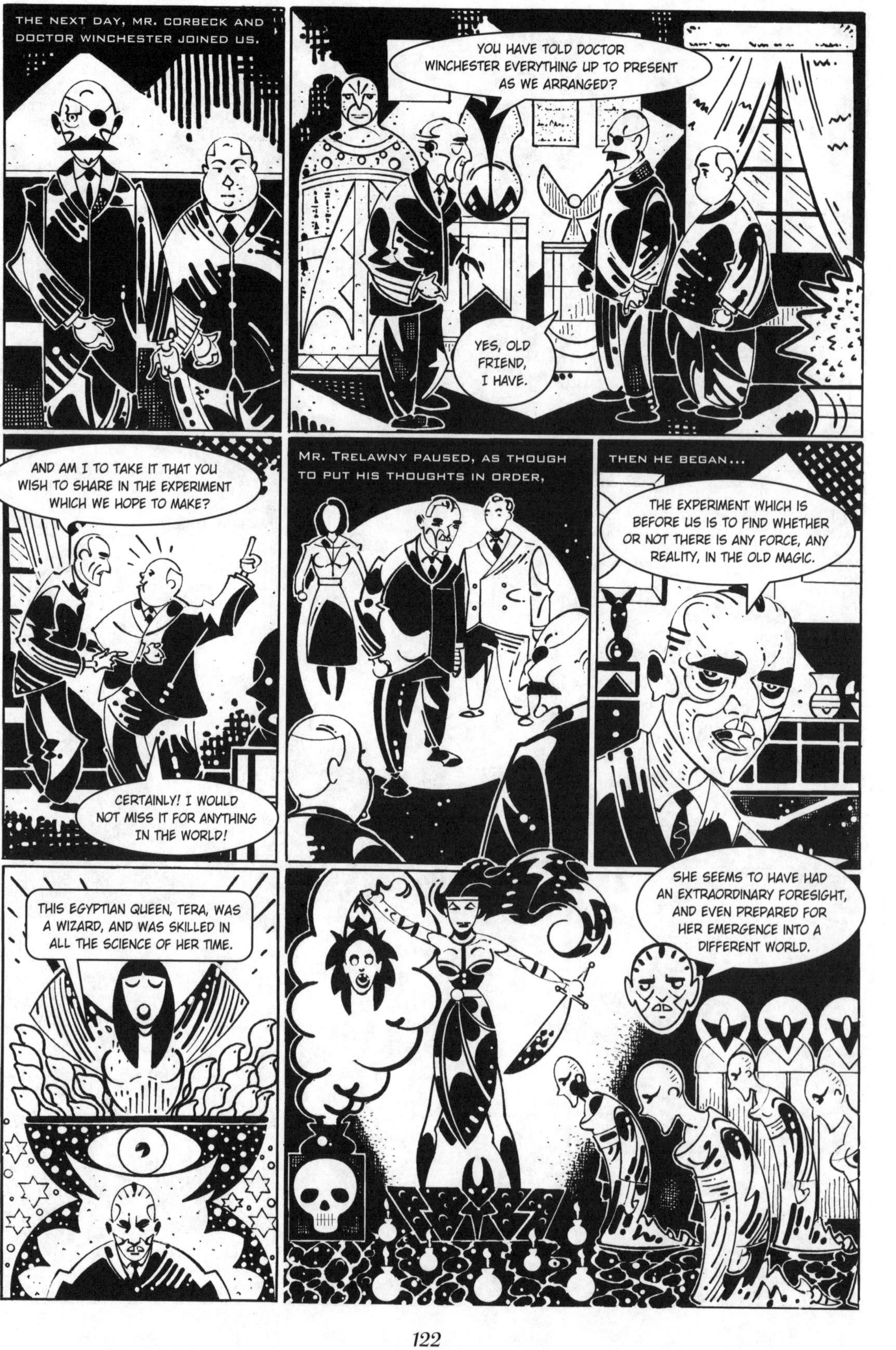
THE NEXT DAY, MR. CORBECK AND DOCTOR WINCHESTER JOINED US.
YOU HAVE TOLD DOCTOR WINCHESTER EVERYTHING UP TO PRESENT AS WE ARRANGED?
YES, OLD FRIEND, I HAVE.
AND AM I TO TAKE IT THAT YOU WISH TO SHARE IN THE EXPERIMENT WHICH WE HOPE TO MAKE?
CERTAINLY! I WOULD NOT MISS IT FOR ANYTHING IN THE WORLD!
MR. TRELAWNY PAUSED, AS THOUGH TO PUT HIS THOUGHTS IN ORDER,
THEN HE BEGAN...
THE EXPERIMENT WHICH IS BEFORE US IS TO FIND WHETHER OR NOT THERE IS ANY FORCE, ANY REALITY, IN THE OLD MAGIC.
THIS EGYPTIAN QUEEN, TERA, WAS A WIZARD, AND WAS SKILLED IN ALL THE SCIENCE OF HER TIME.
SHE SEEMS TO HAVE HAD AN EXTRAORDINARY FORESIGHT, AND EVEN PREPARED FOR HER EMERGENCE INTO A DIFFERENT WORLD.

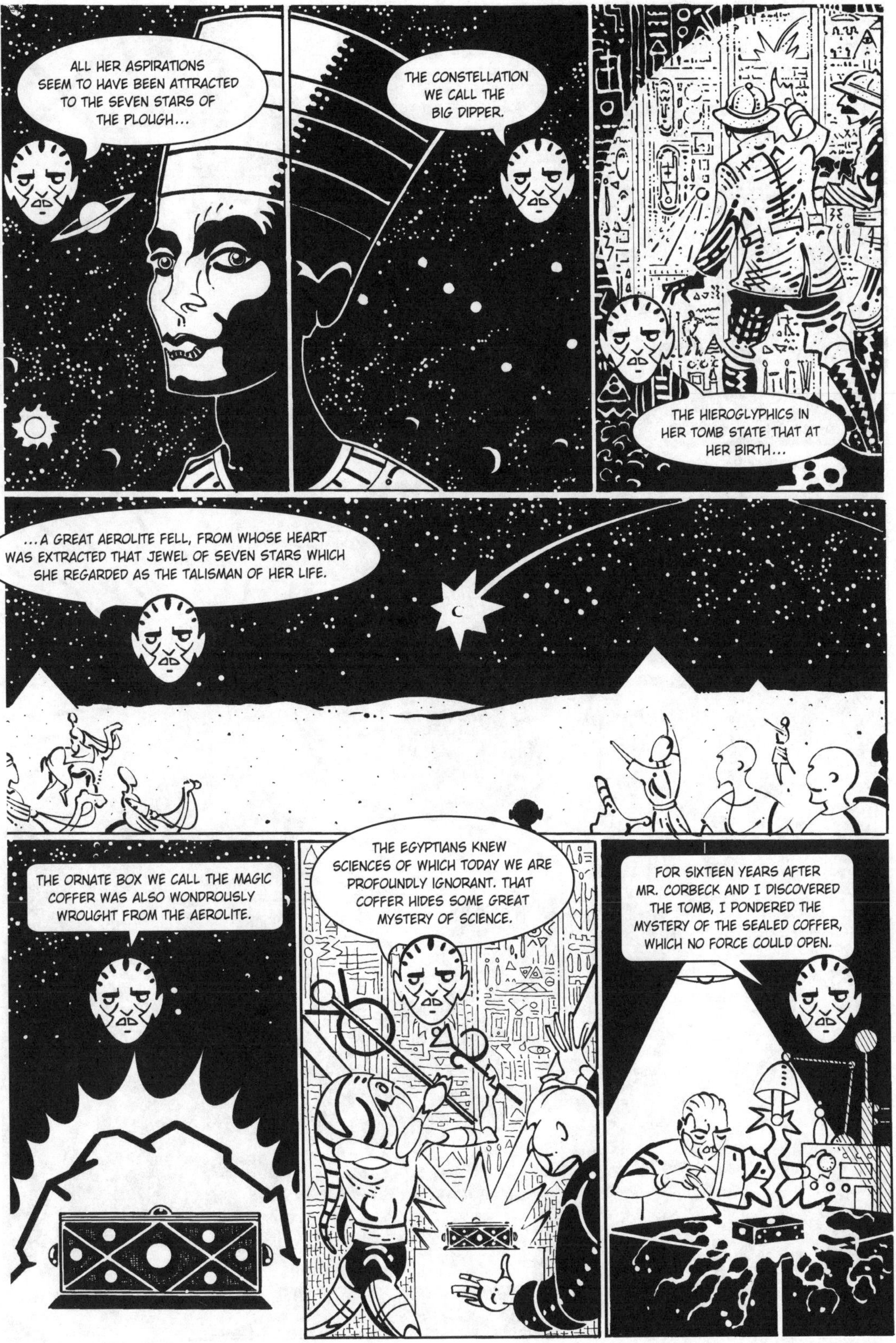
ALL HER ASPIRATIONS SEEM TO HAVE BEEN ATTRACTED TO THE SEVEN STARS OF THE PLOUGH...
THE CONSTELLATION WE CALL THE BIG DIPPER.
THE HIEROGLYPHICS IN HER TOMB STATE THAT AT HER BIRTH...
...A GREAT AEROLITE FELL, FROM WHOSE HEART WAS EXTRACTED THAT JEWEL OF SEVEN STARS WHICH SHE REGARDED AS THE TALISMAN OF HER LIFE.
THE ORNATE BOX WE CALL THE MAGIC COFFER WAS ALSO WONDROUSLY WROUGHT FROM THE AEROLITE.
THE EGYPTIANS KNEW SCIENCES OF WHICH TODAY WE ARE PROFOUNDLY IGNORANT. THAT COFFER HIDES SOME GREAT MYSTERY OF SCIENCE.
FOR SIXTEEN YEARS AFTER MR. CORBECK AND I DISCOVERED THE TOMB, I PONDERED THE MYSTERY OF THE SEALED COFFER, WHICH NO FORCE COULD OPEN.

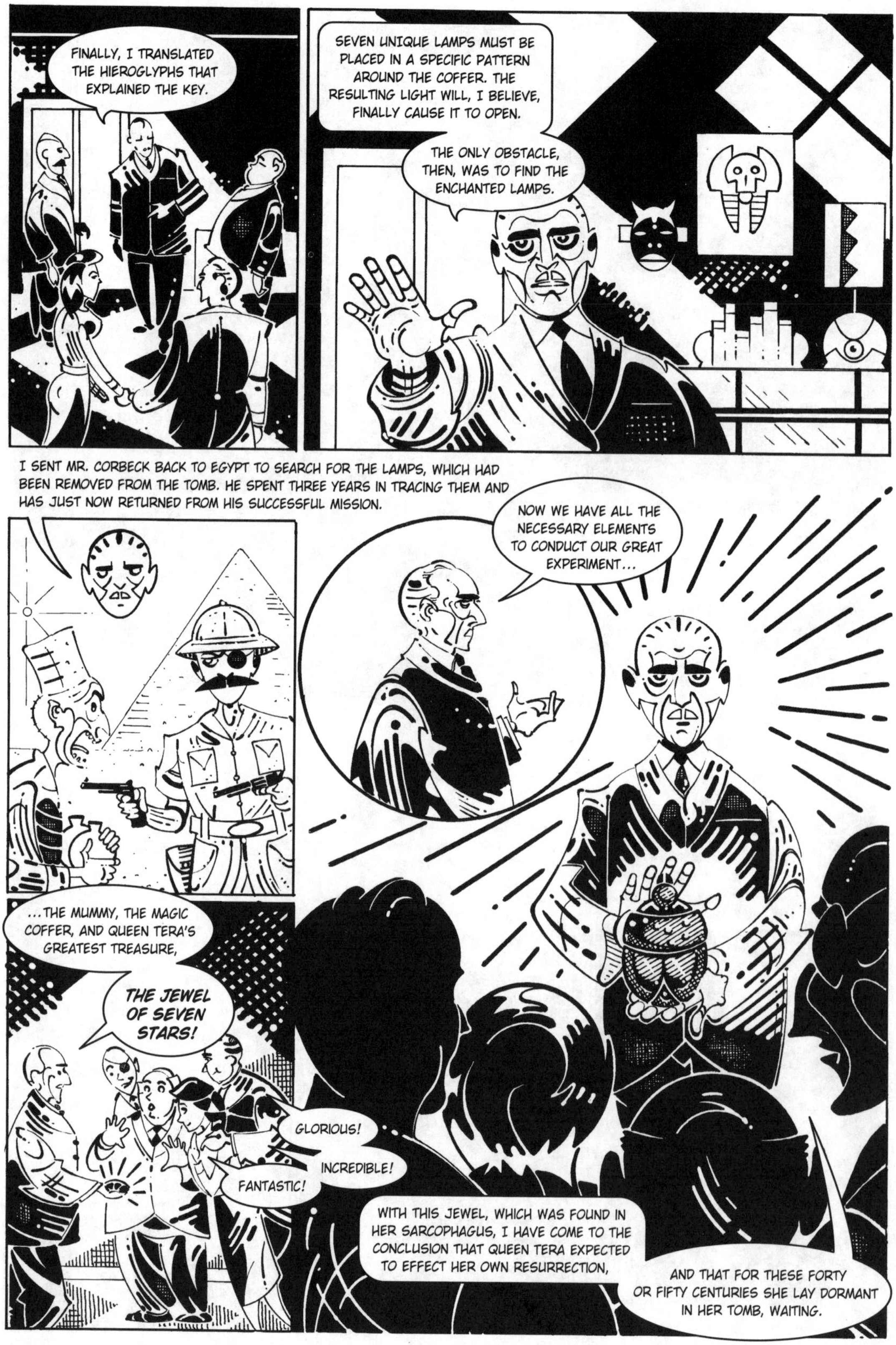
FINALLY, I TRANSLATED THE HIEROGLYPHS THAT EXPLAINED THE KEY.
SEVEN UNIQUE LAMPS MUST BE PLACED IN A SPECIFIC PATTERN AROUND THE COFFER. THE RESULTING LIGHT WILL, I BELIEVE, FINALLY CAUSE IT TO OPEN.
THE ONLY OBSTACLE, THEN, WAS TO FIND THE ENCHANTED LAMPS.
I SENT MR. CORBECK BACK TO EGYPT TO SEARCH FOR THE LAMPS, WHICH HAD BEEN REMOVED FROM THE TOMB. HE SPENT THREE YEARS IN TRACING THEM AND HAS JUST NOW RETURNED FROM HIS SUCCESSFUL MISSION.
NOW WE HAVE ALL THE NECESSARY ELEMENTS TO CONDUCT OUR GREAT EXPERIMENT...
...THE MUMMY, THE MAGIC COFFER, AND QUEEN TERA'S GREATEST TREASURE,
THE JEWEL OF SEVEN STARS!
GLORIOUS!
INCREDIBLE!
FANTASTIC!
WITH THIS JEWEL, WHICH WAS FOUND IN HER SARCOPHAGUS, I HAVE COME TO THE CONCLUSION THAT QUEEN TERA EXPECTED TO EFFECT HER OWN RESURRECTION,
AND THAT FOR THESE FORTY OR FIFTY CENTURIES SHE LAY DORMANT IN HER TOMB, WAITING.

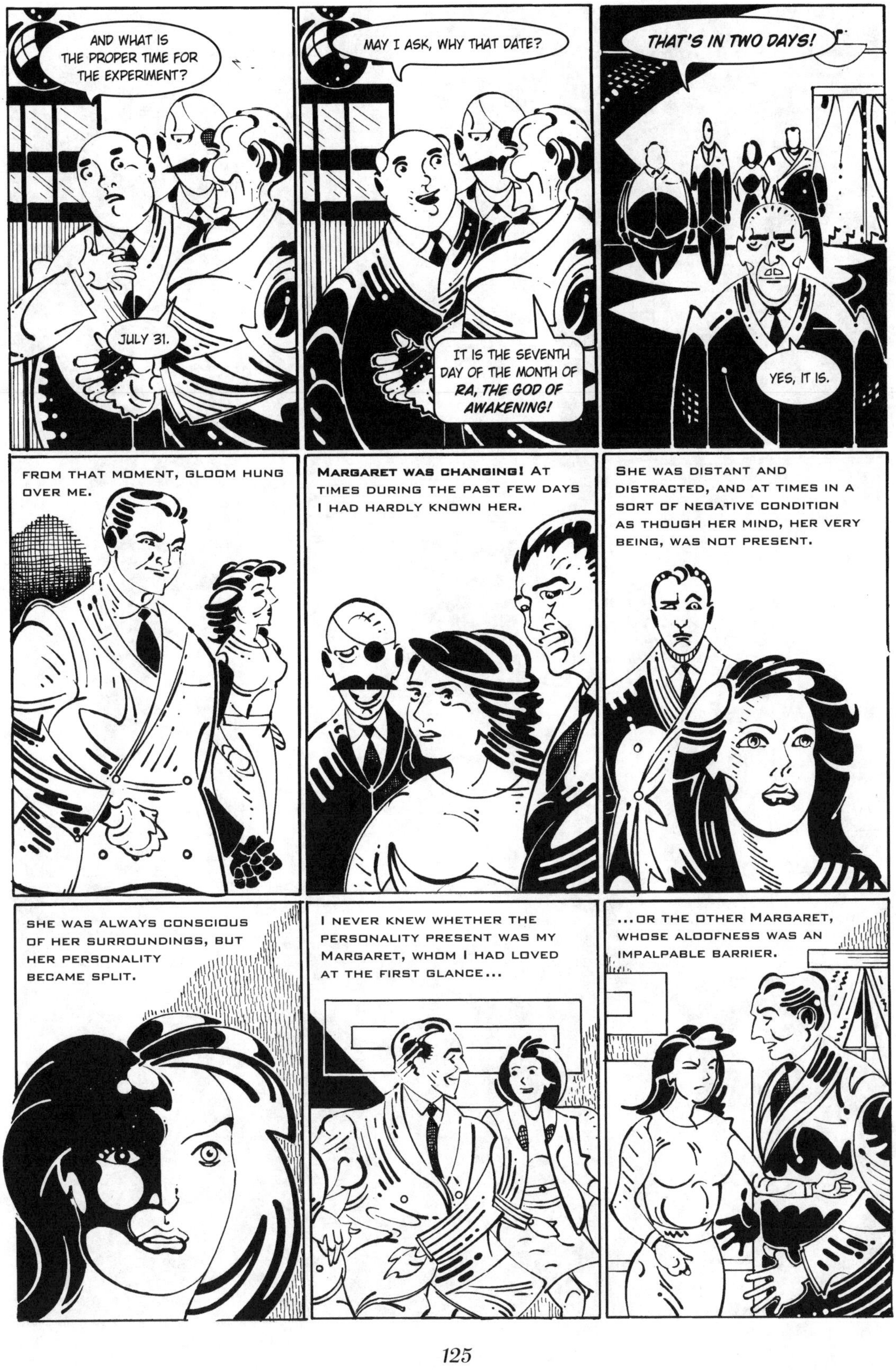
AND WHAT IS THE PROPER TIME FOR THE EXPERIMENT?
JULY 31.
MAY I ASK, WHY THAT DATE?
IT IS THE SEVENTH DAY OF THE MONTH OF *RA, THE GOD OF AWAKENING!*
THAT'S IN TWO DAYS!
YES, IT IS.
FROM THAT MOMENT, GLOOM HUNG OVER ME.
MARGARET WAS CHANGING! AT TIMES DURING THE PAST FEW DAYS I HAD HARDLY KNOWN HER.
SHE WAS DISTANT AND DISTRACTED, AND AT TIMES IN A SORT OF NEGATIVE CONDITION AS THOUGH HER MIND, HER VERY BEING, WAS NOT PRESENT.
SHE WAS ALWAYS CONSCIOUS OF HER SURROUNDINGS, BUT HER PERSONALITY BECAME SPLIT.
I NEVER KNEW WHETHER THE PERSONALITY PRESENT WAS MY MARGARET, WHOM I HAD LOVED AT THE FIRST GLANCE...
...OR THE OTHER MARGARET, WHOSE ALOOFNESS WAS AN IMPALPABLE BARRIER.

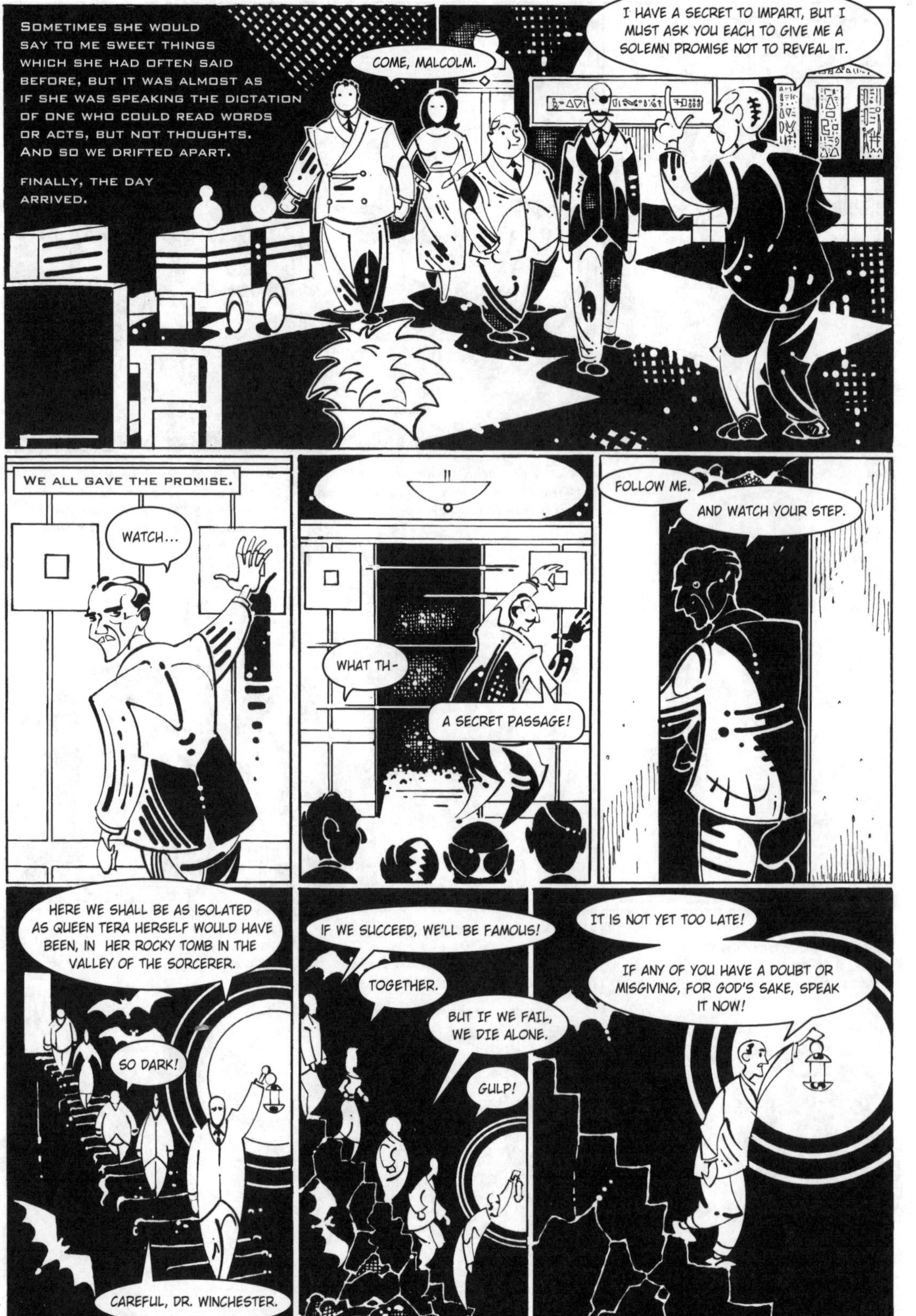
Sometimes she would say to me sweet things which she had often said before, but it was almost as if she was speaking the dictation of one who could read words or acts, but not thoughts. And so we drifted apart.
Finally, the day arrived.
COME, MALCOLM.
I HAVE A SECRET TO IMPART, BUT I MUST ASK YOU EACH TO GIVE ME A SOLEMN PROMISE NOT TO REVEAL IT.
We all gave the promise.
WATCH...
WHAT TH-
A SECRET PASSAGE!
FOLLOW ME.
AND WATCH YOUR STEP.
HERE WE SHALL BE AS ISOLATED AS QUEEN TERA HERSELF WOULD HAVE BEEN, IN HER ROCKY TOMB IN THE VALLEY OF THE SORCERER.
SO DARK!
CAREFUL, DR. WINCHESTER.
IF WE SUCCEED, WE'LL BE FAMOUS!
TOGETHER.
BUT IF WE FAIL, WE DIE ALONE.
GULP!
IT IS NOT YET TOO LATE!
IF ANY OF YOU HAVE A DOUBT OR MISGIVING, FOR GOD'S SAKE, SPEAK IT NOW!

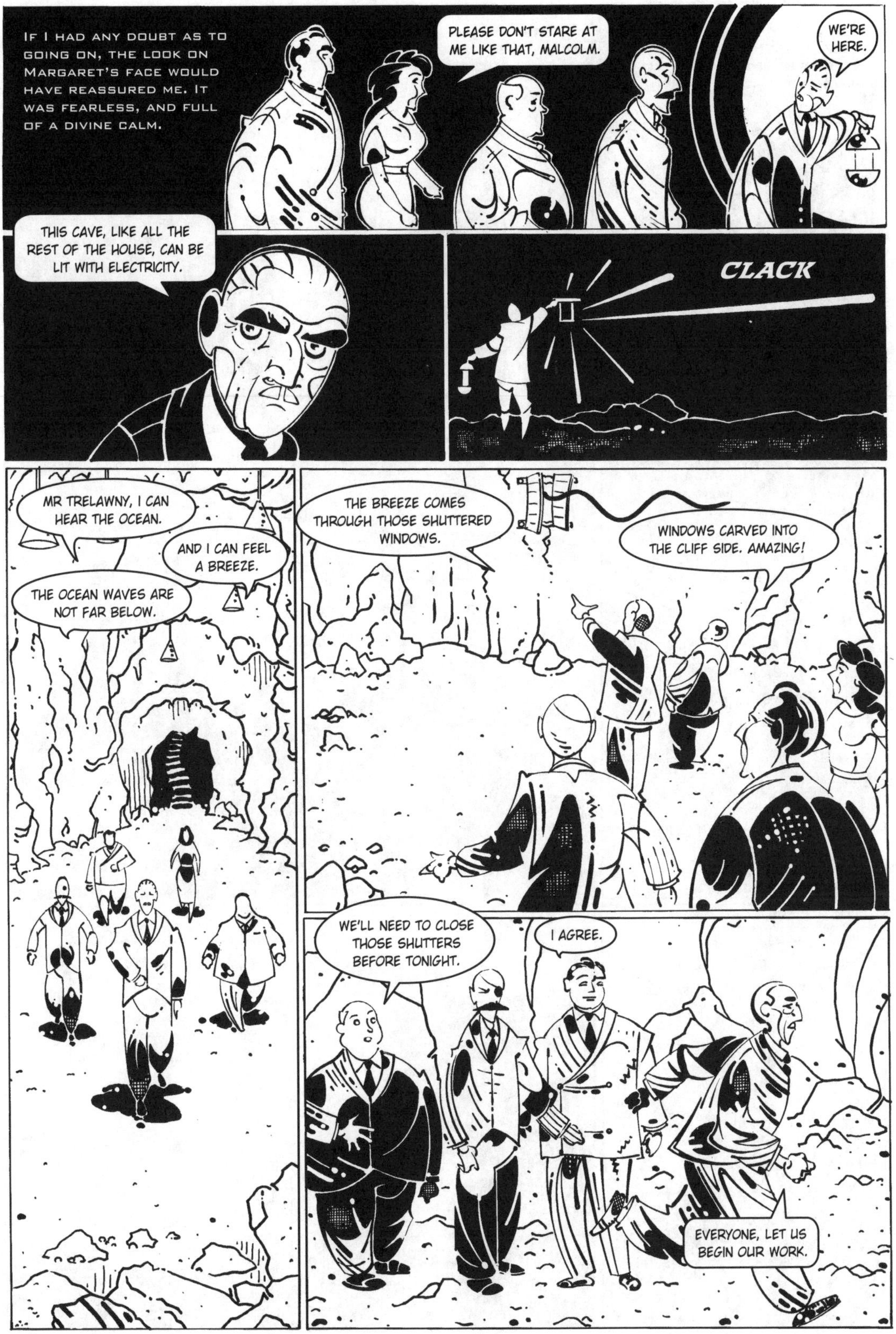
If I had any doubt as to going on, the look on Margaret's face would have reassured me. It was fearless, and full of a divine calm.
Please don't stare at me like that, Malcolm.
We're here.
This cave, like all the rest of the house, can be lit with electricity.
CLACK
Mr Trelawny, I can hear the ocean.
And I can feel a breeze.
The ocean waves are not far below.
The breeze comes through those shuttered windows.
Windows carved into the cliff side. Amazing!
We'll need to close those shutters before tonight.
I agree.
Everyone, let us begin our work.

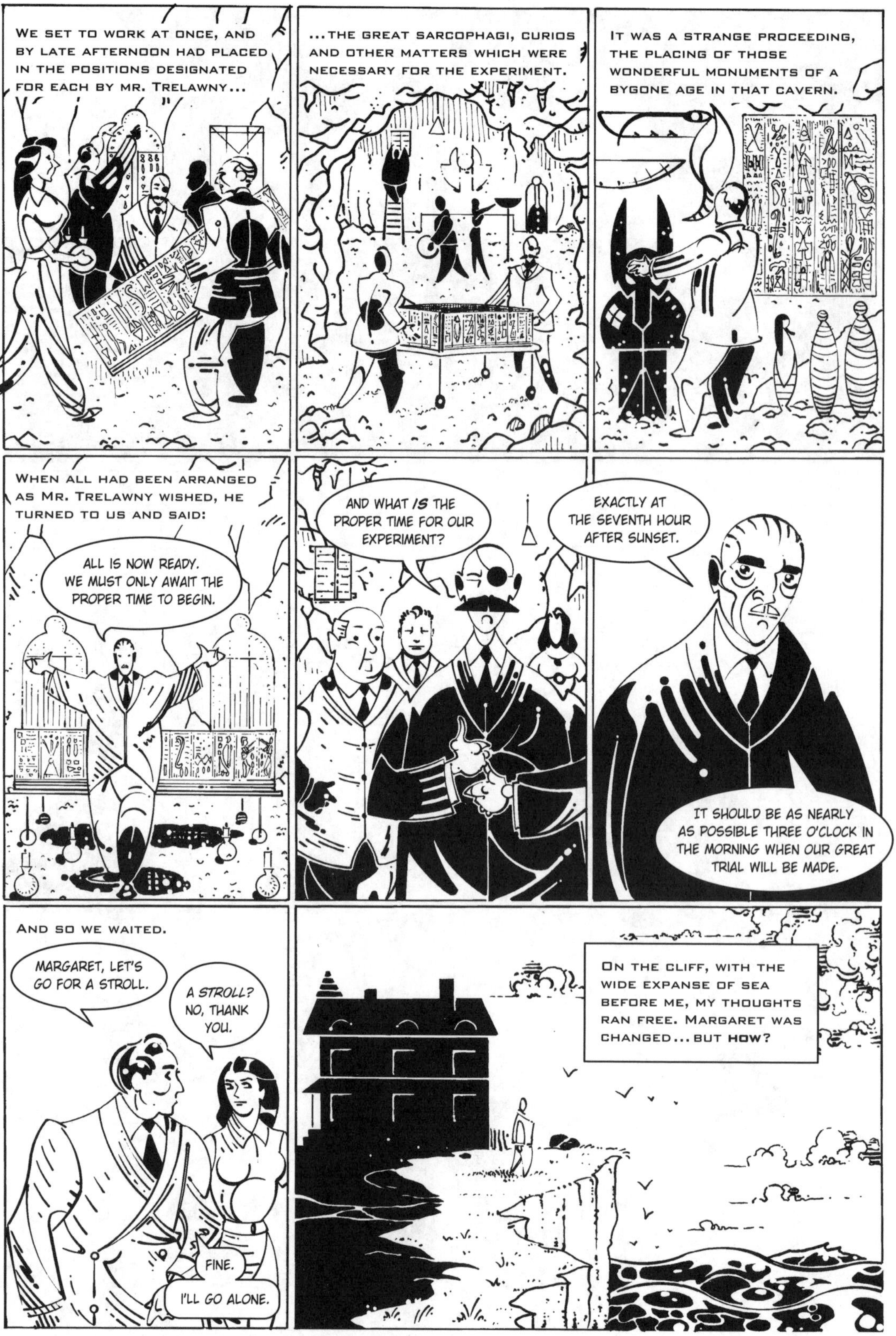
We set to work at once, and by late afternoon had placed in the positions designated for each by Mr. Trelawny...
...the great sarcophagi, curios and other matters which were necessary for the experiment.
It was a strange proceeding, the placing of those wonderful monuments of a bygone age in that cavern.
When all had been arranged as Mr. Trelawny wished, he turned to us and said:
ALL IS NOW READY. WE MUST ONLY AWAIT THE PROPER TIME TO BEGIN.
AND WHAT IS THE PROPER TIME FOR OUR EXPERIMENT?
EXACTLY AT THE SEVENTH HOUR AFTER SUNSET.
IT SHOULD BE AS NEARLY AS POSSIBLE THREE O'CLOCK IN THE MORNING WHEN OUR GREAT TRIAL WILL BE MADE.
And so we waited.
MARGARET, LET'S GO FOR A STROLL.
A STROLL? NO, THANK YOU.
FINE.
I'LL GO ALONE.
On the cliff, with the wide expanse of sea before me, my thoughts ran free. Margaret was changed... but how?

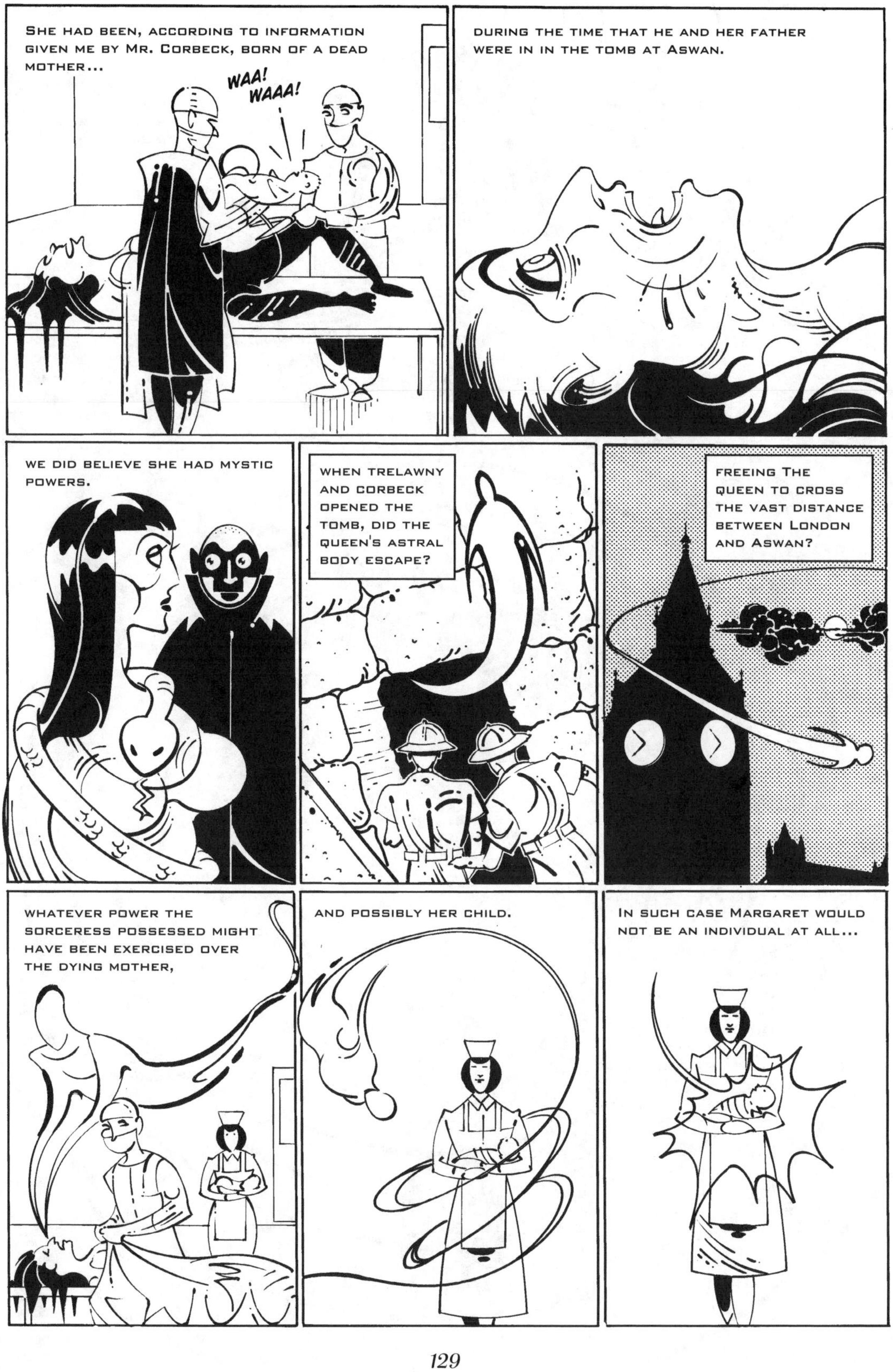
SHE HAD BEEN, ACCORDING TO INFORMATION GIVEN ME BY MR. CORBECK, BORN OF A DEAD MOTHER...
WAA! WAAA!
DURING THE TIME THAT HE AND HER FATHER WERE IN IN THE TOMB AT ASWAN.
WE DID BELIEVE SHE HAD MYSTIC POWERS.
WHEN TRELAWNY AND CORBECK OPENED THE TOMB, DID THE QUEEN'S ASTRAL BODY ESCAPE?
FREEING THE QUEEN TO CROSS THE VAST DISTANCE BETWEEN LONDON AND ASWAN?
WHATEVER POWER THE SORCERESS POSSESSED MIGHT HAVE BEEN EXERCISED OVER THE DYING MOTHER,
AND POSSIBLY HER CHILD.
IN SUCH CASE MARGARET WOULD NOT BE AN INDIVIDUAL AT ALL...

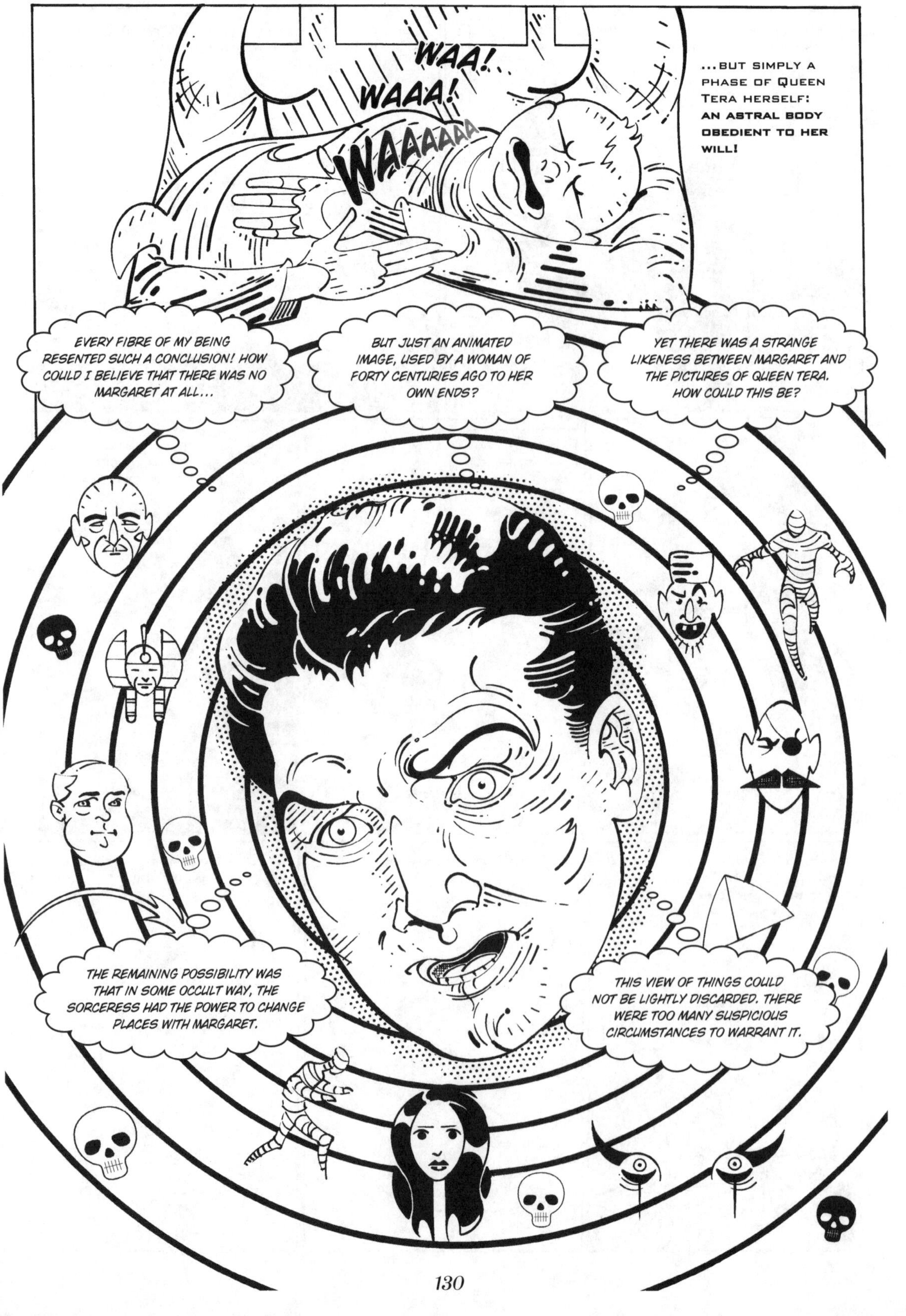
...BUT SIMPLY A PHASE OF QUEEN TERA HERSELF: AN ASTRAL BODY OBEDIENT TO HER WILL!
WAA!
WAAA!
WAAAAAA
EVERY FIBRE OF MY BEING RESENTED SUCH A CONCLUSION! HOW COULD I BELIEVE THAT THERE WAS NO MARGARET AT ALL...
BUT JUST AN ANIMATED IMAGE, USED BY A WOMAN OF FORTY CENTURIES AGO TO HER OWN ENDS?
YET THERE WAS A STRANGE LIKENESS BETWEEN MARGARET AND THE PICTURES OF QUEEN TERA. HOW COULD THIS BE?
THE REMAINING POSSIBILITY WAS THAT IN SOME OCCULT WAY, THE SORCERESS HAD THE POWER TO CHANGE PLACES WITH MARGARET.
THIS VIEW OF THINGS COULD NOT BE LIGHTLY DISCARDED. THERE WERE TOO MANY SUSPICIOUS CIRCUMSTANCES TO WARRANT IT.

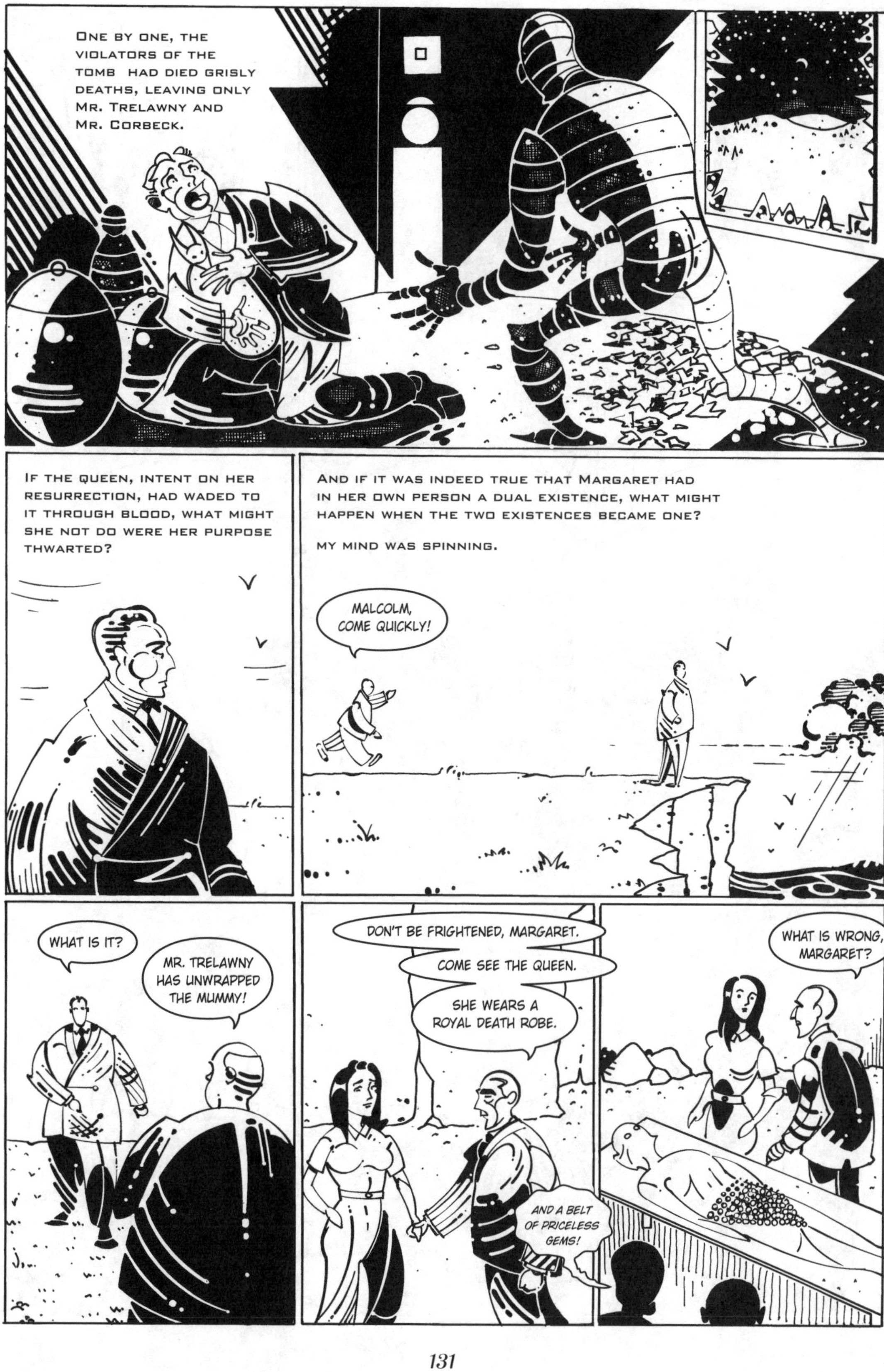
One by one, the violators of the tomb had died grisly deaths, leaving only Mr. Trelawny and Mr. Corbeck.
If the queen, intent on her resurrection, had waded to it through blood, what might she not do were her purpose thwarted?
And if it was indeed true that Margaret had in her own person a dual existence, what might happen when the two existences became one?
My mind was spinning.
MALCOLM, COME QUICKLY!
WHAT IS IT?
MR. TRELAWNY HAS UNWRAPPED THE MUMMY!
DON'T BE FRIGHTENED, MARGARET.
COME SEE THE QUEEN.
SHE WEARS A ROYAL DEATH ROBE.
AND A BELT OF PRICELESS GEMS!
WHAT IS WRONG, MARGARET?

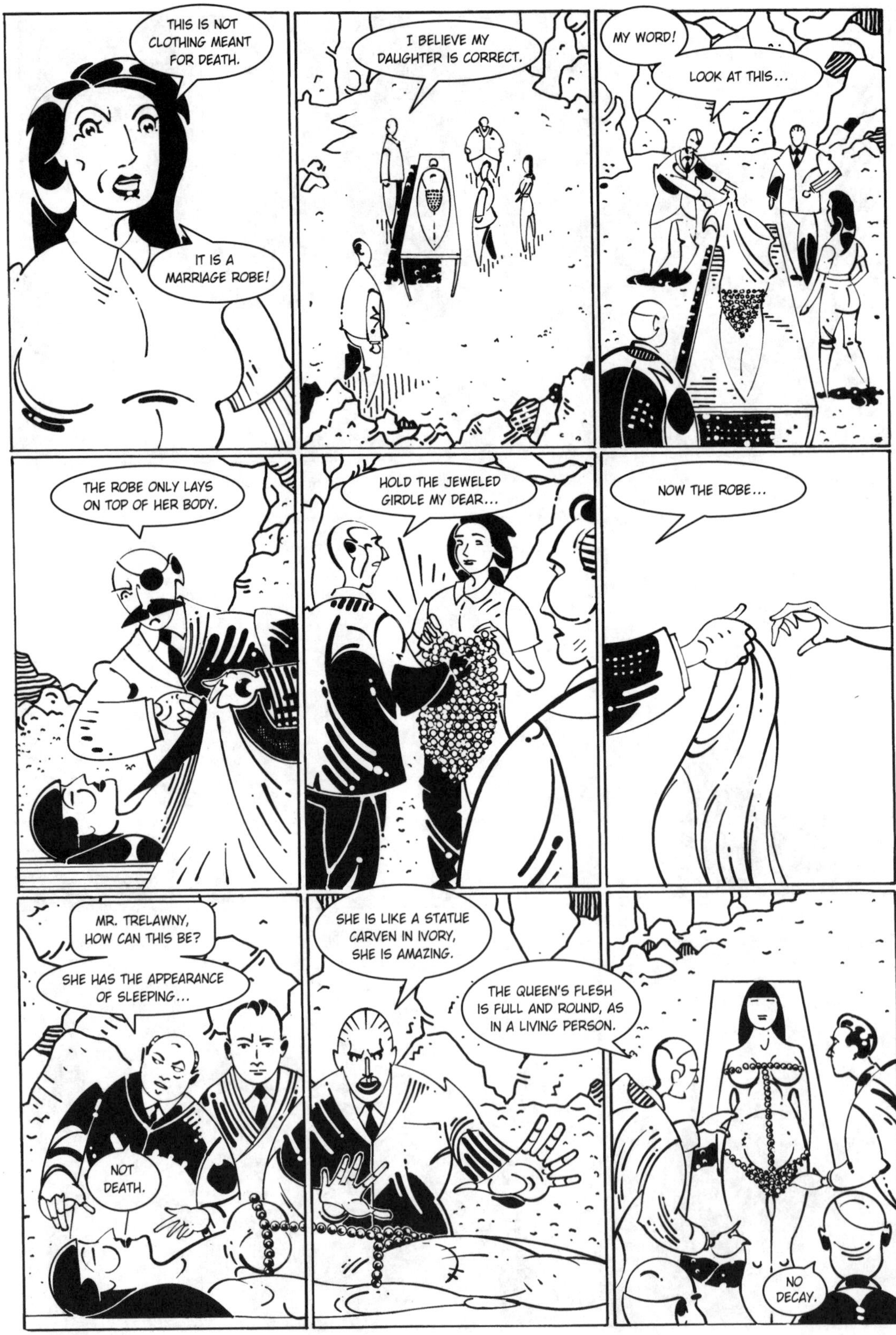
THIS IS NOT CLOTHING MEANT FOR DEATH.
IT IS A MARRIAGE ROBE!
I BELIEVE MY DAUGHTER IS CORRECT.
MY WORD!
LOOK AT THIS...
THE ROBE ONLY LAYS ON TOP OF HER BODY.
HOLD THE JEWELED GIRDLE MY DEAR...
NOW THE ROBE...
MR. TRELAWNY, HOW CAN THIS BE?
SHE HAS THE APPEARANCE OF SLEEPING...
NOT DEATH.
SHE IS LIKE A STATUE CARVEN IN IVORY, SHE IS AMAZING.
THE QUEEN'S FLESH IS FULL AND ROUND, AS IN A LIVING PERSON.
NO DECAY.

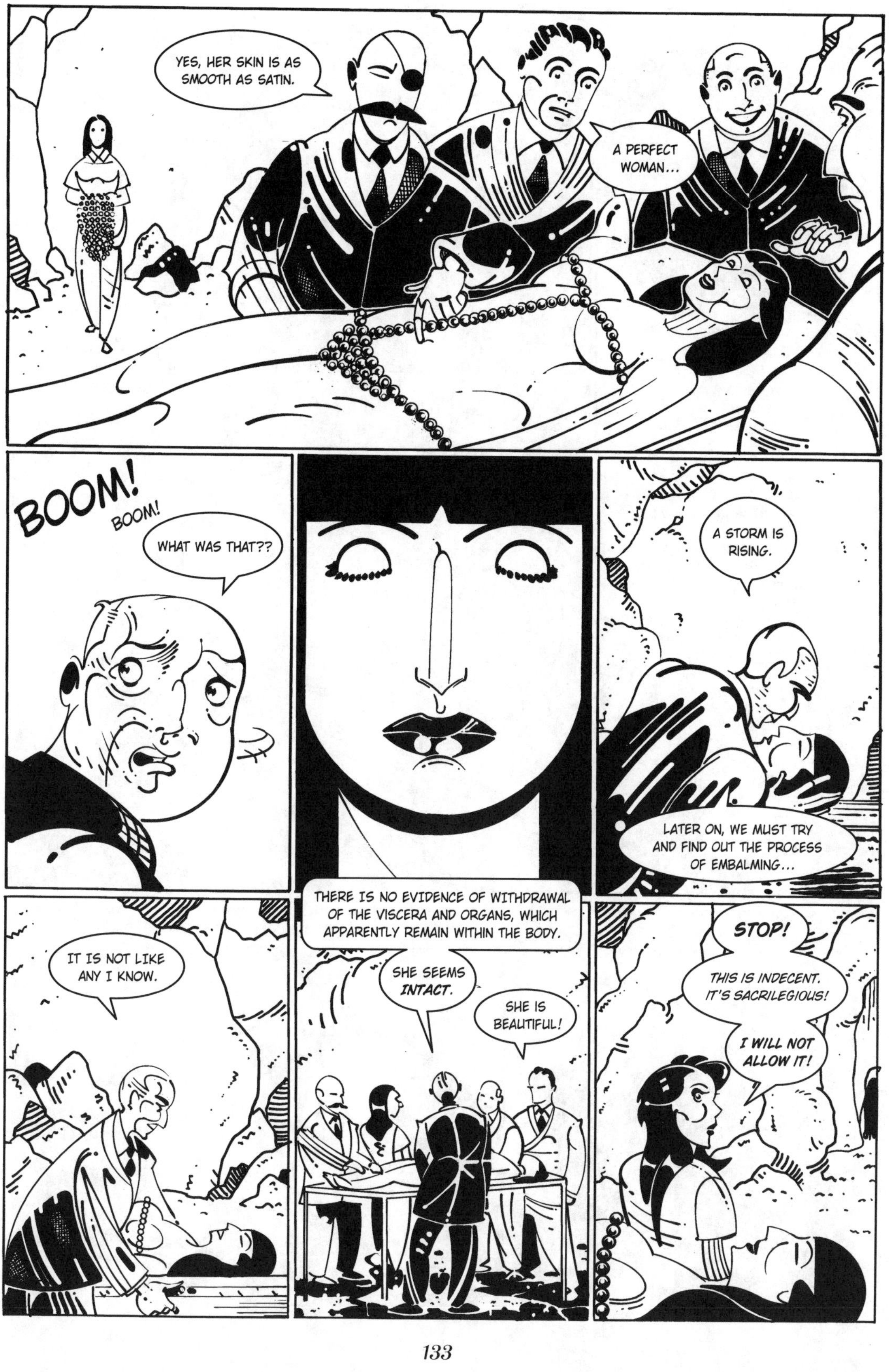
YES, HER SKIN IS AS SMOOTH AS SATIN.
A PERFECT WOMAN...
BOOM!
BOOM!
WHAT WAS THAT??
A STORM IS RISING.
LATER ON, WE MUST TRY AND FIND OUT THE PROCESS OF EMBALMING...
IT IS NOT LIKE ANY I KNOW.
THERE IS NO EVIDENCE OF WITHDRAWAL OF THE VISCERA AND ORGANS, WHICH APPARENTLY REMAIN WITHIN THE BODY.
SHE SEEMS *INTACT*.
SHE IS BEAUTIFUL!
STOP!
THIS IS INDECENT. IT'S SACRILEGIOUS!
I WILL NOT ALLOW IT!

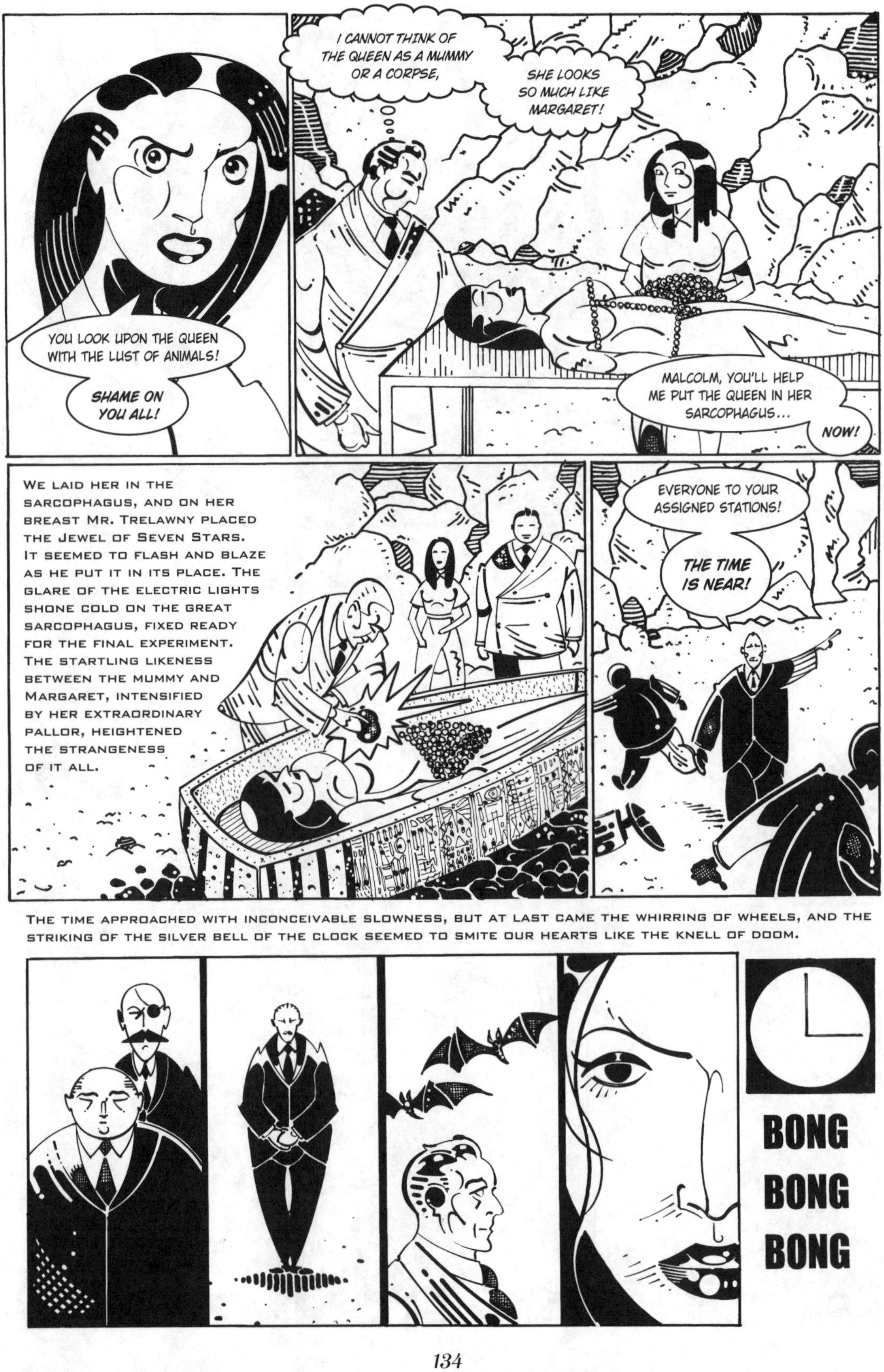
YOU LOOK UPON THE QUEEN WITH THE LUST OF ANIMALS!
SHAME ON YOU ALL!
I CANNOT THINK OF THE QUEEN AS A MUMMY OR A CORPSE,
SHE LOOKS SO MUCH LIKE MARGARET!
MALCOLM, YOU'LL HELP ME PUT THE QUEEN IN HER SARCOPHAGUS... NOW!
WE LAID HER IN THE SARCOPHAGUS, AND ON HER BREAST MR. TRELAWNY PLACED THE JEWEL OF SEVEN STARS. IT SEEMED TO FLASH AND BLAZE AS HE PUT IT IN ITS PLACE. THE GLARE OF THE ELECTRIC LIGHTS SHONE COLD ON THE GREAT SARCOPHAGUS, FIXED READY FOR THE FINAL EXPERIMENT. THE STARTLING LIKENESS BETWEEN THE MUMMY AND MARGARET, INTENSIFIED BY HER EXTRAORDINARY PALLOR, HEIGHTENED THE STRANGENESS OF IT ALL.
EVERYONE TO YOUR ASSIGNED STATIONS!
THE TIME IS NEAR!
THE TIME APPROACHED WITH INCONCEIVABLE SLOWNESS, BUT AT LAST CAME THE WHIRRING OF WHEELS, AND THE STRIKING OF THE SILVER BELL OF THE CLOCK SEEMED TO SMITE OUR HEARTS LIKE THE KNELL OF DOOM.
BONG
BONG
BONG

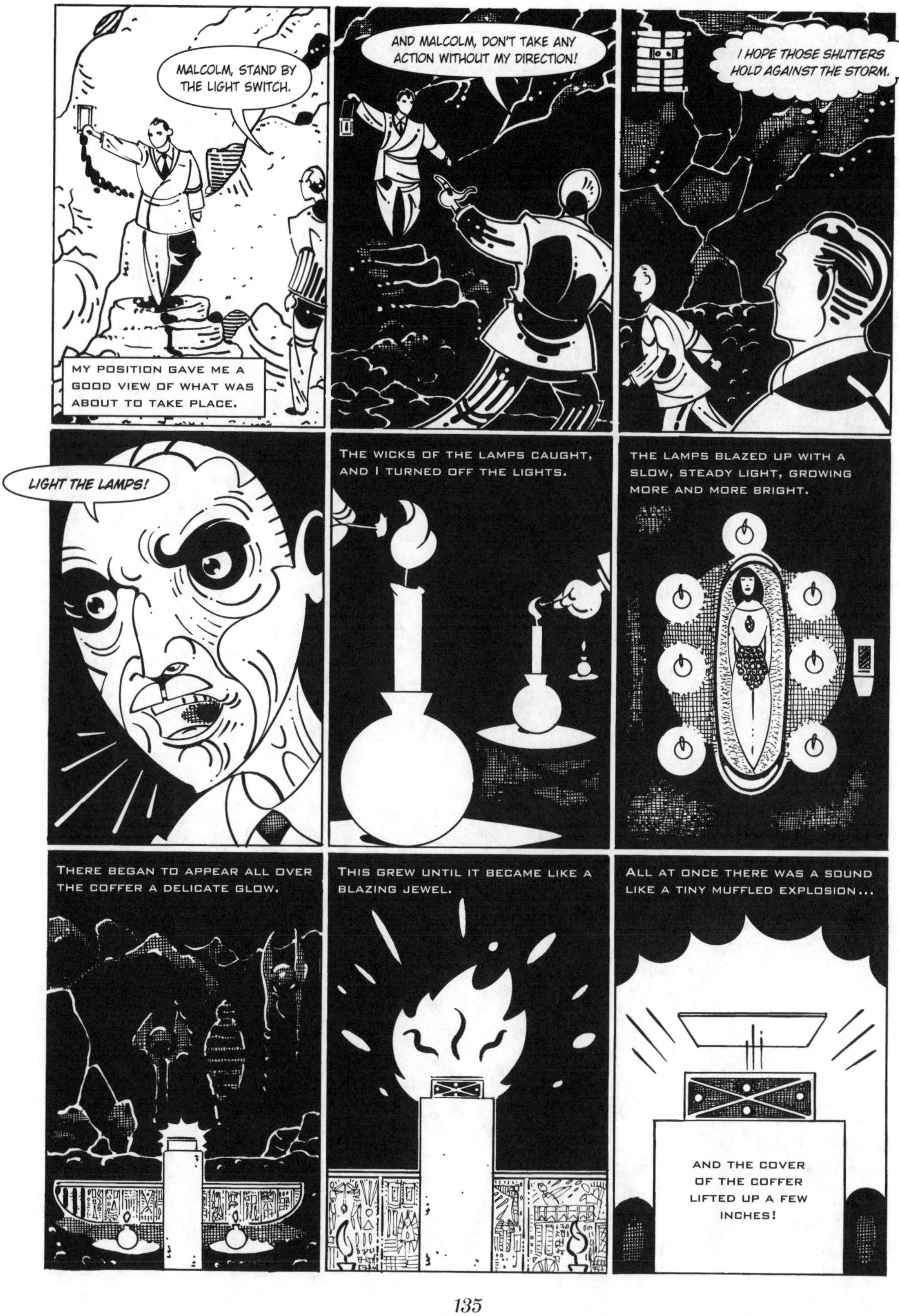
MALCOLM, STAND BY THE LIGHT SWITCH.
MY POSITION GAVE ME A GOOD VIEW OF WHAT WAS ABOUT TO TAKE PLACE.
AND MALCOLM, DON'T TAKE ANY ACTION WITHOUT MY DIRECTION!
I HOPE THOSE SHUTTERS HOLD AGAINST THE STORM.
LIGHT THE LAMPS!
THE WICKS OF THE LAMPS CAUGHT, AND I TURNED OFF THE LIGHTS.
THE LAMPS BLAZED UP WITH A SLOW, STEADY LIGHT, GROWING MORE AND MORE BRIGHT.
THERE BEGAN TO APPEAR ALL OVER THE COFFER A DELICATE GLOW.
THIS GREW UNTIL IT BECAME LIKE A BLAZING JEWEL.
ALL AT ONCE THERE WAS A SOUND LIKE A TINY MUFFLED EXPLOSION...
AND THE COVER OF THE COFFER LIFTED UP A FEW INCHES!

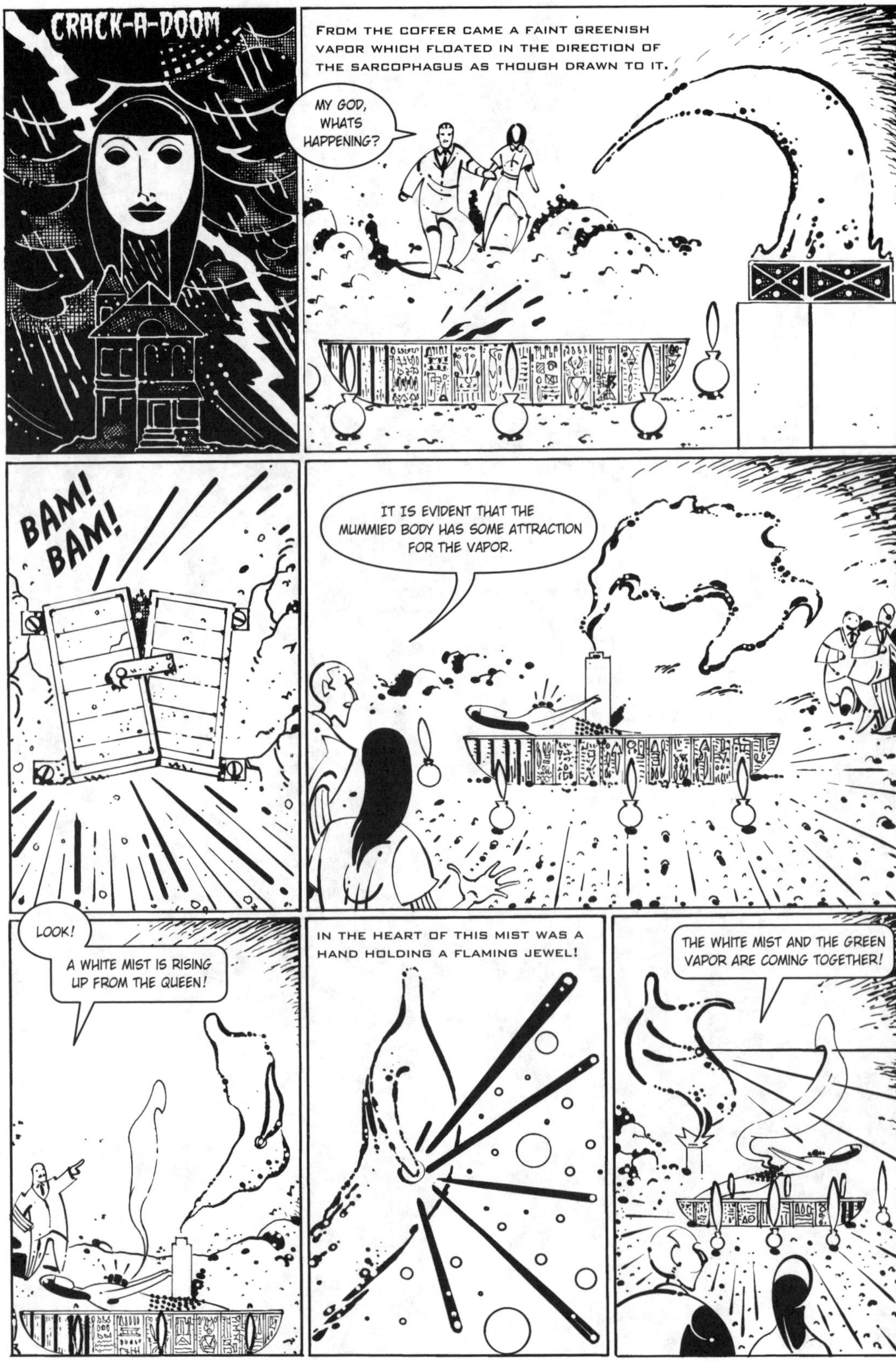
CRACK-A-DOOM
FROM THE COFFER CAME A FAINT GREENISH VAPOR WHICH FLOATED IN THE DIRECTION OF THE SARCOPHAGUS AS THOUGH DRAWN TO IT.
MY GOD, WHATS HAPPENING?
BAM! BAM!
IT IS EVIDENT THAT THE MUMMIED BODY HAS SOME ATTRACTION FOR THE VAPOR.
LOOK!
A WHITE MIST IS RISING UP FROM THE QUEEN!
IN THE HEART OF THIS MIST WAS A HAND HOLDING A FLAMING JEWEL!
THE WHITE MIST AND THE GREEN VAPOR ARE COMING TOGETHER!

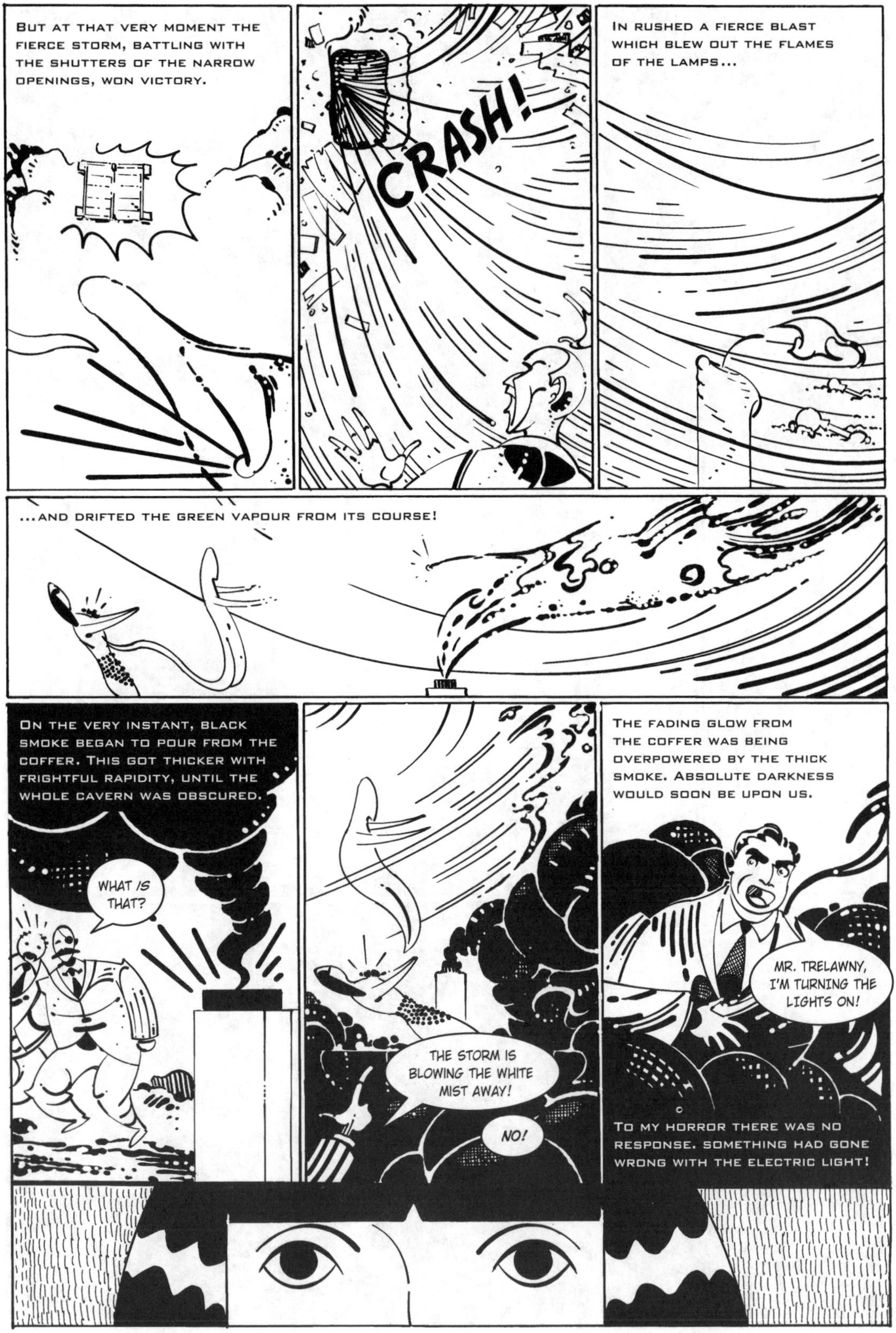
But at that very moment the fierce storm, battling with the shutters of the narrow openings, won victory.
CRASH!
In rushed a fierce blast which blew out the flames of the lamps...
...and drifted the green vapour from its course!
On the very instant, black smoke began to pour from the coffer. This got thicker with frightful rapidity, until the whole cavern was obscured.
WHAT IS THAT?
THE STORM IS BLOWING THE WHITE MIST AWAY!
NO!
The fading glow from the coffer was being overpowered by the thick smoke. Absolute darkness would soon be upon us.
MR. TRELAWNY, I'M TURNING THE LIGHTS ON!
To my horror there was no response. Something had gone wrong with the electric light!

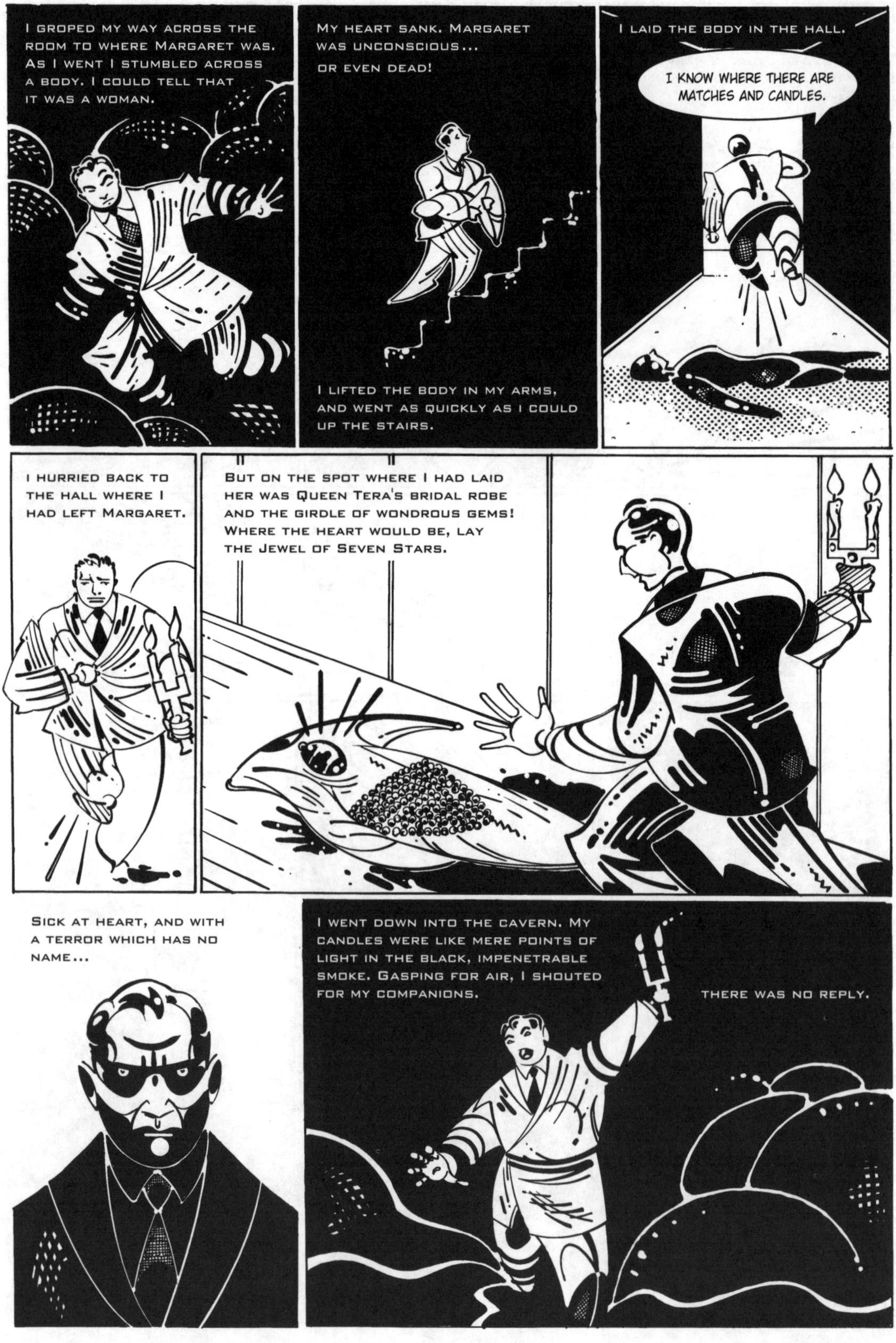
I groped my way across the room to where Margaret was. As I went I stumbled across a body. I could tell that it was a woman.
My heart sank. Margaret was unconscious...
or even dead!
I lifted the body in my arms, and went as quickly as I could up the stairs.
I laid the body in the hall.
I KNOW WHERE THERE ARE MATCHES AND CANDLES.
I hurried back to the hall where I had left Margaret.
But on the spot where I had laid her was Queen Tera's bridal robe and the girdle of wondrous gems! Where the heart would be, lay the Jewel of Seven Stars.
Sick at heart, and with a terror which has no name...
I went down into the cavern. My candles were like mere points of light in the black, impenetrable smoke. Gasping for air, I shouted for my companions.
There was no reply.

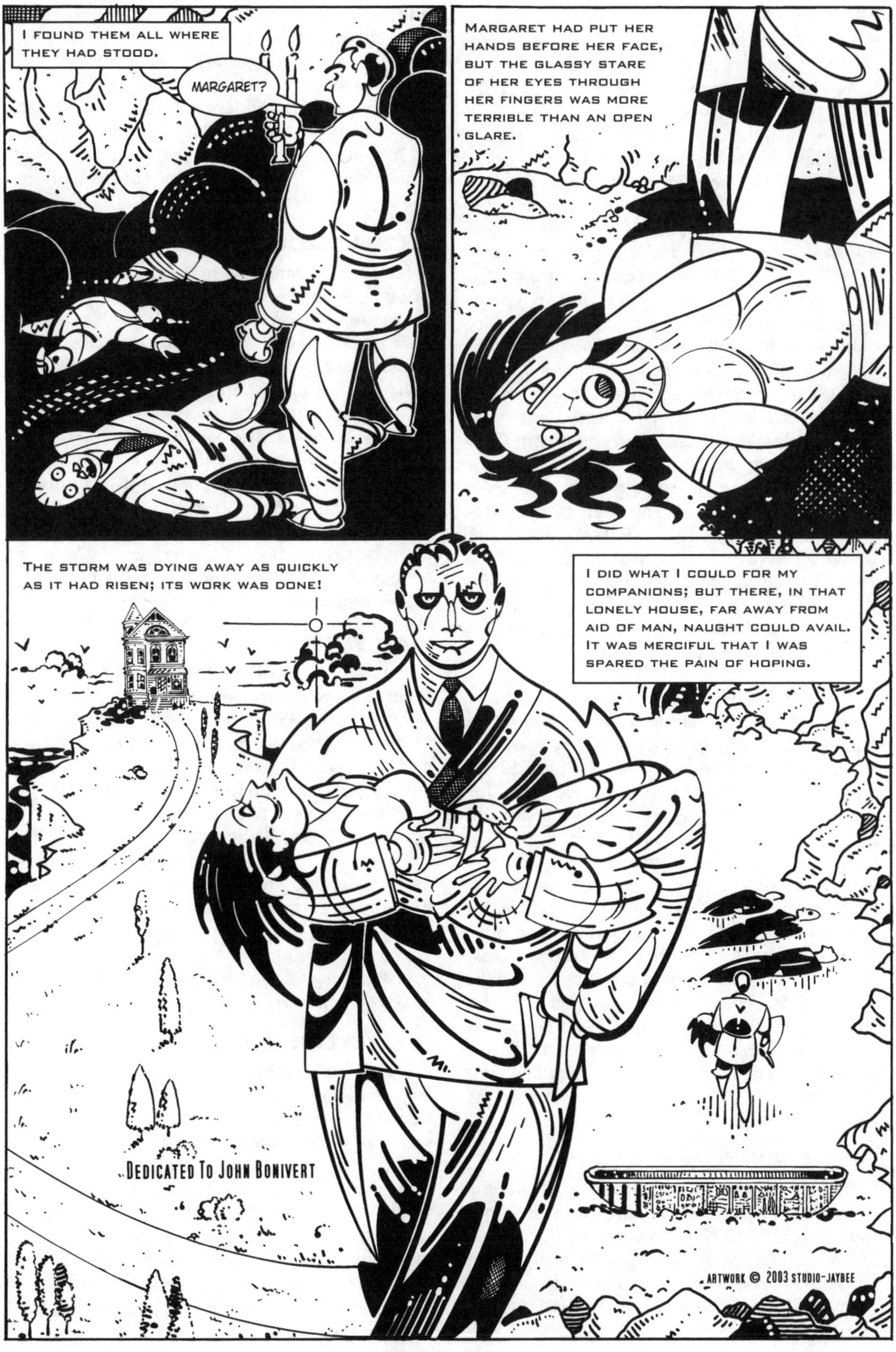
I FOUND THEM ALL WHERE THEY HAD STOOD.
MARGARET?
MARGARET HAD PUT HER HANDS BEFORE HER FACE, BUT THE GLASSY STARE OF HER EYES THROUGH HER FINGERS WAS MORE TERRIBLE THAN AN OPEN GLARE.
THE STORM WAS DYING AWAY AS QUICKLY AS IT HAD RISEN; ITS WORK WAS DONE!
I DID WHAT I COULD FOR MY COMPANIONS; BUT THERE, IN THAT LONELY HOUSE, FAR AWAY FROM AID OF MAN, NAUGHT COULD AVAIL. IT WAS MERCIFUL THAT I WAS SPARED THE PAIN OF HOPING.
DEDICATED TO JOHN BONIVERT
ARTWORK © 2003 STUDIO-JAYBEE

BRAM STOKER

Born in Dublin in 1847, Abraham Stoker was a sickly, bedridden child, whose mother entertained him with stories of the macabre. While his health improved, and he eventually became an athlete at Trinity College, Stoker never lost his fascination for tales of horror. He earned law and mathematics degrees and honors in science, but Stoker's passion for drama won out, and he spent most of his life as the manager of famed Victorian actor Henry Irving's Lyceum Theatre in London. Stoker also served as Irving's secretary and personal manager, and the actor's domineering personality held Stoker in thrall until Irving's death in 1905, and was the inspiration for Stoker's most famous character, Dracula. When Stoker died in 1912, he was known primarily as the author of *Personal Reminiscences of Henry Irving*. Only after his death did his other writings become more broadly known. His eighteen published nonfiction books, novels and short story collections include *The Snake's Pass, Snowbound, Under the Sunset, The Lady of the Shroud, The Jewel of Seven Stars* and *Lair of the White Worm*. But none approached the worldwide popularity of *Dracula*, originally published in 1897 and continuously in print to this day.

GLENN BARR (cover)

Glenn Barr's work has been called "the visual equivalent of a David Lynch film." He uses elements of pop culture set in an alternate 1960s universe. A graduate of the College for Creative Studies in Detroit, Glenn has made the city his home base. His paintings have appeared in galleries from coast to coast, and have been reproduced in art journals including *Juxtapoz* and *Film Threat*. Glenn's work has been featured in *Mad Magazine*, and publications from DC Comics and Paradox Press, as well as in a series of self-published books titled *HEEP*. His animation work includes *The Ren and Stimpy Show*, Bjork's *I Miss You* video and *The New Woody Woodpecker Show*. Glenn's latest books, *Lowlife Paradise* and *The Lowlife Companion*, are available at www.glbarr.com.

KIRSTEN ULVE (page 1)

Kirsten Ulve began her career as a graphic designer and part-time illustrator in Chicago, then relocated to New York in 1996 to devote herself to illustration full time. Since then she has worked in almost every arena of the field, ranging from fashion illustration to caricatures, animated commercials to advertising art, editorial illustration to product embellishment. Her clients include *Entertainment Weekly, Rolling Stone, Cosmogirl, Seventeen, The Village Voice, Nickelodeon*, Mattel, Popsicle, Hasbro and Palty of Japan. She has exhibited her work at the CWC Gallery in Tokyo (August, 2000), and at Sixspace Gallery in Los Angeles (June, 2003). You can find more of her work at www.kirstenulve.com.

ALLEN KOSZOWSKI (page 2)

A former U.S. Marine infantryman and a decorated Vietnam war veteran with a Purple Heart, Allen is one of the most prolific artists in the horror and SF field. Since his first professional sale to *Asimov's SF Magazine* in 1982, he has published more than 2,700 illustrations for hundreds of genre publications such as *Asimov's, The Magazine of Fantasy & SF, Cemetery Dance, Whispers, Fantasy Tales, Weird Tales, The Horror Show* and *The Robert Bloch Companion*. He has won numerous awards, including Best Artist at the 1992 World Fantasy Convention. *Travelers by Twilight*, a collection of his drawings, is available from Magic Pen Press.

HUNT EMERSON (pages 3, 89)

The dean of British comics artists, Hunt Emerson has drawn cartoons and comic strips since the early 1970s. His work appears in publications as diverse as *Fiesta, Fortean Times*, and *The Wall Street Journal Europe*, and he has also worked widely in advertising. Hunt has published over twenty comic books and albums, including *Lady Chatterley's Lover, The Rime of the Ancient Mariner*, and *Casanova's Last Stand*, and his comics have been translated into ten languages. His hilarious adaptation of *Jan, the Unrepentant* appears in *Graphic Classics: Jack London*. You can see lots of cartoons, comics, fun and laffs on Hunt's website at www.largecow.demon.co.uk.

MITCH O'CONNELL (page 4)

Chicago artist Mitch O'Connell continues to lay waste to the axiom that "No one could be that handsome and that talented." Visit his website at www.mitchoconnell.com to see samples of exciting commercial art (from *Newsweek* to MTV), mesmerizing gallery shows (from New York to the UK), tantalizing tattoo designs (from head to toe), breathtaking bobbing head dolls (from up to down and also left to right) and much, much more. In his spare time Mitch says he enjoys yelling at the neighborhood children to stay off his lawn.

MORT CASTLE (page 5)

A writing teacher and author specializing in the horror genre, Mort Castle has written and edited fourteen books and around 500 short stories and articles. His novels and collections include *Cursed Be the Child*, *The Strangers*, *Moon on the Water* and *Nations of the Living, Nations of the Dead*. He has produced an audio CD of one of his stories, *Buckeye Jim in Egypt*, and is the author of the essential reference work for aspiring horror writers, *Writing Horror*. Mort has won numerous writing awards, and he has had several dozen stories cited in "year's best" compilations in the horror, suspense, fantasy, and literary fields. He has been a writer and editor for several comics publishers, and is a frequent keynote speaker at writing conferences. Mort's comics biographies appear in *Graphic Classics: Jack London* and *Graphic Classics: Ambrose Bierce*.

RICO SCHACHERL (page 8)

Rico is a cartoonist and illustrator living and working in Johannesburg, South Africa. Born in Austria in 1966, he claims he was drawing cartoons ever since he was old enough to hold a pencil. After less-than-successful studies in graphic design and architecture during the late 80s, Rico decided to get a real job as a cartoonist. He met writing partner Stephen Francis while working at a publishing company, and together with Stephen, Rico created the comic strip *Madam & Eve*, which has been syndicated in South Africa for over eleven years and published in France, Sweden, Denmark, Britain, Australia and Norway. Rico's media agency now does a wide variety of commercial art and script work for advertising, television and publishing. His first love, however, remains comics, and current projects include the online comics *Vern & Dern* (www.vern-dern.com) and *An Ordinary Day* (www.geocities.com/toucan_comics/od).

ONSMITH JEREMI (page 40)

Onsmith Jeremi (*aka* Jeremy Smith) grew up in a couple of small towns in central Oklahoma, putting in his factory and fast food time while nurturing an interest in small press comics, cartoons, and "zines". He then moved to Chicago, where he started a small press anthology, *Bomb Time for Bonzo*, with fellow artists Ben Chandler and Henry Ng (of the early *Non* anthology). With no formal art education, Onsmith has been producing comics for the past four years. His work has appeared in anthologies including *Expo 2002*, *Studygroup 12* and *Proper Gander*, as well as *Graphic*

Classics: H. P. Lovecraft and *Graphic Classics: Jack London*. To see more of his work, visit www.onsmithcomics.com.

EVERT GERADTS (page 50)

Evert Geradts is a Dutch comics artist living in Toulouse, France. One of the founders of the Dutch underground comix scene, he started the influential magazine *Tante Leny Presents*, in which appeared his first *Sailears & Susie* stories. He is a disciple of Carl Barks, whom he names "the Aesop of the 20th century." Over the years Geradts has written about a thousand stories for Dutch comics of Donald Duck and other Disney characters. He also writes stories for the popular comic series *Sjors & Sjimmie* and *De Muziekbuurters*. He now does all his art on computer, developing the supple vector style he applies to his "kids in space" series *Kos & Mo*. "All my life I have been waiting for the arrival of personal computers with good illustration programs," says Evert. "Adobe Illustrator and my Mac have set me free from the traditional drawing style where the obligatory black outline was always the frontier between color and form."

RICHARD SALA (page 56)

A master of gothic humor in the tradition of Charles Addams and Edward Gorey, Richard Sala creates stories filled with mystery, adventure, femmes fatales and homicidal maniacs. Richard is the artist and author of several collections, *Hypnotic Tales*, *Black Cat Crossing*, *Thirteen O'Clock*, *The Chuckling Whatsit*, plus an homage to Gorey titled *The Ghastly Ones*. His work has appeared in *RAW*, *Blab!*, *Esquire*, *Playboy*, *The New York Times*, *Graphic Classics: Edgar Allan Poe*, *Graphic Classics: Arthur Conan Doyle* and his current, critically-acclaimed comic series, *Evil Eye*. Richard also created *Invisible Hands*, which ran on MTV's animation show, *Liquid Television*. Recent projects include a comic strip written by Lemony Snicket for the upcoming children's book *It Was a Dark and Silly Night* and illustrations for a previously unpublished screenplay by Jack Kerouac titled *Dr. Sax and the Great WorldSnake*. Visit Richard's website at www.richardsala.com for "lots of wonderfully creepy things to look at."

JOHN W. PIERARD (page 58)

John Pierard has had a varied career in illustration. After leaving the bosom of his beloved Syracuse University for New York City, he immediately found work in publications such as *Screw* and *Velvet Touch Magazine*, where he illustrated stories like *Sex Junky*. In a major departure, he then graduated to illustrating children's fiction including Mel Gilden's *P.S. 13* series, and various projects by noted children's author Bruce Coville. He has worked for Marvel Comics, *Asimov's Magazine* and Greenwich Press. John's comics adaptations also appear in *Graphic Classics: H.G. Wells* and *Graphic Classics: Jack London*.

BRANDON RAGNAR JOHNSON (page 76)

Illustrator Brandon Ragnar Johnson grew up under the sweltering sun and bright lights of Las Vegas. From there it was stints in Japan, Taiwan, Mexico and Hollywood before settling in Southern California with his wife and two children. He now works in advertising and as an animation development artist for Disney, MTV, Nickelodeon and other studios. Prints of Ragnar's illustrations of women and monsters, women and chimps, and women and women can be found in galleries, fine retail establishments and at www.littlecartoons.com.

KOSTAS ARONIS (page 77)

In addition to his illustration work, Kostas is an architect in Thessaloniki, Greece and works as a scenographer for the theater, State TV and private channels. He teaches in a school of arts in Thessaloniki and established the theater group "ACHTHOS," to create performances and installations with a comics aesthetic. Kostas organized the first Intervalkanian Comics Festival as part of Cultural Olympiade 2004 and he is now preparing the second one. His illustrations and comics have been published in books, on CDs, and in magazines and newspapers in Greece. His first book, *Between the Legs — Unbelievable Stories*, was published in 2001, and Kostas is finishing his second, as well as preparing his next painting exhibition in Athens. His illustrations in *Graphic Classics: Jack London* were his first works to appear in the United States.

NEALE BLANDEN (page 78)

Neale was born in 1963 in Melbourne, Australia, and started self-publishing in 1988 under the monicker "Beautiful Artform." He has published sixteen comics to date, and has appeared in anthologies in Australia, Canada, Europe and the U.S. He is also an animator, and teaches classes in cartooning. His artwork has been exhibited in galleries in Australia, Canada and Europe. Neale is currently working on two books, one a compilation of past work, and one of new material. He illustrated

two of Bierce's fables in his unique style in *Graphic Classics: Ambrose Bierce*.

SKOT OLSEN (page 79)

While growing up in Connecticut, Skot and his parents spent their summers sailing up and down the coast of New England and all over the West Indies. It was on these long trips that he developed his love for the sea which forms the basis for much of his work. A 1991 graduate of the Joe Kubert School of Cartoon and Graphic Art, Skot now lives on the edge of the Florida Everglades, where he concentrates on paintings which have been featured in numerous publications and exhibited in galleries in Florida, New York and California. A large collection of his work is online at www.skotolsen.com.

MICHAEL MANNING (page 80)

Michael is the creator of the erotic graphic novels *The Spider Garden*, *Hydrophidian*, *In A Metal Web I* and *II*, and *Tranceptor* (all NBM Publishing). He studied at the School of the Museum of Fine Arts in Boston, and began publishing comics in 1987 while working as an animator and director of short films and music videos. A move to San Francisco's Mission District in 1991 coincided with Michael's decision to focus on erotic illustration and gallery shows full-time. His admiration for the Symbolist and Pre-Raphaelite art movements as well as the classical ukiyo-e prints of Tsukioka Yoshitoshi and Unagawa Kuniyoshi has contributed to the formulation of Manning's distinct style. He can be contacted at xeroimage@netscape.net.

JEFF GAITHER (page 81)

Jeff Gaither lives in Louisville, Kentucky and has been practicing his particular blend of horror and rock music for over 25 years. He has created art for The Misfits, Guns-N-Roses, The Undead, Biohazard, Insane Clown Posse, The Accused and many more metal and hardcore bands. He blames it all on his aunt, who in his youth bought him copies of *Famous Monster Magazine* and took him to movies like *The Exorcist* and *Night of the Living Dead*. You can see more of Jeff's monstrous art on his website at www.gaithergraphix.com.

MAXON CRUMB (page 82)

Maxon will be familiar to many readers from his appearance in Terry Zwigoff's 1994 award-winning film, *Crumb*. While his older brother Robert's work may be more well-known, Maxon is equally talented as both a writer and artist. His gritty fantasy story, *Stigmata*, appears in *Crumb Family Comics*, and his illustrated novel of sex, violence and incest, *Hard Core Mother*, was published in 2000 by CityZen Books. Illustrations from his first book, *Maxon's Poe* (1997, Cottage Classics) appeared in *Graphic Classics: Edgar Allan Poe*, and an illustration for Lovecraft's poem, *Fungi from Yuggoth*, in *Graphic Classics: H.P. Lovecraft*.

LISA K. WEBER *(page 84)*

Lisa is a graduate of Parsons School of Design in New York City, where she is currently employed in the fashion industry, designing prints and characters for teenage girls' jammies, while freelancing work on children's books and character design for animation. Other projects include her "creaturized" opera posters and playing cards. Lisa provided the unique cover and illustrations for *Hop-Frog* in *Graphic Classics: Edgar Allan Poe*, and also appeared in *Graphic Classics: H.P. Lovecraft* and *Graphic Classics: Ambrose Bierce*. Illustrations from her in-progress book *The Shakespearean ABCs* were recently printed in *Rosebud 25*. More of Lisa's art can be seen online at www.creatureco.com.

SPAIN RODRIGUEZ *(page 85)*

Manuel "Spain" Rodriguez, born 1940 in Buffalo, New York, first gained fame as one of the founders of the underground comix movement of the 1960s. After drawing comics in New York for the *East Village Other*, he moved to San Francisco where he joined Robert Crumb and other artists on *Zap Comix*. Spain's early years with the Road Vultures Motorcycle Club and his reportage of the 1968 Democratic Convention in Chicago are chronicled in the comics collection, *My True Story*. Along with autobiographical stories and politically-oriented fiction featuring his best-known character, Trashman, Spain has produced a number of historical comics, and his story of Poe's astonishing choice for a posthumous literary agent, *The Inheritance of Rufus Griswold*, appeared in *Graphic Classics: Edgar Allan Poe*. Spain's work can also be seen in the online comic *The Dark Hotel* at www.salon.com, and in *Graphic Classics: Jack London*.

TODD SCHORR *(page 86)*

Todd Schorr lives in the realm of the Pop Surreal, expressing his visions on large-scale canvasses. His first book, *Secret Mystic Rites*, was published by Last Gasp of San Francisco in 1998, and the much-anticipated second

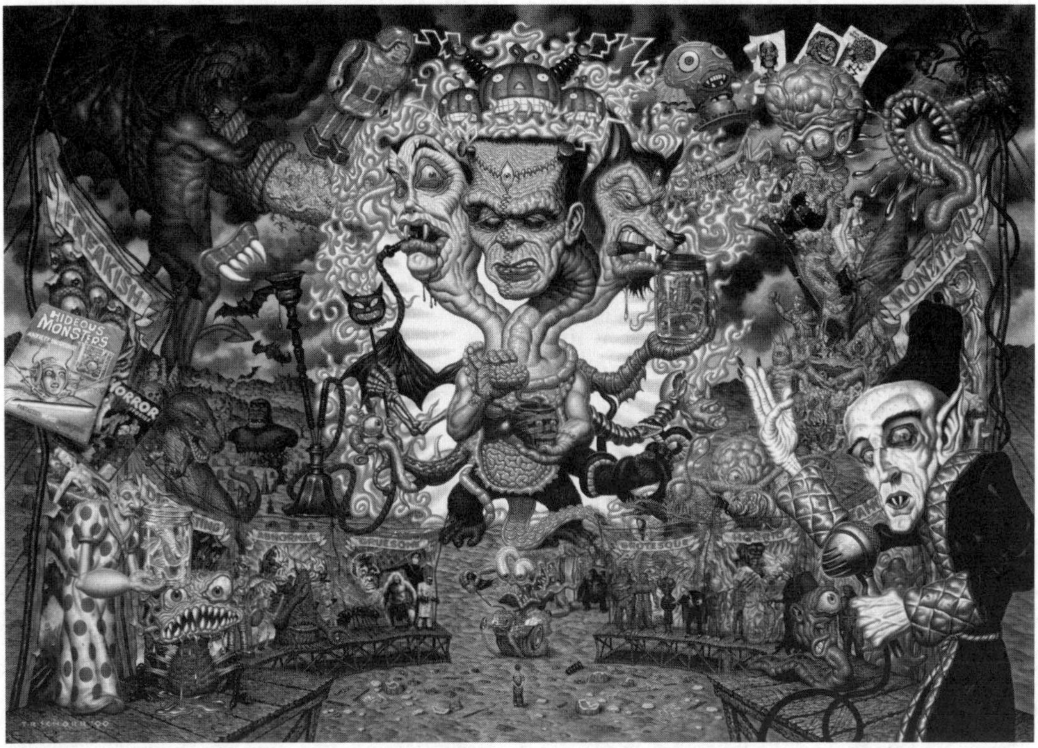
FREAKISH
HIDEOUS MONSTERS
HORROR

Complete view of Tod Schorr's ***Spectre of Monster Appeal****, 60"x 84", acrylic on canvas, 2000*

book of his acclaimed paintings entitled *Dreamland* will be published by Last Gasp in 2003. His "H.P. Lovecraft's Seafood Cart" was reproduced on the cover of *Graphic Classics: H.P. Lovecraft*. Visit www.toddschorr.com to see more.

ANTON EMDIN (page 87)

Anton is a freelance illustrator living and working in Sydney, Australia. Since finishing his Fine Art degree in 1997 ("I learned a hell of a lot about drinking beer") his work has been featured in many major publications, as well as appearing in exhibitions and books both in Australia and abroad. His influences include early *Mad* artists Will Elder, Harvey Kurtzman, and Jack Davis, and contemporary comic book legends Charles Burns, Kaz, Peter Bagge and Dave Cooper. Anton is heavily involved in the Australian underground comix scene, and publishes his own title, *Cruel World*, a collection of offbeat strips and stories about "love, death, gap-toothed girls and squirrels." You can see Anton's work on the cover of *Graphic Classics: Ambrose Bierce*, and online at www.antongraphics.com.

TODD LOVERING (page 88)

Todd was born on the East coast, and "moved out to the Northwest at 21 years of age, took a few classes at the School of Visual Art and stuck my feet into illustration. Got out and into throwing pizza. A dear friend turned me on to the video game industry and I've been working in it to this day." Todd is also an editorial and commercial illustrator and has shown his paintings in several galleries in the Northwest. He says his strongest influences are Robert Williams, Rick Griffin, Jamie Burton, Jim Blanchard and "all the talented cats I work with." Contact him at tlovering@attbi.com.

LESLEY REPPETEAUX (page 94)

Lesley (*aka* Black Olive) is a Los Angeles-based illustrator whose work has appeared in numerous publications including *Amplifier Magazine*, *Adventure Cyclist*, *Bitch*, *Delaware Today*, *Graphic Classics: Jack London* and *Graphic Classics: Ambrose Bierce*. Between freelance assignments, she exhibits her paintings in galleries nationwide, and is the creative force behind *Outlook: Grim*, a spooky new comic book series published by Slave Labor Graphics. When she is "not overexerting herself or being a busy little bumblebee," she is updating her website which you can check out at www.reppeteaux.com.

GERRY ALANGUILAN (page 102)

Gerry Alanguilan is a licensed architect who chooses to write and draw comic books. In his native Philippines he has created comics including *Timawa*, *Crest Hut Butt Shop*, *Dead Heart* and *Wasted*. *Wasted* has received acclaim abroad from writers like Warren Ellis and Steven Grant, and is now currently being shot as in independent film in the Philippines. In America, he has contributed inks on such titles as *X-Men*, *Fantastic Four*, *Wolverine*, *X-Force*, *Darkness*, *Stone* and *High Roads*, working with pencillers Leinil Francis Yu and Whilce Portacio. He is currently inking *Superman: Birthright* for DC Comics and is putting together *Komikero*, a portfolio of his sketches, illustrations and comics. Gerry's illustrations also appear in *Graphic Classics: H.P. Lovecraft* and *Graphic Classics: Jack London*.

J.B. BONIVERT (page 119)

Jeffrey Bonivert is a Bay Area native who has contributed to independent comics as both artist and writer, in such books as *The Funboys*, *Turtle Soup* and *Mister Monster*. His unique adaptation of *The Raven* appears in *Graphic Classics: Edgar Allan Poe*. His art is published in *Graphic Classics: Arthur Conan Doyle*, *Graphic Classics: Jack London* and *Graphic Classics: Ambrose Bierce*, and he was part of the unique five-artist team on *Reanimator* in *Graphic Classics: H.P. Lovecraft*. Jeff's biography of artist Murphy Anderson appears in *Spark Generators*, and *Muscle and Faith*, his Casey Jones / Teenage Mutant Ninja Turtles epic, can be seen online at www.flyingcolorscomics.com.

CHRISTOPHER MISCIK (back cover)

Chris claims to have "always been drawing, since a very young age," influenced by his mother, aunt, and grandmother, all of whom are amateur artists. Of course, he could still be considered in his "young age," as Chris is currently an art student at Madison (Wisconsin) Area Technical College. His main focus has been illustration and concept art, and he plans a second degree in animation. Chris has done freelance advertising and videogame work and exhibited his art locally, but *Graphic Classics: Bram Stoker* presents his first published editorial illustration.

TOM POMPLUN

The designer, editor and publisher of *Graphic Classics*, Tom has a background in both fine and commercial arts and a lifelong interest in comics. He designed and produced *Rosebud*, a journal of fiction, poetry and illustration, from 1993 to 2003, and in 2001 he founded *Graphic Classics*. Tom is currently working on the eighth book in the series, *Graphic Classics: Mark Twain*, scheduled for release in January 2004. You can see previews of this and all the previous volumes on the *Graphic Classics* website at www.graphicclassics.com.